Fighting Terrorism on Global Front

TEENA SARAN

AKANSHA PUBLISHING HOUSE
NEW DELHI - 110002 (INDIA)

AKANSHA PUBLISHING HOUSE
4649-B,Ansari Road,
Daryaganj, New Delhi-110002
Phones:23268193, 9811582579, 09435116718
Email: ektabooks@yahoo.com
visit us: www.akanshapublishinghouse.com

Fighting Terrorism on Global Front

First Published 2009

ISBN 978-81-8370-201-0

PRINTED IN INDIA

Published by Akansha Publishing House, New Delhi-110002
and Printed at Mehra Offset Press, Delhi.

Dedicated
to
My Respected Aunty
Smt. Rajbeeri Devi

Contents

Preface

Terrorism is the main concern every nation-state in the world is currently inflicted with. After terrorist attacks on America's WTC and Pentagon only its grimness is being felt by every one. India is the worst victim of cross-border terrorism. After attack on Indian Parliament followed by a series of other incidents, recently attack on Mumbai on 26 November 2008 have attracted world attention.

Terrorism now has become a worldwide phenomenon. During the last two decades the world has been marked by an increasing number of terrorist attacks. Its recent manifestation have been described in countless books, articles, plays, novels and films on all possible levels of sophistication; terror has fascinated the metaphysicians as much as the popular novelists. This work grew out of a study of *Fighting Terrorism on Global Front* and the root causes of terrorism.

The purpose of this study is to highlight the meaning of terrorism. Where does it occur mostly? Who provide finance to encourage terrorists in their action? What are the main motives of terrorism and its impact on world peace? In chapter-4 I have discussed about the methods adopted by the terrorists and the possibilities of the new adventures. The last two chapters in this book consider how to counter terrorism. Nations, affected by terrorism, have long tried to cope with it as best they could and in a piecemeal fashion. The need now is for international, decisive action to deal with terrorism and so the study concludes with a brief account of the Counter-Terrorism measures.

In this research work most of the material was obtained from different Libraries (e.g., I.D.S.A., I.C.W.A., U.S.I. Meerut

College etc), Newspapers and Magazines. ›ome of the data and pictures have been retrieved from the ꓷifferent websites.

Based on primary and secondary sources of information, the present empirical study portrays world terrorism in pros and cons. The issue is taken in entirety. Causes of emergence of terrorism, its nature, types, magnitude, strategy and tactics, continent-wise profile of major terrorist outfits, consequences of terrorism, and remedial measures :o combat terrorism on global front are given an elaborate treatment.

Amidst plenty of literature, this book will delight and enlighten one and all concerned—be they academics, administrators, policy-makers or any serious reader.

—Teena Saran

Acknowledgements

This study is the part of my long journey to fulfill my dreams in academic field of Defence Studies. I have not traveled in a vacuum in this journey. A journey is easier when you travel together. Interdependence is certainly more valuable than independence. This work is the result of three years of work whereby I have been accompanied and supported by many people. It is a pleasant aspect that I have now the opportunity to express my gratitude for all of them.

To begin with, I thank the most merciful and compassionate, the Almighty God as I believe that God always guides us from darkness to the path of light.

I would also like to gratefully acknowledge the support of some very special individuals and to thank them for a many reasons.

At the outset I am deeply beholden to my supervisor Dr. Somnath Mishra, Reader, Dept. of Defence Studies, Meerut College, Meerut, whose great knowledge and experience proved beneficial to me since I began at C.C.S. University. His encouragement and sound advice has played a large part in helping this study and my career more generally to develop. I owe him lots of gratitude for having me shown this way of research. I also had an opportunity to work with him, he rendered his services as a Coordinator of Defence Studies Deptt. in C.C.S. University. I got this precious opportunity to work as a teacher in the Deptt. which gave me an exposure to interact with the academician of different fields.

It is with great sincerity and a humble sense of gratitude that I acknowledge my beloved Aunty Smt. Rajbeeri Devi, she has been my guiding lamp who showed me the way throughout. She has always been there for me, supporting me, inspiring me and guiding me as and when required, even when I lost my ground and hope. I shall forever be indebted to her for her critical evaluation towards perfection which has sculptured me and made to be things which I would never dream of.

I would like to thank my sister Dr. Reetu and my brother Dr. Abhishek for discussions and advice and tips that helped me a lot in staying at the right track.

On the personal front I would like to thank my loving, caring parents—my father Mr. Sadhu Saran, Mother Mrs. Neelam Saran who formed part of my vision and taught me the good things that really matter in life.

I would also like to thank my relatives Mrs. Radha Gupta, Mrs. Harbeeri Devi, Ch. Ranveer Singh, Mrs. Sangeeta Malik, Rahul Dev Nain and Kunal Chaudhry for their constant support, sacrifice and blessings. They have been there for me during the tough hour of this work, constantly encouraging me to complete this study. My bhaiya Mr. Sundeep Saran and bhabhi Mrs. Pinky Saran for their encouragement and timely support.

I would like to express my fond appreciation for my loving sister Sweta who have supported me in all my steps and endeavours throughout my life.

I am very thankful to my friend Amita who has always stood like a pillar in all the times of difficulties. My acknowledgement would be incomplete without mentioning the help and blessings of my sisters Sonika, Anila, and Naina whose constant support worked as an impetus to complete this work.

Finally, I am thankful to Mr. M.P. Misra, Akansha Publishing House, New Delhi for undertaking publication of this work.

—Teena Saran

Terrorism is

T = Theory of Violence for political gains.

= Terrorises thousands by killing one.

E = Evolution of psychological aspirations.

= Evolution of voice of depressed masses.

R = Revenge against ruler.

= Revolutionary character of guerilla warfare.

R = Redress fails, terrorism grows.

= Results in to mass destruction of national property.

O = Open defiance of law and order.

= Opportunists operate for self gains.

R = Result of liberal democracies and failure of timely action against anti-national elements.

= Requires recognition of common cause by masses and their support for its success.

I = Ideology of supressed & aggrieved.

= Ideology of Communism.

S = System for seeking political demand by violence.

= Strategy of violence for Coup'd'etate, Insurrection, Guerrilla war & terrorism.

M = Method of a group for realization of their aims.

= Movement of politically, economically and ethinical aspired people.

1

Introduction

Terrorism is a curse to mankind. This insanity is perpetuated by fanatic acts of deranged barbarians who have no value for human life. Thousands of innocent persons, having no link with knowledge of terrorist have lost their lives in terrorist attack. The evil of terrorism has even crippled life in several states and countries which are riddled with devastation, causing economic breakdown leading to unemployment, hunger and untold misery. We, as responsible citizens and policy makers must, from our heart and actions, declare war on this specter of savagery, which is bound to paralyze the economic and social fabric of society. But before we endeavour to take any step in this direction, we must be aware of the nature and dimensions of this problem.

National security is concern of everyone. There were time when the defence of the country and its people was the sole responsibility of a ruler or the government and the military. But the 20th Century has been the most violent and destructive period that humankind has experienced within one generation, we were subjected to two 'world war' and 'cold war'.[1]

As we enter the 21st century, it is appropriate to take stock of the security situation around us and assess what the future holds for succeeding generations. Given the right assessments and evaluations and the institution of appropriate corrective measures, it may be possible to make the world a safer place than it is at present.

. The concept of security has been one of the 'Core' issues that have dominated the study of International Relations (IR) as an academic discipline although the concept itself has undergone significant change over the last two decades or so.

> "National security is the preservation of the core values critical to the nation or state from external and internal threats".[2]

A nation has security when it does not have to sacrifice its legitimate interest to avoid war and is able, if challenging, to maintain them by direct or indirect use of 'force' our history of the last 53 years tells us that we cannot ever take peace and security and territorial integrity for granted.[3]

> "National security can be most fruitfully defined as the ability of a nation to protect its internal values from external threats"[4]

The concept of security itself is undergoing a change. No longer do threat originate only from outside the country's border but also from within the country. Internal change in the society, technological changes, population growth, poverty, economic instability, unemployment, widespread urbanisation, diseases, environmental degradation, energy and resources depletion etc. can destabilise a country and be a source of threat to national security.

The security of a nation can be threatened in three ways:

- The *First Category* of threat is external threat from a nation or group of nations.
- The *Second Category* of threat is internal one arising out of communal case, linguistic, ethnic and organized criminal elements. Tensions and violence arising out of these factors and disrupt good governance which is essential for sustained economic, social political and culture progress of a nation, are wrecked by violence and intimidation then that polity would have a very serious setback. Countries like India, which are multi-religious, multi-lingual and multi-ethnic are particularly

vulnerable to this category of national security threat. Most of the wars that are taking place today in the world are internal wars arising out of ethno-nationalist factors.

- The *Third Category* of national security threat is where the external and internal factors interact with each other.

An adversary nation helps various dissident and anti-national elements in a country to endanger its national security and hamper its progress. In the case of India, it is hardly realised by our own ruling class that this country faces all three categories of threat.

Bary Buzan was the first to draw attention to the need for developing a holistic view of security encompassing the three levels of the security problem: the individual, the state and the international system.[5] While he was right in arguing that the concept of security binds these three levels together, he had failed to distinguish between the security concerns of the third world states and those of the developed state, although he did take note of some of these in developing the nation of 'security complex', in the context of the study of regional security in particular, we agree with the panel's view that development and security are closely linked.

The tension in some part of the country, especially in the tribal areas, due to a perceived threat to their identity is not new, but the rise of so many violent movements is a relatively recent development. In the border sates these movements become secessionist because of the support they received from the hostile neighbouring states.

Internal and external security challenges are not confined to any one area. In today's world, 'a threat to one is a threat to all'. The interconnection of threats to international peace and security is more evident than ever before. There are Six Cluster of threats with which the world must be concerned now in the decades ahead:[6]

1. War between states,

2. Violence within states, including civil wars; large-scale human rights abuses and genocide,
3. Poverty, infectious diseases and environmental degradation,
4. Nuclear, radiological, chemical and biological weapons,
5. Terrorism, and
6. Transnational organised crime.

Threats may come in different forms some are waxing, some are waning; some are old and other are very new. It can occur anywhere, in which terrorists appear to be increasingly successful because they are targeting relatively unprotected public individuals. They want to make government docile in responding to the cause of the public's safety. Meeting the challenges of today's threats means getting serious about prevention; the consequences of allowing latent threats to become manifest, or of allowing existing threats to spread, are simply too severe.

Development issues are closely linked to global security. Perceptions of injustice due to extreme poverty and lack of opportunity to improve living conditions often provide fertile breeding grounds for terrorism, civil unrest, intrastate and inter state-conflict.

Internal security now encompasses both external and internal threats to a country, besides law and order problems. Time has come not only to redefine the term but also to enlarge its scope to include all the elements, which endanger internal security in the present conditions.

In the current environment the term internal security should encompass the following:

- Terrorism.
- Insurgency and guerrilla warfare.
- Narco terrorism and connected smuggling activities.
- Nexus between politicians and criminals.

- Organized crime.
- Religious conflicts.
- Threats from Hijackers.
- Employment of weapons of mass destruction by terrorists.
- Deliberate attempt to destabilise the country politically and economically, by a hostile country or its surrogates.
- Piracy.

More than 2300 years ago, Chanakya in his *Arthashastra* had said that internal troubles are more serious and should be put down promptly.[7]

The domestic conflicts and involvement of external agencies-both states and non-states actors have thus endangered the security of state as well as of individuals living within the state. What is even more alarming is that the different separatist groups such as the LTTE in Sri Lanka, the ULFA in Assam and etc. Ever since Independence, India has been facing all types of violent conflicts based on religious caste, language, ethnicity and regional loyalties.

Proxy wars, low intensity conflicts, infiltration across the border, small arms proliferations, drug trafficking, and terrorism have become household words. Threats to national security would not be confined to external military threats or internal subversion only. In order to weaken the nation and ultimately jeopardise its sovereignty, socialist, secular and democratic character and even disintegrate it, other threats could be posed. Such threats include diplomatic pressure, economic deprivation, distruction of ecological balance, flooding of fake currency, smuggling of drugs and narcotics and so on.

It is worth to quote *Panchatantra* here which states "of all the gifts that a king can give, it is not the gift of gold, nor the gift of land, nor the gifts of cows, which is important, but the gifts of security".[8]

Further, "today, the gravest threat to world peace", is not from national standing armies, but terrorism."[9]

The biggest threat that world faces today is undoubtedly terrorism which is widespread geographically and diverse ideologically. The threat is multi-country and multinational and hence its menacing aspect to international peace and security.

At present, the war against terrorism holds the center stage. The evolution of events since September 11 and December 13 terrorist attacks on World Trade Center and Indian Parliament, the symbol of the largest multi-ethnic democracy in the world, has challenged nations about security, vulnerability and strategy. New aspect of threat-including the rise of global terrorist network and the potential for terrorist use of nuclear, biological or chemical weapons-require new responses.

These events have sensitized them to the threats posed by terrorism, which Indian had long since identified as the principal destabilising factors of the world order.

An effective multilateral system is essential to cope with the challenges of today's world. No individual state can protect itself from global threat. Therefore a common understanding is needed on the future of collective security and the necessary institutional reforms. Having this in mind, we will actively participate in the efforts towards more effective policies and in adapting the U.N. system to the realities of today's world.

TERRORISM

Terrorism poses the most serious threat to our territorial integrity and internal security. Terrorists attacks are becoming increasing lethal, and they now aim to kill maximum number of people. This trend reflects the changing motivations of terrorist groups and easy availability of sophisticated weapons, around the world.

Massacre of innocent people is considered perfectly

legitimate in the current terrorist ideologies. The targets are chosen for their symbolic value, the assassinations of political opponents or the massacre of the innocent women and children, witnessed in the U.S., were calculated to spread anger and despair throughout the world. Many terrorist groups are in a position to use biological, radiological or nuclear weapons. These weapons of mass destruction can cause very large number of casualties; immense material damage and can even lead to political destabilization of a targeted regime. No single ministry or national agency can handle such a challenge in isolation, as it can take varied forms, from random terrorism to mass scale destruction, from jihad terrorism, Narco terrorism and so on. Now, the states of the world should realise the gravest nature of the threat that they are facing at present.

The present research work is an attempt to elucidate the concept of terrorism, which is assuming serious proportions with every successive terrorist strike. And which has become a common threat for the world.

Terrorism is a crime against humanity; it endangers the lives of innocent people. It creates a climate of hate and fear; it fuels global divisions along ethnic and religious lines. Terrorism constitutes one of the most serious violations of peace, international law and the values of human dignity. Terrorism is an attack on democracy and human rights. No cause justifies the targeting of civilians and non-combatants through intimidation and deadly acts of violence.

Over the last two decades there has been a significant increase in the number of terrorist attacks. Despite the efforts of much government to combat terrorism, it appears to be on the increase and getting more deadly. Terrorism has been spreading its tentacles to all aspects of human life thus eroding the quality of life. Hardly a day passes without a terrorist incident somewhere or the other part of the globe. Terrorism is used as a strategic weapon in creating disorder and anarchy in the international system. Globally organized crime, that is terrorism is now recognised as a threat to human and national security.

There is a close nexus between terrorist organisations and organised crime groups. The LTTE is reportedly running its own shipping services, which is used not only to supply arms to its cadres in Sri Lanka, but also generate revenue out of illegal trade.[10] However, by now LTTE is reportedly crushed completely by the Sri Lankan Government. The intelligence and security agencies of many countries, including India, have been very concerned about such threats. Terrorism constitutes a threat to all: What is being inflicted on one country today can be inflicted on another tomorrow.

Meaning of Terrorism

In the autumn of 2001 the word 'terrorism' was on all lips. It was a term prominent in the press and on television. Everybody used it but nobody explained it. The terrible events in New York and Washington on September 11, 2001 were constantly recounted in an atmosphere of incredulity and horror.

Here the question arises, in the most straightforward words, what does the term 'terrorism' really means?

Almost certainly, terrorism has a different meaning for different people and for those in authority who are responsible for peace, order and security. But before we explain the concept of terrorism we must briefly investigate the general characteristics of the extremist the foundation of terrorism. An important step toward defining terrorism is to develop an understanding of the sources of terrorism. In order to identify these sources, one must first understand the important role of extremism as a primary feature underlying all terrorist behaviour. One must keep in mind, however, that although terrorism is a violent expression of these beliefs it is by no means the only possible manifestation of extremism.

Meaning of Extremism

Extremism is a precursor of terrorism—it is an overarching belief system that is used by terrorists to justify their violent behaviour. Extremism is characterized by what a person's beliefs are as well as how a person expresses his or her beliefs. Thus, no matter how offensive or reprehensible one's thoughts or words are, they are not by themselves acts of terrorism. Only persons who violently act out their extremist beliefs are labeled as terrorists.

Two examples illustrate this point:

First, example of extremist behavior: - Daniel and Philip Berrigan were well known members of the Roman Catholic Pacifist Left and were leaders in antiwar and antinuclear movements in the United States during the 1960s and 1970s. What they believed in was an uncompromising commitment to pacifism. How to express their beliefs was by committing a series of symbolic, and often illegal, protest actions. During one such action on May 17, 1968 they and seven other Catholic men and women entered the Baltimore Selective Service Board, stole selective service classification forms, took them outside to a parking lot, and burned several hundred of the documents with a homemade napalm-like gelled mixture of gasoline and soap flakes. This was certainly extremist behaviour, but it falls short of terrorism.[11]

Second, an example of extremist speech: - The American knights of the Ku Klux Klan (AK-KKK) were an activist faction of the KKK that operated mostly in the Midwest and east during the 1990s. What they believed in was racial supremacy. How they expressed their beliefs was by holding a series of rallies at government sites, often country courthouses. They were known for their vitriolic rhetoric. The following remarks were reportedly taken from a speech delivered by the Imperial Wizard of the AK-KKK in March 1998 at rally held at the country courthouse in Butler, Pennsylvania, near Pittsburgh. The language used were internationally racist, hateful and inflammatory, and yet it falls short of advocating violence or revolution.[12]

From the above example we have come to know that extremism is a quality that is "radical in opinion, especially in political matters".[13] It is characterized by intolerance toward opposing interests and divergent opinions, and it is the primary catalyst and motivation for terrorist behavior. Extremists who cross the line to become terrorists always develop nobe arguments to rationalize and justify acts of violence directed against enemy nations, people, religions or other interests. When terrorists adopt a religious belief system, their worldview becomes one of a struggle between supernatural forces of good and evil. They view themselves as living a righteous life in a manner that fits with their interpretation of God's will. Therefore, extremists thus become a special elite who have discovered a hidden agenda and who have become targets of that agenda.

Defining Terrorism

In the past four decades, much has been written about terrorism and terrorists, some of it focused on the psychological profile of who the terrorist is, what his or her motives are for engaging in terrorism how government should respond to it[14] and what exactly terrorism means?

In fact, terrorism is a nebulous term. Terrorism means different things to different people. The nature of terrorism has changed over the course of history. Violent activity at one point in time may be called terrorism. Definition may depend upon circumstances and attitudes and these alter with time, definition of terrorism bears a grotesque finality. It leads to denial of life of liberty, of privacy, of human rights.

Hundreds of definitions of terrorism are offered in the literature. Some focus on the perpetrators, others on their purposes, and still others on their techniques. No definition of terrorism can possibly cover all varieties of terrorism that have appeared throughout history. One of the primary reasons that terrorism is difficult to define is that the meaning changes within social and historical contexts. However, defining terrorism is not such a simple process. Experts have for some time grappled with designing (and agreeing upon) clear definition of terrorism; the issue has in fact, been at the center of an ongoing debate. The result of this debate has been a remarkable variety of approaches and definitions. Defining terrorism is more than an academic exercise. The definition inevitably determines the kind of data we collect and analyze, which in turn influences our understanding of trends and our predictions about the future. How we define terrorism profoundly influences how we respond to it.

Tracing the Roots of the word as a Label: Indeed, where did the word terrorism come from? The original use of the word in English is often believed to have derived from the Latin word "Terrere", meaning, "to tremble", when combined with the French suffix isme, referencing "to practice", or "to cause or create the trembling". Trembling here obviously is another word for fear, panic and anxiety—what we mean today is terror. A group of revolutionaries called the Jacobins in France used the term when self-reflexively describing their own actions and justifications in the French Revolution. The meaning of this word in France was mentioned in 1798.[15] Robespierre, the high priest of the 1789 revolution declared that 'a democratic France would be 'terrorised' France.[16]

The English version of word as terrorism owes to an Englishman's characterization of the bloodshed he had observed from a far in France, where the same revolution was underway using an Anglicized version of the same word he had understood the Jacobins to use in describing their own behaviour, Sir Edmund Burke wrote of the revolution in France and warned about "thousands of those hell hounds called 'terrorists'" who were creating havoc and panic in the country.[17] Though Burke did not himself define terrorism or terrorist in his reflections, he as much as provided the definition by operationalizing it in several ways.

In Burke's view, a terrorist was a fanatic; therefore, it could be inferred that a terrorist does not follow any means of logic or reason to justify his or her actions. Moreover, a terrorist was an assassin, a murderer, a thief, and a fraud not to mention an oppressor.[18] Burke had begun the process of defining terrorism and terrorists and delegitimizing their behaviour, but as the reader may have noticed, the word terrorism and terrorist as Burke employed them were perhaps more labels than definition.

Government has developed definitions of terrorism, individual agencies within government have adopted definitions, private agencies have designed their own definitions and academic experts have proposed and analyzed dozens of definitions.

"Terrorism" as a concept is difficult to define. Even political scientists and strategists have found it difficult to arrive at an agreed definition of the term. This term has actually been defined by different persons in different ways at different times. Between 1936 to 1986 at least 115 definitions of terrorism have been provided.[19] The word 'terrorism' is a phenomenon which is easier to describe than to define.

Leiser states that:

> "Terrorism is an organized set of acts of violence designed to create an atmosphere of despair or fear, to shake the faith of ordinary citizens in their government regime whose popular support is shaky. It is a policy of seemingly senseless, irrational and arbitrary murder, assassination sabotage, subversion, robbery and other forms of violence all committed with dedicated indifference to existing legal and moral codes or with claims to special exemption from conventional social norms. The policies of terrorists are pursued with the conviction that the death and suffering of innocent persons who have no direct connection with the causes to which the terrorists are dedicated are fully justified by whatever success terrorists may enjoy in achieving their political ends."[20]

Academic Definitions

Over time, academicians and theorists have suggested literally hundreds of different definitions for the word. Though many of these definitions are similar, they are subtly different, often projecting an agenda for the author.

For example Martha Crenshaw has written that 'Terrorism is a conspiratorial style of violence calculated to alter the attitudes and behaviour of multitude audiences. It targets the few in a way that claims the attention of the many. Terrorism is not mass or collective violence but rather the direct activity of small groups'.[21]

Though Crenshaw's definition recognizes that terrorism is directed to certain audiences, she also limits her definition to small group activity, effectively predicting and discussion of state based terrorism.

- Walter Laqueur, whose book *'The Age of Terrorism'* is considered by many to be a classic on the history of terrorism, has suggested that terrorism is the use or the threat of the use of violence, a method of combat, or a strategy to achieve certain targets. It aims to induce a state of fear in the victim that is ruthless and does not confirm with humanitarian rules. Publicity is an essential factor in the terrorist strategy.[22]

  'Countries that endured terrorist campaigns have written official definitions of 'Terrorism'.

- *In Europe* :- They have defined terrorism as "the use or threat, for the purpose of advancing a political, religious or ideological cause of action which involves serious violence against any person or property".

- The European Union defines terrorism as an carried out intentionally with the aim of :- "destabilising or destroying basic political, constitutional, economic and social structures. It includes crimes, such as making threats of death or destroying physical integrity of persons, taking hostages, hijacking of aircraft, explosions etc".[23]

  In 1976, the European definition known under the name TREVI (Terrorism, Radicalism, Extremism and Violence) was established. The literature contains an explanation that the abbreviation TREVI was derived from the name of a fountain in Rome near the building of the European Ministry of Justice and Internal Affairs. According to this definition "terrorism is defined as the use of violence or intimidation to use violence by a consistent group of violent persons, other than soldiers in a war, for the purpose of gaining political profits".[24]

- *In Germany*: Terrorism has been described as an "enduringly conducted struggle for political goals, which are intended to be achieved by means of assaults on the life and property of other persons, especially by means of severe crime".
- *In United States*: The United States has not adopted a single definition of terrorism as a matter of government policy, instead relying on definitions that are developed from time to time by government agencies. The definitions reflect the United States traditional law enforcement approach to distinguishing terrorism from more common criminal behaviour. The US government has not yet issued a unified definition of terrorism. The following definitions are the official U.S approach toward defining terrorist behaviour.

The CIA proposed the first definition of terrorism in 1976, which was amended several time afterwards. The version from the year 1980 reads as follows:

> "The threat or the use of violence in order to achieve political goals, carried out by individual or groups acting in opposition or for governmental authorities, provided such actions serve the purpose of intimidating large group of population, bigger than the group of actual victims".[25]

The American army used in 1983 the following definition:

"Planned use of violence or threat to use violence for the purpose of achieving political or ideological profits, carried out by means of intimidation, violent forcing or producing fear".[26]

The Department of Defence defines terrorism as:

"The unlawful use of, or threatened use of force or violence against individuals or property to coerce and intimidate government or societies, often to achieve political, religious, or ideological objective".

The Federal Bureau of Investigation (FBI) has defined terrorism as:

"The unlawful use of force or violence against persons or property to intimidate or coerce a government, the civilian population, or any segment there of, in furtherance of political or social objectives".

U.S Law defines terrorism as:

"Premeditated, politically motivated violence against non combatant targets by sub-national groups or clandestine agents".

This definition focuses on violence that is done intentionally by groups at a substrate level.

In 1984 the Foreign Affairs Department of the U.S. formulated another definition, which describes terrorism as:

"Premeditated, politically motivated violence perpetrated against non-combatant targets by sub-national groups or clandestine agents, usually intended to influence an audience".[27]

In 1794, M. Robespierre (the high priest of the 1789 French Revolution) stated in his declaration to excuse the brutal acts of the revolutionists:

"Terror is nothing else than immediate justice, cruel and unchangeable: it is an execution of power which is less a specific principle than a consequences of the general principle of democracy used in a moment, when the homeland is in utmost exigency".

- According to British Government:

"The use of threat, for the purpose of advancing a political, religious or ideological course of action which involves serious violence against any person or property".[28]

➢ India had officially defined the terms 'terrorist and terrorism' in the annulled Terrorist and Disruptive Activities Prevention Act 1985:

"Terrorist is as one who with the intent to overawe the government or to strike terror in the people or any section thereof or to alienate any section or adversely affect the harmony among different sections of the people, does anything using bombs, dynamite or other explosives of inflammable substances or firearms or lethal weapons or poisons or noxious gases or other chemicals or any other substances, biological or otherwise in such a manner as to cause death or damage or destroy property or disrupt supplies or services essential to the life of the community."

➢ *International Definitions*

Globally, the community of nation-states is no closer to consensus on this definition than we are at home in the United States. For example, the United Nation's has long struggled to define the concept. In 1937, the original "League of Nations" (the predecessor to the modern UN) drafted a definition of terrorism as "all criminal acts directed against a state and intended or calculated to create a state of terror in the minds of particular persons or a group of persons or the general public".[29]

Yet, the formulation of a universally acceptable definition is an urgent imperative and the first vital step for all nations. It may be qualified by use of adjuncts to specify particular types of terrorism.

A broadened definition of terrorism is given below:-

"Unlawful acts under conventions of international or national law, of individuals or group or organizations (indigenous, externally sponsored and international), either unlawful or sponsored or lawful, and/or abetted by external power as an instrument of proxy war, against selected targets, innocent civilians or security forces or properties, to gain political, social, economic, technological, environmental and military objectives, which constitute threats to human, national, regional, international and global security."[30]

Attempts to Synthesize a Consensus Definition (Jenkin's Definition)

Brain Jenkins has worked for many years as a consultant on terrorism and counter-terrorism security. He proposed what may be the simplest definition of terrorism, synthesizing what he believed were the most basic components of all definitions on the subject.

Jenkins suggested that terrorism is the use or the threatened use of force designed to bring about a political change.[31] This definition, popular with many who look at terrorism and security issues, side steps the complexities of the many different definitions by simplifying and reducing the term to violence or threats of violence for political gain.

Using these definitions, the following common elements can be used to construct a composite American definitional model: Terrorism is a premeditated and unlawful act in which groups or agents of some principal engage in a threatened or actual use of force or violence against human or property targets. These group or agents engage in this behaviour with an underlying political objective.

These common elements indicate that the United States has adopted a fairly narrow and legalistic approach to defining terrorism.

According to Walter Reich: "A strategy of violence designed to promote desired outcomes by instilling fear in the public at large".[32]

According to Paul Johnson: "The deliberate, systematic murder, maiming, and menacing of the innocent to inspire fear in order to gain political ends. Terrorism is intrinsically evil, necessarily evil, and wholly evil".[33]

According to Peter Sederberg: International terrorism is the threat or use of violence for political purposes when (1) such action is intended to influence the attitude and behaviour of a target group wider than its immediate victim, and (2) its ramification transcend national boundaries.

Reich (a psychiatrist) emphasises the intimidatory strategy, which instills widespread fear and a sense of personal vulnerability in the civilian population.

According to the standard definition quoted by Noel O'Sullivan (*Terrorism Ideology and Revolution*), political terrorism occurs when "a group, whether holding governmental office or outside government, resolve to pursue set of ideological objectives by methods which not only subvert or ignore the requirement of domestic and international law, but which rely for their success primarily upon the threat or use of violence".

The "less coherent" nature of warfare particularly applies to what Jeanne J. Kirkpatrick has called "terrorist war, (that) is part of a total war which sees the whole society as an enemy, and all members of a society as appropriate objects for violent action".[34]

According to Richard Clutter Buck, "Guerrilla warfare and terrorism, rural and urban, internal and international, has undoubtedly become the primary form of conflict of our time".[35]

International terrorism is not a new phenomenon, although it may be difficult to find a definition of terrorism that 'international terrorism' was coined in the 1950s to refer to activities of the Soviet Union that were designed to promote instabilities in the west. However, later the base of international terrorism shifted to West Asia and Africa because of historical reasons. It is not without significant that of the 13 major terrorist groups out of a list of 40 mentioned in the U.S. State Department report "Patterns of Global Terrorism 1995" (released in April 1996) as many as 7 were rooted in West Asia. The present concern about terrorism related to the activities of groups or organizations, having their roots in South Asia and in the regions adjacent to it, who advocate indiscriminate violence in support of their goal, and are inspired by religious dogma.[36]

In a dozen's definitions the common ground is obvious. More 'official' definitions stress and institutional attitude to offences against persons and property.

Despite numerous incidents of what often appear to be brutal and mindless violence, terrorism is the premeditated, calculated use of force to achieve certain objectives. Terrorism in the sense, we will use it here is never the use of violence for its own ends (to satisfy some personal vendetta to eliminate an opponent), but always has some ulterior aim focused ultimately on the political process.

Terrorism is a direct and serious threat to social an economic development, democracy and human rights.

Whereas Terrorism is defined in dictionary as:

> "The unlawful use or threatened use of force or violence by a person or an organized group against people or property with the intention of intimidating or coercing societies or government, often for ideological or political reasons".

Thus 'Terrorism' may be explained as under:

A surprise attack, generally on innocent civilians, historical monuments, means of transportation (such as Railways, Buses and some time Air ways) crowded markets, pickets of armed forces and center of entertainments to terrorizing a much large group to obtain their goal. It should come as little or no surprise that the controversy over defining terrorism is long standing in both the academic and the geopolitical senses. For decades academicians and theorists have fared no better at defining the world.

Why is Terrorism so Difficult to Define?

Hoffman's understanding of terrorism is that it is inherently political and that it is a calculated process. He describes shifts in the meaning of the terms and changes, in the way that terrorist organizations regard themselves and in their modes of behaviour whether it is domestic or international violence.

Use pejoratively the term terrorism is often confused with guerrilla warfare (Insurgency) or ordinary criminality.

Thus viewed in a broader perspective, terrorism and insurgency are two distinct phenomenons. As both believe in violence, they are sometime construed as one and the same, but in reality they are not alike, they are significantly different from each other. The objective of insurgence is invariably political it is a revolt against authority. Terrorism is merely a strategy to obtain certain objectives.[37]

The term insurgency has been in frequent usage in the realm of journalism, government, politics and administration, but it is less understood in its multidimensional spectrum. S. B. Bhattacharya defines insurgency "as a prolonged armed struggle carried out immaculately step by step in order to achieve specific objective leading finally to overthrow of the existing order. He further endeavours to refine the concept by suggesting that it is an action process in which one or more organization pursue strategy of violence to bring change in society in accordance with some ideology".[38]

Undoubtedly, both insurgency and terrorism are means for violent revolutionary change yet they differ in many respects.

1. Insurgency is regional while Terrorism is international by character.
2. The action of the insurgents seldom affect the international community, whereas the terrorist perpetrate violence far and wide, there by evoking international concern.
3. Terrorists do not belong to a particular area but come from different parts of the world while Insurgency involves local people.
4. Both wage a violent struggle or war to overthrow the existing constitutional government. Insurgency is operated with the support of a section of the local people, where as terrorism may or may not have that

support. Insurgency in a sense is a miniature and localized form of terrorism or militancy.

Characteristics of Terrorism

It is difficult to give an exact definition of terrorism. However, its main characteristics can be summed up as follows.

1. It is an organized, planned and deliberate act of selective violence carried out by a handful of people.
2. It is politically motivated violence with a sole motive to overthrow or challenge the existing order.
3. It uses violence to create a psychological impact for making their demand accepted.
4. It is always unlawful, inhuman and anti-democratic.

However, it should be noted that all types of violence are not the terrorist acts. Only that violence, which is motivated by some political and ideological consideration, falls within the purview terrorism.

The study evaluates terrorist's success in obtaining political goals and the conditions, which affect their ability to materialize their objectives. Whereas the mode of struggle adopted by insurgents is dictated by circumstances rather than by choice. Guerrilla is a diffuse type of war, fought in relatively small formations, against a stronger enemy. In some guerrilla doctrines, final victory is expected to result from wearing out the enemy. The principal is always to prevent the government forces from employing its full might in the contest.[39]

Historical Development of Terrorism

The term 'terrorism' has shifted in meaning through the centuries. Words still used today by way of condemnation zealot, thug, assassin illustrate the changing stress terrorists have placed upon their objectives.

The origins of terrorism are lost in antiquity. As Hacker (1977, ix) points out, terror and terrorism "are as old as the human discovery that people can be influenced by intimidation". The use of threat or violence to achieve political aim was already familiar to the ancesstors of Brutus, Cassius and the rest of the conspirators who assassinated Julius Caesar. (The assassination of Julius Caesar in 44 B.C with which we trace the genesis of murder diplomacy is a classic example of terrorism).

But the terms terrorism and terrorist are comparatively recent; they can be traced to the period of the French Revolution. More precisely, they are associated with the so-called "Reign of Terror" which some historians date from September 4, 1793, the day that Barere's motion was carried "to place the terror on the order of the day". Other historians have identified the terror with all popular violence after the Tennis Courts Oath of June 20, 1789. There is general agreement, however that the terror ended with the death of Robespierre on the nint of Thermidos.[40]

We can trace the history of terrorism as far back in time as we are willing to go. During the first and second centuries of the Roman empire, Jewish insurgents used techniques of coercion and intimidation that do not differ appreciably from those used in that part of the world today but the term terrorism dates from the latter part of the 18th Century, when thousands of French were victimized by the political convulsions of the French revolution.[41]

The history of terrorism really does start a long time ago. Certainly philosopher's theologians have debated the question of whether it is justifiable to kill a political opponent for over 2000 years.

Early Antecedents

The first documented examples of terrorism were the activities of the Zealots in Palestine during 66-73 A.D. (1st Century AD). The Jewish Zealot movement fought against the harsh and oppressive rule of Rome. The Sicarri,[42] a religious sect whose member were active within the Zealot struggle in Palestine, employed terrorist tactics that were also directed against Jewish moderates between 66 and 73 A.D the Sicarri and Zealots managed to polarize the Jewish population by the act of violence from the Roman military government: imprisonment of Jewish religious leaders, desecration of religious symbols, use of excessive military force to break up demonstration and similar measures. Rapoport and Alexander (1983) have noted that the Sicarri-a term derived from Sica, the short sword that was the favorite weapon of the sect members chose to intensify the histrionic effects of their violence by making it a point to attack their targets, Roman soldiers or administrators and Jewish moderates, in broad daylight, especially when their victims were surrounded by supporters and friends, to demonstrate that no circumstances could guarantee immunity from assault.[43] There were nationalistic and religious element in their activities, as there are innumerous terrorist initiatives today. They were zealous in their harassing of Roman officialdom and of Jews whose orthodoxy was tainted with heresy. What in modern language is described as 'religious fundamentalism' played a part in the twelve hundred years of terror that the Thugs brought to central and northern India.[44]

The Thugs, a secret brotherhood of stranglers and followers of the Hindu goddess Kali, were active throughout India from the 13th Century until the Mid-1800s. Their existence had long been suspected, but it was the investigative work of a British administrator, Sir William Sleeman, the finally revealed the extent of their activities. 'Thugs' were born into the profession, membership passing from father to son. One Thug leader's confession stated that he led 20-30 men who infested the high road between Agara and Benares. The Thugs strangled travelers as a tribute to Kali but were allowed to keep some of the taking for themselves.[45]

The 1866, the Ku Klux Klan (KKK) was formed in the southern part of United States as a means of keeping the blacks in line after the civil war had freed them from slavery. Over the next 60 years, the KKK was responsible for extra-judicial killings of blacks, often with official connivance. The KKK peaked in membership during the 1920s depression, when there was increased poverty and competition for jobs. The KKK still exists today, with small international chapters, but is an organization much reduced in influence.[46] Special branches exist today in many British Commonwealth countries. Their role is to monitor and counter-security threats to the state, which in today's world means that there main focus is on the threat from terrorism.

The Anarchist Heritage

The modern era of terrorism can be said to have begun with the Anarchist movement in Europe during the nineteenth century. During the later part of the 19th Century and the early part of the 20th Century, there was an increase in assassination activity by revolutionaries and anarchists. In the 1880s and 1890s it included the assassination of Tsar Alexander II of Russia, the President of France and Italy, The king of Portugal and Italy, the Prime Minister of Spain and the Empress of Austria. There were also attempts on the German Kaiser and Chancellor. In 1901, an assassin killed President McKinley of the United States.[47]

The targets in this period were almost always government officials, rather than civilians. During the last part of 19th Century, Russia experienced a spurt in terrorism—the Narodnaya Voly Movement (C 1878-1881) The Irish, Macedonian, Serb and American dissident groups used terror tactics in pursuit of autonomy or national independence. Narodnaya Volya assassinated Czar Alexander II of Russia. Narodnaya Volya bears the dubious distinction of having been the first terrorist organization to use dynamite on a wide scale. Indeed, it was crude bomb containing dynamite that ended Czar Alexander's life.

The assassination of the Czar set the stage for a meeting in London of the International Congress of Anarchists on July 14, 1881.[48] Here the leading Anarchists met to assert their belief that a revolution could be brought about only through illegal means. Terrorism was to be the means for awakening people throughout the world from their tranquility. Anarchism had its theorists, such as Bakunin and Kropotkin, who were sincere, dedicated, and humanitarian in their ideas and aims.

Michael Bakunin

One of the most influential anarchists was Michael Bakunin. Ironically enough Bakunin, who was living in exile from Russia, lost control of the first, international to Karl Marx, who did not share Bakunin's an other anarchists contempt for organization and discipline.

In tracing the development of Bakunin's revolutionary thought, Draper (1978) observes that he was heavily influenced by Pirre Joseph Prudhon recognized among historians as the "father of anarchism".

Anarchism is a product of revolt against oppression and is seen more as a natural reaction than as an ideological conviction. The target against which anarchists direct their attacks is the state itself, or some group or object that symbolizes state authority. Bakunin believed that the state will always be an instrument of the capitalist ruling class for domination and exploitation. A recurrent theme throughout Bakunin's doctrine of anarchism is the nation of 'Pan-destruction'.[49]

Peter Kropotkin

The most eminent anarchist after Bakunin was Prince Peter Kropotkin, a revolutionist. During the course of his wanderings throughout the world, Kropotkin aligned himself with a secret revolutionary committee, which led to his imprisonment when its existence was discovered. Kropotkin is credited with having maintained that the perfection of the human condition was impeded by the inertia of those who have a vested interest in existing conditions.

Although contemporary acts of terrorism occur within a wide range of contexts, anarchist violence at the turn of the century was principally confined to bombings and assassinations one of the first major anarchist bombings was a domestic incident that occurred in May of 1885, during the Haymarket Square riot in Chicago.[50]

The riot started as a strikers meeting; during the course of the meeting, there was a clash between the strikers and strike breakers. Called in to quell the disturbance, the police fired in to the crowd, killing two people. The next day August Spies, editor of Chicago's German Language anarchist newspaper, *Arbeiter Zeitung* called a protest meeting in Haymarket Square. The police responded to disperse the crowd, and a bomb of unknown origin was thrown. The eight men who participated in the bombing were sentenced to death. Three later had their sentence commuted to prison terms, one committed suicide on the eve of his execution, and the remaining four, including August Spies, were hanged on November 11, 1887.

- At the Opera House in Barcelona, Spain on November 8, 1893, during a performance of William Tell,[51] the theme of which deals with revolt against tyranny two bombs were tossed over the balcony in to the crowd. Twenty-two people were killed and fifty injured. In January of the following year, a man named Santiago Salvador claimed responsibility for the bombing and was arrested and subsequently executed. Another bombing immediately followed Salvador's arrest, for which his fellow anarchists of Barcelona took credit. This pattern follows the contemporary cycle of action reaction (Shaw, Hazelwood, Hayes and Harries, 1977) in which terrorists and government engage in a series of exchange in a series of exchange of force, each seeking to emerge the victor in the struggle for public support.

- One of the most notorious bombing incidents occurred in March, 1893, when August Valliant detonated a homemade explosive device in the French Parliament's Chamber des deputes in Paris Valliant hurled his bomb on to the debate floor from his seat in the public gallery.[52] Fortunately, although several people were injured, the explosive charge was non-lethal. Valliant's motivation was simply to end his life so that he would not have to see his family suffer in a society ruled by a government

> that was rife with scandal and corruption. During his trial, Valliant stated that if he had really wanted to kill, he would have used a heavier explosive charge and bullets instead of nails. Nevertheless, he was given the death penalty. This incident was the first time in the nineteenth century that anyone was sentenced to capital punishment for a crime that did not result in the death of a victim.

A number of anarchist inspired assassination occurred in Europe during this period. The first and most important was the assassination of President Sadi Carnot of France who was fatally stabbed by an Italian named Santo Caserio on June 24, 1894. Caserio was Italian born; and after aligning himself with anarchist factions in Milan, a center of anarchist activity, he eventually emigrated to France, where he befriended a group of anarchists who called themselves "Les Coeurs de Chene" (Hearts of Oak) Caserio was angered by Carnot's refusal to pardon Valliant for his bombing of the chambre des Deputes. When Caserio learned that Carnot would be arriving in Lyons shortly, he made arrangements to be in that city during Carnot's visit. While riding in an open carriage through the crowds that had assembled for the exhibition, Carnot was approached by a man holding a rolled up newspaper, which the guards assumed contained flowers. Concealed in the newspaper was the knife that Caserio used in fatal stabbing. Obsessed with anarchist philosophy, Caserio described the assassination as "Propaganda of the deed".

There followed the assassination of premier Antonio Canovas del Castillo of Spain in 1897; Empress Elizabeth of Austria in 1898; King Umberto of Italy in 1900; President of McKinley of the United States in 1901; and Premier Jose Canejas of Spain in 1912, all at the hands of avowed anarchists. There is an interesting link between the assassination of King Umberto and of President McKinley. The American newspaper accounts of Umberto's murder were read avidly by a twenty year old Polish American Leon Czolgosz. After having been laid off during a strike, Czolgosz aligned himself with a group of workers dedicated to socialism, anarchism and political radicalism. Among the topics discussed in their meetings was "Presidents and that they were no good". In 1898, Czolgosz contract an illness that left him depressed. On September 6, 1901, at the Pan American Exposition in Buffalo, New York, he passed through the receiving line in front of McKinley and shot the President with a gun concealed in a handkerchief wrapped around his hand. In his confession, Czolgosz stated: "I killed President McKinley because I did my duty, because he was enemy of the good working people".[53] He also indicated that he had been inspired by a lecture given by anarchist leader Emma Goldman, whose central theme was that "all rulers should be exterminated". Czolgosz went on to say that "I don't believe we should have any rulers. It is right to kills them" (Tuchman, 1966, 106).[54]

The assassination of McKinley marked the end of anarchist political murder in the western democracies. Anarchism survived as a moment in Russia until World War I, and in Spain until the beginning of World War II, but the force of anarchist passion flowed into the more realistic combat of the syndicates or trade unions. Anarchists achieved their greatest success in the U.S. with the founding of the International workers of the world (World War I) in 1905. Labour unions were seen as the cutting edge of revolutionary struggle and the chief instrument for bringing about a stateless industrial society. As its energy passed in to syndicalism anarchism added its qualities of violence and extremism to the struggle for power of organized labour.

The 20th century witnessed great changes in the use and practice of terrorism. Terrorism became the hallmark of a number of political movements stretching from the extreme right to the extreme left of the political spectrum. Technological advances such as automatic weapons and compact, electrically detonated explosives gave terrorists a new mobility and lethality.

Terrorism was adopted as virtually a state policy, though an unacknowledged one, by such totalitarian regimes as those of Nazi Germany under Adolf Hitler and the Soviet Union under Joseph Stalin. The terror, which overtook the Jews under Nazi Germany and Stalin's Russia, was the worst example of state terror in the history of modern world. The total count of mass murder will never be known. When Mao got in to power in China on October 1, 1949 he made use of terror on a bigger scale than Stalin.[55]

Origin of Terrorism in India

In a mighty country like India terrorism has had its faint beginnings only in the 20th century as we see it today. Internal terrorism or International terrorism had its openings in India in the assassination of two Prime Ministers of India—Indira Gandhi and Rajiv Gandhi. Historically speaking the Sungan Coup de'tat of overthrowing the Mauryas staged by Pushyamitra Sunga appears to be the first act of terrorism in ancient India.[56]

Murder diplomacy was the order of medieval Indian history as well. The planned murder of Jalaluddin Khalji the Sultan of Delhi by his nephew Alauddin Khalji (1296 A.D). Medievalism in India is marked by military might and as such brother, sister, uncles, father, sons etc. were brutally murdered for the security of the throne.[57] Might proved right in those days. These were all acts of terrorism of the old type.

Today, the terrorists around the world are operating on international linkages based on nationality, religion, race or political ideology. They are financed, trained, equipped and inspired by agencies outside the countries of their operation. As a result of international collaboration, the incidence of terrorism has grown alarmingly in recent years.

Terrorism is a disturbing phenomenon. We must understand that terrorism is now international and has no regard for international frontiers. The real sponsors of international terrorism are economically sound powers who have concealed objective. The groups may belong to one country, be financed by a second, trained in a third, may have equipment from a fourth and may operate in a fifth.

A Brief Historical Chronology of Terrorism: Some Important Dates

Date or Time Period	*Description*	*Type of Terrorism*
200 B.C.E	Imperial Rome uses destruction (Punitive war) to control populations and state it has conquered. There is brutalization of populations, servitude and tortue in the name of bringing order to the empire.	**State sponsored terrorism under guise of war**
63-72 C.E	Radical Jewish assassins (Sicarri in Latin) called zealots, known for their fervent commitment to the Torch, kill Roman soldiers and suspected Jewish Collaborates in an attempt to drive Rome from ancient Palestine.	**Liberation Terrorism**
1000-1200	A group called assassins emerges among Shiite muslims; they murder Muslim leaders whom they accuse of responsibility for corrupting Islam; the assassins resent the passing of Islamic leadership from Mohammad's family to others.	**Terroristic assassinations**
1789-1799	The **French Revolution** (1789-99) brings maxim lien de Robespierre (1758-1794) to power as an enemy of the French monarchy and an advocate of democratic reforms. He urges the guillotine execution of king Louis XVI and later eliminates members of both moderate and extremist political factions, instituting a "Reign of Terror". He is subsequently overthrown his position as president of the national convention; he & 99 of his supporters are beheaded by the very instrument with which he terrorized the people of France	**State-sponsored terrorism**
1879-??	An ideological group in Russia called **Narodnaya Volya** (The people's will) is formed to bring about revolution and the downfall of the Czarist official and others in their efforts.	**The beginning of modern terrorism**
Sept. 6, 1901	President **McKinley** is shot in Buffalo New York, by Leon Czolgosz,	**Anarchy terrorism**

	an anarchist. Mc Kinely dies from the wounds on Sept. 14, 1901.	
June 28, 1914	Serbian nationalist, belonging to a group known as the Serbian Black Hand Society, led by Gaurilo Princip, assassinate Francis Ferdinand, Archduke of Austria and his wife in Sarajevo Bosina. The assassination invites World War I.	**Political terrorism**
Sept. 1-3, 1923	In the wake of the great Tokyo-Yokohama earthquake, Emperor Hirohito of Japan Commands his special private organization (The Black Dragon Society) to round up 4,000 Koreans and behead them. The Koreans are blamed for the earthquake. Hirohito also uses the occasion to murder some political critics. The black dragon society was founded in the 1890s by Mitsuru Toyama as a criminal terrorist organisation. It has been succeeded in modern times by Yakuza.	**State-sponsored terrorism under the guise of protecting national security; Criminal & political terrorism**
1936-1945	Nazi Germany begins the eradication of all Jews through mass executions at various concentration camps. More than 6 million Jews are killed in what has come to be known as the Holocaust.	**Genocidal Terrorism**
Dec. 21, 1988	Pan Am Flight 103 is destroyed by a bomb over lockerbie, Scotland, killing 259 people in the air and 11 on the ground; a libyan terrorist is convicted of the crime.	**Modern day State Sponsored international terrorism**
Feb. 26, 1993	The World Trade Center is damaged from a car bomb planted in its underground garage by Islamic terrorists who are follower of Omar Abd al-Rahman. Six people die and more than 1,000 people are injured.	**International Sub-state terrorism**
March 20, 1995	The religious and political cult, Aum Shinri Kyo (Supreme Truth), under the leadership of Shoko Asahara, attempts to poison the Tokyo Subway passengers using Sarin gas; 12 die and 5,500 are injured.	**Religious extremist terrorism**
Sept. 11, 2001	Civilian airplanes are flown in to the World Trade Center (WTC) and the Pentagon in an attack attributed to al-Qaeda; almost 3,000 people were killed.	**International Sub-State Terrorism**

Though it is rarely taught in this way, the perspective of history can turn massacres in to heroic victories and murderers in to martyrs. The perspective of history also numbs our immediate horror at actions, turning them into stories almost too ancient to seem real. Sometimes the judgment of history take a long time to change our perceptions; few would deny that many of the actions of the French revolutionaries were clearly brutal but perhaps even fewer would denounce them, now as terrorism. From a historical perspective, the overthrow of the ancient regimes seems almost inevitable and reasonable. At other times history is much quicker, as in the case of the French resistance in the World War II, whose status was quickly changed from that given them by the vichey government, although their methods were in some senses terrorist. In the present era, terrorism is a diffused concept as it has ever been and prefixes frequently get attached.

Faced with this national security threat the world has to be a member of collective coalition against terrorism, realistically in such broad coalition it is not possible to expect that any country can counter it individually.

Its Impact on Peace and Security

Terrorism has become a widespread phenomenon in most of the contemporary political system of world. It poses a challenge not only to the state power but also to the national security. There is hardly a day passes when a dozen or more innocent persons do not fall to the bullets of terrorists, women are raped, children starved, the elderly freezed to death and human being kidnapped and made hostage and property—public or private—destroyed or looted.

REFERENCES

1. Lt. General (Retd.) Satish Nambiar, *National Security, New Approach 2001*, Sekhar Basu Publication, Kolkata, 2001, p. 37.

2. Jasjeet Singh, *Strategic Analysis*; Nov. 1987, p. 886, IDSA

3. General (Retd.) V.P. Malik, *National Security, New approach 2001*, Sekhar Basu Roy Publication, Kolkaka. p. 38.

4. Cited in *Strategic Analysis*, November 1987, Vol. XI, No. 8, p. 885.

5. Bary Buzan, *People state & fear : The National Security Problem in International Relation*. The University of Carolina Press, Chapel Hill, 1983, p. 43.

6. *Strategic Digest*, Volume 35, No. 1, January 2005; IDSA. p. 16.

7. Gen (Retd.) K. V. Krishna Roy; *National Security, New Approach* 2001; Sekhar Basu Roy Publication, Kolkata, p. 38.

8. K. Subrahmanyam; *National Security New Approach*, 2001, Sekhar Basu Roy Publication Kolkata, p. 38.

9. Brig. G.B. Reddy; *Nation is Crisis Dimensions of National Security & Terrorism*, Volume 1; AuthorsPress Publication, New Delhi, 2001, p. 455.

10. Brig G.B. Reddy, *op.cit.*, p. 464.

11. Gus Martin, *The Nature of the Best: Defining Terrorism; Understanding Terrorism*; Sage Publication London; Year 2003; p. 29.

12. *Ibid.*

13. Gus Martin; *Terrorism A Conceptual Review*; *Understanding Terrorism Challenges, Perspective & Issues*; Sage Publication London, 2003; p. 6.

14. J Margolin; ed. Yonah Alexander & Seymour Maxwell Finger; "*Psychological Perspective in Terrorism; Interdisciplinary Perspective*; John Jay Press, New York; 1977, p. 5.

15. Joseph S. Tuman, *Communicating Terror the Rhetorical Dimensions of Terrorism*; San Francisco State University Sage Publications, London; 2003, p. 2.

16. David J. Whittaker, *Terrorism Understanding the Global Threat*; Longman Publishers, Great Britain; 2002, p. 14.

17. Edmund Burke, *Reflection on the Revolution in France*; (ed. CCO Brien, 1790); London; Penguin Books, 1969.

18. Joseph S. Tuman, *Communicating Terror the Rhetorical Dimensions of Terrorism*; San Francisco State University; Sage Publication, New York; 2003; p. 3.

19. B.P. Singh Sehgal, *Global Terrorism : Socio Politico and Legal Dimensions*; Deep & Deep Publication, New Delhi; 1995; pp. 329-330.
20. Cited in Burton M. Leiser. "Terrorism, Guerrilla Warfare and International Morality", *Stanford Journal of International Studies*, Vol. 12 Spring 1977, p. 39.
21. Joseph S. Tuman, *Communicating Terror the Rhetorical Dimensions of Terrorism*; San Francisco State University; Sage Publications London; 2003; p. 5.
22. Walter Laqueur, *The Age of Terrorism*; 2nd ed. Bosten; Little, Brown; 1987; p. 143 (Walter Laqueur who invested his life time research effort in exploring this phenomenon expressed now difficult it is to define it).
23. R. C. Mishra, *Terrorism Implications of Tactics and Technology*; Authorspress, New Delhi; 2004, p. 24.
24. *Ibid.*
25. R. C. Mishra, *Terrorism Implications of Tactics and Technology*; Authorspress, New Delhi; 2004, p. 24.
26. *Ibid*, pp. 25-26.
27. *Ibid.*
28. David J. Whittaker; *Terrorism Understanding the Global Threat*; Publication Longman Publishers Great Britain, 2002, p. 22.
29. Brig G. B. Reddy; *Nation in Crisis Dimensions of National Security and Terrorism*; Authorspress Publication; 2001, p. 472.
30. *Ibid.*
31. Joseph S. Tuman; *Communicating Terror the Rhetorical Dimensions of Terrorism*; San Francisco State University Sage Publications London; 2003; p. 13.
32. David J. Whittaker; *The Terrorism Reader*; Routledge Taylor & Francis Group, New York; 2001, p. 3.
33. *Ibid.*
34. Jeanne J. Kirkpatrick, "Defining Terrorism", *Catholicism in Crisis*; September 1984; Washington D.C. 25 June; p. 56.

35. Stephen Sloan, *Beating International Terrorism An Action Strategy for Preemption & Punishment*; Air University Press Maxwell Air Force Base, Alabama: Dec. 1986; p. 3.

36. Anatony of fear "Essay on India's Internal Security" (ed.) Purusottam Bhattacharya, Tridib Chakraborti Shibashis Chatterjee; Lance's Books Pub; 2004; p. 4

37. S. K. Ghosh, *Terrorism: World Under Siege*, Ashish Publishing House, New Delhi, 1995; p. 4

38. AAKROSH; Oct. 04 Vol. 7, Number 25; Forum for Strategic and Security Studies; *Insurgency in India*; Anil Kumar Singh; p. 52.

39. Terrorism as a Strategy of Insurgency; *Terrorism & Political Violence*; Vol 5, No 4 (Winter 1993); pp. 213-25, Frank Cass, London.

40. Harold J. Vetter, Gary R. Perlstein (Administration of Justice Department Portland State University); *Perspectives on Terrorism*; Brooke/Cole Publishing Company Pacific Grove, California; 1991; p. 29

41. *Ibid.*

42. It can certainly be doubted whether this group was actually a terrorist organization or simply a group of violent.

43. Harold J. Vetter, Gary R. Perlstein (Administration of Justice Department Portland State University); *Perspective on Terrorism*, Cole Publishing Company, Pacific Grove, California; 1991, p. 30.

44. David J. Whittaker, *Terrorism Understanding the Global Threat*; Longman Publishers, Great Britain, 2002. pp. 13-14.

45. Clive Williams,*Terrorism Explained the Facts about Terrorism and Terrorist Groups*; New Holland Publishers, Australia, 2004, p. 7.

46. *Ibid.*, p. 8.

47. Clive Williams; *op. cit.*, p. 16.

48. Harold J. Vetter, Gary R. Perlstein; *Perspective on Terrorism*; Brooke Cole Publishing Company, Pacific Grove, California, 1991, p. 32.

49. Harold J. Vetter, Gary R. Perlstein, *op. cit.*, p. 33
50. *Ibid*, p. 34.
51. *Ibid.*
52. *Ibid.*
53. *Ibid.*
54. *Ibid.*
55. S. K. Ghosh, *Terrorism: World Under Siege,* Ashish Publishing House, New Delhi, 1995, p. 7.
56. Romila Thapar, *Ancient India,* Pelican Publication, Delhi, 1973, p. 27.
57. G. Gopa Kumar, *International Terrorism & Global Order in the 21st Century,* Kanishka Publication & Distributors, New Delhi, 2003, p. 18.

2

Various Terrorist Organizations Operating in the World and Their Nature of Working

Terrorism has grown threateningly over centuries to infect human life in form and peace. This masquerader projection is being channeled as a legitimate revolutionary weapon in some societies. In such, men to achieve their selfish, political and religious gains, propagate violence by means of bullets and bombs to impose their negotiations. Modern terrorist, with their unique attributes, interest and methods can be segregated in to various terror propelling organization. While studying terrorism, the precise classification is vital to understand the characteristic sources and causes of terrorism in more details. Further enabling the search for efficient means to successfully implement counter terrorist operations.

Here we categorize terrorism on criteria basis of sources and originators, extent causes, attack targets and prospects.

Types of Terrorism

1. According to the originators or participants terrorism can be classified as:

(a) *State Terrorism*

Which means open or hidden application of terrorist methods by state power against its domestic and foreign opponents. The targets of such terror might be ethnical minorities, religious groups, dissidents etc. The aim of state terrorism is to terrorize the people to enforce their obedience to the regime and strength its authority over them. State terrorism can strike state institutions directly or the individuals.[1] State terrorism has been used in by many regimes in many countries to exercise colonial, racial and apartheid policies. State terrorism also includes government support by sponsoring terrorist groups, which act in conjunction with government policy.

(b) *Non-State Terrorism*

Which means the use of violence by extremist organizations sponsored usually from non-governmental and sometimes from politically motivated sources. It is the use of "inappropriate" methods, pressure and threats by various illegal secret group or legally existing extra-governmental organization going beyond the limits of legal activity and putting the governmental authorities under undue pressure.[2]

2. According to the extents of terrorist activity, terrorism can be distinguished as:

(a) *International Terrorism or State-sponsored Terrorism*

International or state-sponsored terrorism is an act of terrorism that has clear international consequences and includes incidents in which terrorists indulge in terror and violence by going abroad to strike their targets[3] in other words it includes international components, such as attacks carried out on the territory of another country, support of other governments by the terrorist group, attacks against the citizens of another country.

(b) *Intrastate Terrorism*

Affecting only internal affairs of a particular country, on the territory of which the terrorist attacks take place. It might be, for example, a consequence of a conflict between two political parties or interest or nationalist groups. Its consequences do not go beyond the border of that particular country, but sometimes the conflict might escalate.

3. According to the cause of terrorism and its spread the following types of terrorism exist.

(a) *Political Terrorism*

Which is caused by fierce political fight, usually between extremist political parties, with the aim to gain or maintain power in the country.[4] Terrorist actions have the aim to physically destroy the political opponents, to discriminate them, criminalise them or to terminate their legal existence.

(b) *Ideological Terrorism*

Which is caused by the conflicts between different ideologies (either religious or civilisations), with the aim to gain or maintain influential position within the target territory. Recently, religious terrorism has been very strong, which was however; often intentionally interpreted as nationalist or political terrorism.[5] Terrorist actions have the aim to physically destroy the political opponents, to discriminate them, criminalize them. It ranks among the most resistant types of terrorism.

(c) *Social Terrorism*

Which is usually the privilege of terrorist organization from the far left or far right on the political spectrum. It might be based on various philosophical concept and perspectives. Its existence is stimulated by bad economic situation resulting in to social tension.

(d) *Criminal Terrorism*

They usually pursuing criminal objectives (gaining of money, property, materials of any kind, information, etc) but its consequences may reach into political area. This type of terrorism includes drug terrorism. Political terrorist resort to criminal terrorist acts in order to raise funds and procure arms.[6]

(e) *Nationalist Terrorism*

Which is caused by conflicts between different races,

nationalities, ethnic groups or as a demonstration of intolerance against another nationality or race. It takes the form of verbal and physical attacks, restriction of free movement, destruction of property or extermination of members of other nationalities or races. Its existence is often related to bad economic situation and big difference between different ethnics and nationalities. It may have political, ideological or purely separatist goals and very deep historical roots.

(f) *Psychopathological terrorism*[7]

The originators are psychologically disturbed individual with sadistic inclination or religious fanatics. Recently, the world witnessed several cases, when extremist religious sects or groups indicated all or some of their members to collective suicide. The motives were fanatic religious conviction and efforts to take possession of the property of the sect members, who bequeathed it to the sect before the suicide. Another group in this category may consist of mentally disturbed persons, which were simply used or misused to carry out the terrorist attack. To this category we may well add persons, the mind of whom was manipulated deliberately by various means, combining psychiatric methods, administration of narcotics and etc. Such mentally disturbed, dependent and easy-to-manipulate persons are used by the terrorists for assassinations or suicide attacks.

All types of terrorism mentioned above are not disjunctive. Terrorist activities have usually a combined form exhibiting the features of different types of terrorism.

The national and international dimensions of terrorism are two sides of the same coin. Terrorism knows no borders or barriers; it usually spills over from one country to another set. Terrorism is a dangerous phenomenon not only because of the immediate spillover effects from one country to another but also because the states, in combating terrorism, take measures which adversely affect human right and fundamental freedoms.

Various Types of Organizations Operating in the World

Our contemporary world continues to be infected with a parasital growth of many terrorist organizations. It is not easy to compile a list of those (force of evil), which terrorize us most since the tally worldwide never stays static. There are highly feared organizations with dynamic leaders propitiating consistently dreaded strategies. Many of these have been thriving for years and the counter-terrorist institutions have well recorded information on them. There are some organizations with ever changing reigns of leadership strength, motives, and political action. Their goals and intentions may be difficult to comprehend. But it is possible to select and briefly survey some of the threatening better-known terrorist groups out of the fifty-sixty notorious lot swarming our world globally. A strategic way of doing this would be highlight the groups within the operating countries in various continents.

The following list is far from comprehensive but it does show 21st centuries terrorism as both technically diverse and far-flung.

The following list elucidates the organizational names and national affiliation or locales.

Organizations	*National affiliation (or locales)*
1. Abu Nidal Organization (ANO)	Lebanon
2. Abu Sayyaf Group (ASG)	Philippines
3. Al-Gama'a al-Islamiyya (The Islamic Group, IG)	Egypt
4. African National Congress	Africa
5. Al-Fatah	Lebanon
6. Al-Ittihad al-Islami (AIAI)	Kenya
7. Al-Jehad (AJ)	Cairo

8. Allied Democratic Forces (ADF)	Uganda
9. Al-Qaeda (The Base)	Afghanistan
10. Ansar al-Islam (Al)	Iraq
11. Armed Islamic Group (GIA)	Algeri
12. Asbat al Ansar	Lebanon
13. Basque Fatherland and Liberly (ETA)	Spain
14. Chukaku-Ha (Nucleus or Middle Corefaction)	Japan
15. Democratic Forces for the Liberation of Rawanda (FDLR)	Congo
16. Democratic front for the Liberation of Palestine (DFLP)	Palestine
17. Gama'a al-Islamiyya (IG)	Europe
18. HAMAS	Palestine
19. Harakat ul-Jihad-l-Islami (HuJi)	Afghanistan
20. Harakat ul-Ansar	Pakistan
21. Harakat ul-Mujahidin (HUM)	Pakistan
22. Hizballah (Party of God)	Lebanon
23. Hizbul-Mujahedin (HM)	Pakistan
24. Irish Republican Army	Northern
25. Islamic Jihad Group (IJG)	Ireland
26. Jamaat ul-Fuqra	Central Asia,
27. Japanese Red Army (JRA)	North America
28. Jaish-e-Mohammed (JEM)	Pakistan
29. Kach and Kahane Chai	Asia

30. Kurdistan Worker's Party (PKK)	Pakistan
31. Lashkar e-Tayyiba (LT)	Pakistan
32. Lashkar i Jhangvi (LJ)	Turkey
33. Liberation Tigers of Tamil Eelam (LTTE)	Sri Lanka
34. Libyan Islamic Fighting Group (LIFG)	Karachi
35. Lord's Resistance Army (LRA)	Uganda
36. Manuel Rodriquez Patriotic Front (FPMR)	Libya
37. Morazanist Patriotic Front (FPM)	Sudan
38. Mujahedin-e khalq organization (MEK)	Chile
39. National Liberation Army (ELN)	Honduras/Iran
40. New Red Brigades/Communist Combatant Party (BR/PCC)	Colombia/ Italy
41. Palestine Liberation Front (PLF)	Lebanon
42. Palestine Liberation Organization (PLO)	Middle East
43. People's Liberation Army (EPL)	Colombia
44. Popular Front for the Liberation of Palestine (PFLP)	Palestine
45. Popular Struggle Front (PSF)	Syria
46. Real IRA (RIRA)	Northern Ireland
47. Red Brigades (BR)	Italy/ Colombia
48. Revolutionary Armed Forces of Colombia (FARC)	Greece
49. Revolutionary organization 17 November	Turkey
50. Revolutionary people's liberation front (DHCF)	Turkey

51. Revolutionary People's Struggle (ELA)	Greece
52. Shining Path (SL)	Peru
53. Sikh Terrorism	Northern India
54. Sipah-i-Sahaba/ Pakistan (SSP)	Pakistan
55. Tanzim Qa'idat al-jihad fi Bilad al-Rafidayn (QJBR)	Iraq
56. Tunisian Combatant Group (TCG)	Afghanistan
57. Turkish Hizballah	Turkey
58. Ulster Freedom Fighters (UFF)	Northern Ireland
59. United Liberation Front of Assam (ULFA)	India
60. Zviadists	Russia.[8]

From the above noted list of terrorist organization, some of the prominent organizations are being explained continental wise in detail as under.

1. Africa
2. Asia
3. Europe
4. Middle East
5. South America

AFRICAN TERRORIST ORGANIZATIONS

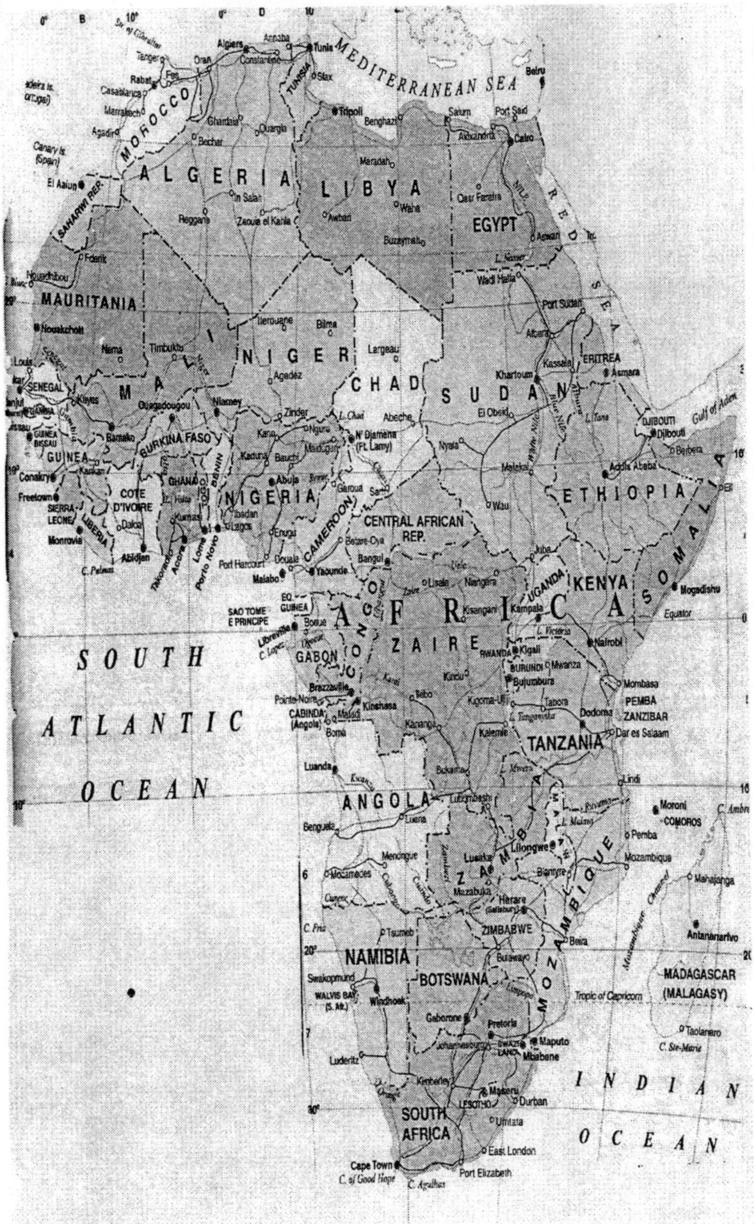

S.No.	Location	Name	Other Name	Leaders	Classification
1	Somalia, Ethiopia	Al-Ittihad al-Islami (AIAI)	Islamic Union; Islamic Unity	Aweys; Sheikh Hassan Dahir	Religious
2	Western Uganda and Congo	Allied Democratic Force (ADF)	Unknown	Unknown	Religious
3	Algeria, Mali, Mauritania, Niger	Armed Islamic Group (GIA)	Al-Jama'ah; al-islamiyh; al Musallah.	Abdullah Ahmed Abu; Ahmed, Mourad Sid; Zitouni Djamel Zouabri, Antar	Religious
4	Congo	Democratic Forces for the liberation of Rawanda (FDLR)	Former Armed Forces (Ex-FAR), Army for the liberation of Rawanda; Interahamwe	Unknown	Unknown
5	Southern Egypt	Al Gama'a al-Islamiyya (GAI)	Islamic Group; Jamaatal-Islamiyya	Abdel Rehman Hamdi; Ahmed, Rifai; Ibrahim Nageh; el-zomor, Aboud	Religious
6	Libya	Libyan Islamic Fighting Group (LIFG)	Al-Jama'a al-Islamiya al Muqatilah bi-Libya, Libyan Islamic Group; Fighting Islamic Group.	Rashed, Omar Sebai, Anas	Religious
7	Northern Uganda; Southern Sudan	Lord's Resistance Army (LRA)	Unknown	Koney, Joseph; Odhiamdo okot; Ongwen Deminic; Otti Vincent	Religious

PROFILES OF INTERNATIONAL AFRICAN TERRORIST GROUPS

1. Al-Ittihad al-Islami (AIAI)

Other Name: Islamic Union, Islamic Unity

Classification: Religious

Description

AIAI rose to prominence in the Horn of Africa in the early 1990's, following the downfall of the Siad Barre regime and the subsequent collapse of the Somali nation state in to anarchy. AIAI was not internally cohesive and suffered divisions between factions supporting moderate Islam and more puritanical Islamic ideology. Following military defeats in 1996 and 1997, AIAI evolved into a loose network of highly compartmentalized cells, factions and individuals with no central control or coordination. AIAI elements pursue a variety of agendas ranging from social services and education to insurgency activities in the Ogaden.[9] Some AIAI-associated Sheikhs espouse a radical fundamentalist version of Islam, with particular emphasis on a strict adherence to Sharia (Islamic Law), a view often at odds with Somali emphasis on clan identity. A small number of AIAI-associated individuals have provided logistical support to and maintain ties with al-Qaeda; however, the network's central focus remains the establishment of an Islamic government in Somalia.

Key Leader

Aweys, Sheikh Hassan Dahir - (No known aliases)

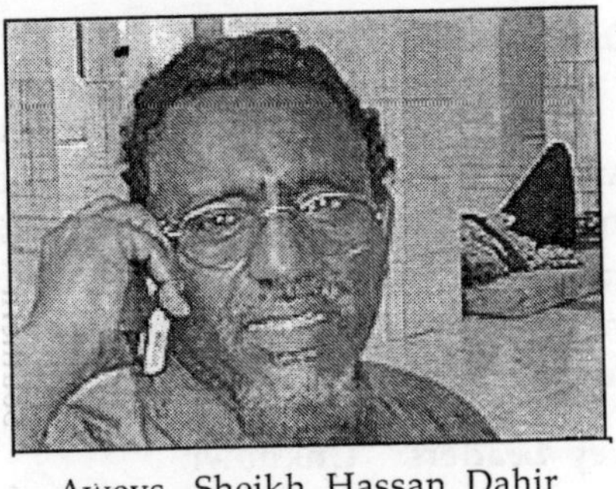

Aweys, Sheikh Hassan Dahir

Activities

Elements of AIAI may have been responsible for the

kidnapping and murder of relief workers in Somalia and Somaliland in 2003 and 2004, and during the late 1990s. Factions of AIAI may also have been responsible for a series of bomb attacks in public places in Addis Ababa in 1996 and 1997. Most AIAI factions have recently concentrated on broadening their religious base, renewed emphasis on building businesses, and undertaking "hearts and minds" actions, such as sponsoring orphanage and schools and providing security that uses an Islamic legal structure in the areas where it is active.[10]

Strength

The actual membership strength is unknown but has been estimated at 2000 plus reserve militians.

Location/Area of operation

Primarily in Somalia, with a presence in the Ogaden region of Ethiopia, Kenya and possibly Djibouti.

External Aid

Receives funds from Middle East financiers and Somali Diaspora communities in Europe, North America and the Arabian Peninsula. May maintain ties to al Qaeda. Past weapons deliveries from Sudan.

2. ALLIED DEMOCRATIC FORCES (ADF)

Other Name: Unknown

Classification: Unknown

Description

A diverse coalition of former members of the National Army for the Liberation of Uganda (NALU), Islamists from the Salaf Tabliq group, Hutu militiamen, and fighters from ousted regimes in Congo. The conglomeration of fighters formed in 1995 in opposition to the government of Uganda president Yoweri Museveni.[11]

Key Leaders: Unknown

Activities

The ADF seeks to use kidnapping and murder of civilians to create fear in the local population and undermine confidence in the Government. The group is suspected to be responsible for dozens of bombings in public areas. A Uganda military offensive in 2000 destroyed several ADF camps, but ADF attacks continued in Kampala in 2001.

Strength

A few hundred fighters.

Location/Area of operation

Western Uganda and Eastern Congo.

External Aid

Received past funding, supplies, and training from the government of Sudan. Some funding suspected from sympathetic Hutu groups.[12]

3. ARMED ISLAMIC GROUP (GIA)

(Designated as a Foreign Terrorist Organization.)

Other Name: Al-Jama'ah, al-Islamiyah, al Musallah.

Classification: Religious

Description

An Islamist extremist group the GIA aims to overthrow the Algerian regime and replace it with a fundamentalist Islamic state. The GIA began its violent activity in 1992 after the military government suspended legislative elections in anticipation of an overwhelming victory by the Islamic Salvation Front, the largest Islamic opposition party. First designated in October 1997.

Key Leaders

- Abdallah, Ahmed Abu (Aliases : Sherif Ghousmi)

- Ahmed, Mourad Sid (Aliases Djafaar al-Afghani)
- Oukali, Rachid (Aliases: Abou Tourab, Rachid Abou Tourab)
- Zitouni, Djamel, (Aliases Abou Abderrahmane Amine)
- Zouabri, Antar (Aliases Anter Zowabri)

Anter Zowabri

Activities

The GIA has engaged in attack against civilians and government workers. Starting in 1992, the GIA conducted a terrorist campaign a Civilian massacres, sometime wiping out entire villages in its area of operation, and killing tens of thousands of Algerians.[13] GIA's brutal attacks on civilians alienated them from the Algerian populace. Since announcing its campaign against foreigners living in Algeria in 1992, the GIA has killed more than 100 expatriate men and women, mostly Europeans, in the country. The group uses assassinations and bombings including car bombs, and it is known to favour kidnapping victims and slitting their throats. The GIA hijacked an Air France flight to Algiers in December 1994. In late 1999 a French court convicted several GIA members for conducting a series of bombing in France in 1995. In 2002, a French court sentenced two GIA members to life imprisonment for conducting a series of bombings in France in 1995. The GIA's most recent significant attacks were on August 31, 2001.

Strength

Precise numbers are unknown, but probably fewer than 100.

Location/Area of Operation

Algeria, Sahel (i.e. Northern Mali, Northern Mauritania, and Northern Niger), and Europe.

External Aid

Algerian expatriates, some of whom reside in Western Europe, provide some financial and logistic support. In addition, the Algerian Government has accused Iran and Sudan of supporting Algerian extremists.[14]

4. DEMOCRATIC FORCES FOR THE LIBERATION OF RWANDA (FDLR)

Other Name: Army for the Liberation of Rwanda (ALIR), Former Armed Forces (Ex-Far), Interahamwe.

Classification: Unknown

Description

The Democratic Forces for the Liberation of Rwanda (FDLR) in 2001 supplanted the Army for the Liberation of Rwanda (ALIR), which is the armed branch of the PALIR, or the Party for the Liberation of Rwanda. ALIR was formed from the merger of the Armed Forces of Rwanda (FAR), the army of the ethnic Hutu-dominated Rwanda regime that orchestrated the genocide of 5,00,000 or more Tutsis and regime opponents in 1994, and Interahamwe, the civilian militia force that carried out much of the killing, after the two groups were forced from Rwanda into the Democratic Republic of Congo (DRC-then Zaire) that year. Though directly descended from those who organized and carried out the genocide, identified FDLR leaders are not thought to have played a role in the killing.[15] They have worked to build bridges to other opponents of the Kigali regime, including ethnic Tutsis.

Key Leaders: Unknown

Activities

ALIR sought to topple Rwanda's Tutsi dominated Government, reinstitute Hutu domination, and, possibly, complete the genocide. In 1999, ALIR guerrillas critical of US-UK support for the Rwandan regime kidnapped and killed eight foreign tourists, including two U.S citizens, in a game park on the Democratic Republic of Congo-Uganda border. Three suspects in the attack are in US custody awaiting trial. It established the ADRN Igihango alliance in 2002, but it has not resonated politically in Rwanda.

Strength

Exact strength is unknown, but several thousand FDLR guerrillas operate in the eastern DRC close to the Rwandan border. In 2003, the United Nations, with Rwandan assistance, repatriated close to 1,500 FDLR combatants from the DRC.[16] The senior FDLR military commander returned to Rwanda in November 2003 and has been working with Kigali to encourage the return of his comrades.

Location/Area of operation

Mostly in the eastern Democratic Republic of the Congo.

External Aid

The Government of the Democratic Republic of the Congo provided training, arms and supplies to ALIR forces to combat Rwandan armed forces that invaded the DRC in 1998. Kinshasa halted that support from several local congolese warlords and militias (including the Mai Mai).

5. AL-GAMA'A AL-ISLAMIYYA (GAI)

(Designated as a foreign Terrorist Organization)

Other Name: Islamic Group, al-Gama'a al-Islamiya, Jamaat al-Islamiyya.

Classification: Religious

Description

The GAI, Egypt's largest militant group, has been active since the late 1970s and is a loosely organized network. It has an external wing with supporters in several countries. The group's issuance of a cease-fire in 1997 led to a split into two factions : One, led by Mustafa Hamza, supported the cease-fire, the other, led by Rifa'i Taha Musa, called for a return to armed operations. The IG issued another ceasefire in March 1999, but its spiritual leader, Shaykh Umar Abd al-Rahman, sentenced to life in prison in January 1996 for his involvement in the 1993 World Trade Center bombing[17] and incarcerated in the United States, rescinded his support for the cease-fire in June 2000. IG has not conducted an attack inside Egypt since the Luxor attack in 1997.[18] In February 1998, a senior member signed Osama Bin Laden's fatwa calling for attacks against the United States. In March 2002, members of the group's historic leadership in Egypt declared use of violence misguided and renounced its future use, prompting denunciations by much of the leadership abroad. IG members are still dedicated to violent jihad, their main or primary goal is to overthrow the Egyptian government and replace it with an Islamic State in Egypt. Since allying themselves with al Qaeda however, the faction likely has broader objectives, including attacks on the U.S.

Key Leaders

- Abdel-Rehman, Hamdi
- Ahmed, Rifa'i (Aliases: Abu-Yasir, Rifai Taha, Ahmed Taha)
- el-Dawalibi, Fouad (No known aliases)
- el-Zomor, Aboud (No known aliases)
- Ibrahim, Nageh (No known aliases)

Ahmed, Rifa'i

Activities

IG conducted armed attacks against Egyptian security and other government officials, and Egyptian opponents of Islamic extremism before the cease-fire. After the 1997 cease-fire, the faction led by Taha Musa launched attack on tourists in Egypt, most notably the attack in November 1997 at Luxor. IG also claimed responsibility for the attempt in June 1995 to assassinate Egyptain President Hosni Mubarak in Addis Ababa, Ethiopia.

Strength

Unknown. At its peak IG probably commanded several thousand hardcore members and a like number of sympathizers. The 1999 cease-fire, security crackdowns following the attack in Luxor in 1997 and, more recently, security efforts, following September 11 probably have resulted in a substantial decrease in the group's numbers.

Location/Area of operation

Operates mainly in the al-Minya, Asyut, Qina and Sohaj Governorates of Southern Egypt. Also appears to have support in Cairo, Alexandria and other urban locations, particularly among unemployed graduates and students. Has a worldwide presence, including in the United Kingdom, Afghanistan, Yemen and various locations in Europe.

External Aid

Unknown. There is some evidence that Osama bin Laden and Afghan militant groups support organization. IG also may obtain some funding through various Islamic non-governmental organization (NGOs).

6. LIBYAN ISLAMIC FIGHTING GROUP (LIFG)

(Designated As A Foreign Terrorist Organization)

Other Name: Al-Jama'a al-Islamiyyah al-Muquati Loh bi-Libya, Fighting Islamic Group, Libyan Fighting Group, Libyan Islamic Group.

Classification: Religious.

Description

The Libyan Islamic Fighting Group (LIFG) emerged in the early 1990s among Libyans who had fought against Soviet forces in Afghanistan and against the Qadhafi regime in Libya. The LIFG declared the Government of Libyan leader Muammar Qadhafi un-Islamic and pledged to overthrow it. Some members maintain a strictly anti-Qadhafi focus and organize against Libyan Government interests, but others are aligned with Osama Bin Laden and believed to be part of al-Qaeda's leadership structure or active in the international terrorist network.[19]

Key Leaders

- Rashed, Omar (No known aliases)
- Sebai, Anas (No known aliases).

Activities

Libyans associated with the LIFG are part of the border international jihadist movement. The LIFG is one of the group believed to have planned the Casablance suicide bombing in May 2003.[20] The LIFG claimed responsibility for a failed assassination attempt against Qadhafi in 1996 and engaged Libyan security forces in armed clashes during the 1990s. It continues to target Libyan interests and may engage in sporadic clashes with Libyan security forces.

Strength

Not known, but probably has several hundred active members or supporters.

Location/Area of Operation

Probably maintains a clandestine presence in Libya, but since the late 1990s many members have fled to various Asian, Persian Gulf, African, and European countries, particularly the United Kingdom.

External Aid

Not known. May obtain some funding through private

donations, various Islamic non-governmental organizations, and criminal acts.

7. LORD'S RESISTANCE ARMY (LRA)

Other Name: Unknown

Classification: Religious

Description

The LRA was formally established in 1992, succeeding the ethnic Acholi-dominated Holy spirit movement and other insurgent groups LRA leader Joseph Kony has called for the overthrow of the ugandan Government and its replacement with a regime run on the basis of the Ten Commandments. More frequently, however, he has spoken of the liberations and honor of the Acholi people, whom he sees as oppressed by the foreign government of Ugandan President Museveni. Kony is the LRA's undisputed leader. He claims to have supernatural powers and to receive messages from spirits, which he uses to formulate the LRA's strategy.[21]

Key Leaders

- Kony, Joseph (No known aliases)
- Lukwiya, Raska (No known aliases)
- Odhiambo, Okot (No known aliases)
- Ongwen, Dominic (No known aliases)
- Otti, Vincent (No known aliases).

Activities

The Acholi people, whom Kony claims to be fighting to liberate, are the ones who suffer most from his actions. Since the early 1990's, the LRA has kidnapped some 20,000 Ugandan children, mostly ethnic Acholi, to replenish its ranks. Kony despises Acholi elders for having given up the fight against Museveni and relies on abducted children who can be brutally indoctrinated to fight for the LRA. The LRA forces kidnapped children and adult civilians to become soldiers, porters, etc. for LRA leaders. The LRA prefers to attack camps for internally

Kony, Joseph

Ongwen, Dominic

displaced persons and other civilian targets, avoiding direct engagement with the ugandan military. Victims of LRA attacks sometimes have their hands, fingers, ears, noses or other extremities cut off. The LRA stepped up its activities from 2002 to 2004 after the Ugandan army, with the Sudanese government's permission, attacked LRA positions inside Sudan. By late 2003, the number of internally displaced had doubled to 1.4 million, and the LRA had pushed deep into non-Acholi areas where it had never previously operated.[22] During 2004, a combination of military pressure, offers of amnesty, and several rounds of negotiation markedly degraded LRA capabilities due to death, desertion, and defection of senior commanders.

Strength

Estimated in early 2004 at between 500 and 1,000 fighters, 85 percent of whom and abducted children and civilians, but numbers have since declined significantly.

Location/Area of Operation

Northern Uganda and Southern Sudan.

External Aid

Although the government of Sudan in the past has supported the LRA, the Sudanese now appear to be cooperating with the government of Uganda in a Campaign to eliminate LRA sanctuaries in Sudan.[23]

Asia's Terrorist Organizations

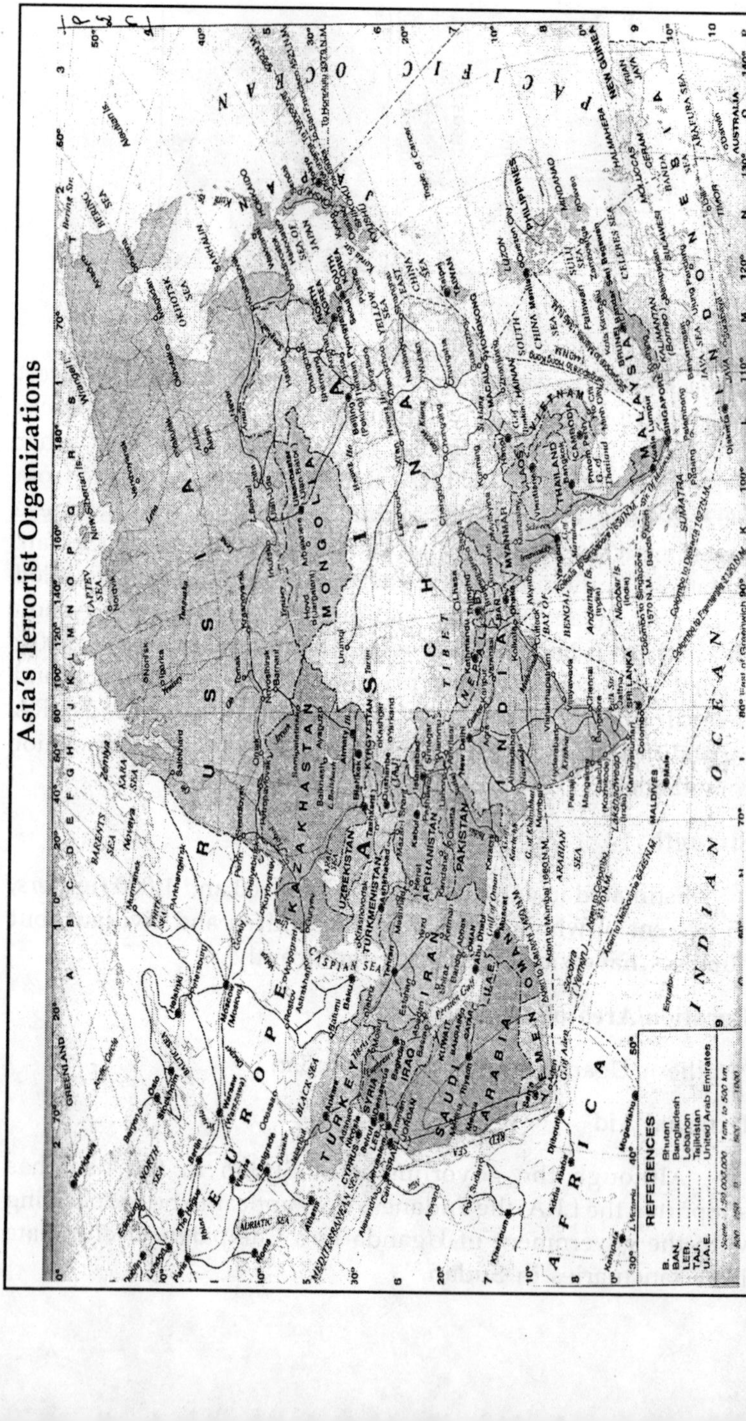

Asia's Terrorist Organizations

S.No.	Location	Name	Other Name	Leader's	Classification
1	Zamboanga Peninsula.	Abu Sayyaf Group (ASG)	Al Harakat Al-Islamiyyah; Bearer of the Sword.	Janjalani, Abdulrajik Abu-bakar; Abubakar Janjalani Khadaffy	Nationalist; Separatist, Religion.
2	Japan ; Russia	Aum Shinrikyo (AUM)	Aum Supreme Truth, Aleph	Asahara, Shoko; Hayashi IKUO; Ouchi, Toshiyaso.	Religious
3	Pakistan; Muzaffarabad, Rawalpindi, Kashmir; Afghanistan	Harakat ul-Mujahidin (HUM)	Harakat Ul-Ansar	Azhar, Maulana Masood; khalil Farooq Kashmiri; Khalil, Fazlur Rehman; Khalil, Maulana Saadatullah	Religious / Separatist Nationalist;
4	Eastern Afghanistan; Pakistan	Hizb-I Islamic Gulbuddin (HIG)	Unknown	Hikmatyar, Gulbuddin.	Religious
5	Pakistan; Jammu & Kashmir	Hizbul Mujahedin (HM)	HM of the Jamaat e-Islami	Dar, Abdul Majeed; Shah Ghulam Rasool; Shah Mohammed Yusuf.	Nationalist / Separatist
6	Central Asia; South Asia	Islamic Jihad Group (IJG)	(IJU) Islamic Jihad Union.	Unknown.	Religious / Separatist

(Contd...)

Asia's Terrorist Organization *(contd.)*

7	Pakistan; Religious Afghanistan	Jaish e-Mohammed (JEM)	Army of Mohammed Tehrik; Ul-Furquaan; Khuddamul Islam.	Azhar, Maulana Masood; Ahmed, Maulana Qari Mansoor Saeed, Sheikh Omar; Usman, Maulana Sajjad.	Nationalist/ Separatist
8	Indonesia ; Malaysia; Philippines	Jemaah Islamiya Organization (JI)	Islamic Community Islamic Group	Bashir, Abu Bakar; bin Husin, Azahari; Dujana, Abu	Religious
9	Muridke (near lahore) and Muzaffarabad	Lashkar e-Tayyiba (LT)	Lashkar-e-Toiba; al Mansooreen; Army of righteous ; Army of pure	Iqbal, Zafar; Kashmiri, Maulana Abdul Wahid; Saeed, Hafiz Mohammad Saifullah.	Religious, Nationalist/ Separatist
10	Punjab; Karachi; Pakistan and Afghanistan	Lashkar i Jhangvi (LJ)	Army of Jhangvi; Lashkar E Jhangvi (LEJ)	Ajmal Muhammad; Asif, Choto; Basra Riaz; Hai, Qari Abdul; Ishaque, Malik	Nationalist/ Separatist
11	Northern and Eastern Coastal area of Sri Lanka	Liberation Tigers of Tamil Eelam (LTTE)	The Tamil Tigers; The Ellalan Force; World Tamil Association (WTA); The Federation of Association of Canadian Tamil (FACT)	Kausalyan, E; Prabakharan, Vellupillai	Nationalist/ Separatist.
12	Pakistan	Sipah-i-Sahaba/Pakistan (SSP)	Unknown.	Unknown.	Unknown.

PROFILES OF INTERNATIONAL ASIAN TERRORIST GROUPS

1. ABU SAYYAF GROUP (ASG)

(Designated as a Foreign Terrorist Organization)

Other Name: At-Harakat Al-Islamiyyah, Bearer of the Sword.

Classification: Nationalist / Separatist, Religious.

Description

The ASG is primarily a small, violent Muslim terrorist group operating in the Southern Philippines. Some ASG leaders allegedlly fought in Afghanistan during the Soviet war are students and proponents of radical Islamic teachings.

The group split from the much larger Moro National Liberation Front in the early 1990s under the leadership of Abdurajak Abubakar Janjalani, who was killed in a clash with Philippine police in December 1998. His younger brother, Khadaffy Janjalani, replaced him as the nominal leader of the group and appears to have consolidated power.[24] First designated in October 1997.

Key Leaders

- Janjalani, Abdulrajik Abubakar
- Janjalani, Khadaffy Abubakar (Aliases: Abu Muktar; Khadafi Montanio.)

Janjalani, Khadaffy Abubakar

Activities

The ASG engages in kidnapping for ransom, bombings, beheadings, assassinations and extortion. The group's stated goal is to promote an independent Islamic state in Western Mindanao and the Sulu Archipelago (areas in Southern Phillipines heavily populated by Muslims) but the ASG has primarily used terror for financial profit. The group's first large scale action was a raid on the town of Ipil in Mindanao in April 1995.[25] In April 2000 an ASG faction kidnapped three U.S. persons, including 10 Western tourists from a resort in Malaysia. On May 27, 2001, the ASG kidnapped three US citizens and 17 Filipinos from a tourist resort in Palawan, Philippines. Several of the hostages, including US Citizen Guillermo Sobero, were murdered. During a Philippine military hostage rescue operation on June 7, 2002, US hostage Gracia Burnham was rescued, but her husband Martin Burnham and Filipina Deborah Yap were killed. Philippine authorities say that the ASG had a role in the bombing near a Philippine military base in Zamboanga in October 2002 that killed a US servicemen.[26] In February 2004, Khadaffy Janjalani's faction bombed Super Ferry 14 in Manila Bay, killing approximately 132 people.[27]

Strength

At least 1000 individuals motivated by the prospect of receiving ransom payment for foreign hostages had allegedly joined the group but membership now estimated at 200 to 500 fighters.

Location/Area of Operation

The ASG was founded in Basilan Province and operates there and in the neighbouring provinces of Sulu and Tawi Tawi in the Sulu Archipelogo. The group also operates on the Zamboanga peninsula, and members occasionally travel to Manila. In mid-2003, the group started operating in the major city of Cotobato and on the coast of Sultan Kudarat on Mindanao. The group expanded its operational reach to Malaysia in 2000 when it abducted foreigners from a tourist resort.

External Aid

Largely self-financing through ransom and extortion; has received support from Islamic extremists in the Middle East and may receive support from regional terrorist groups.

2. AUM SHINRIKYO (AUM)

(Designated as a Foreign Terrorist Organization)

Other Name: Aum Supreme Truth, Aleph.

Classification: Religious

Description

A cult established in 1987 by Shoko Asahara, the Aum aimed to take over Japan and then the world. Approved as a religious entity in 1989 under Japanese law, the group ran candidate in a Japanese parliamentary election in 1990. Overtime, the cult began to emphasize the imminence of the end of the world and stated that the united would initiate Armageddon by starting World War III with Japan.[28] The Japanese Government revoked its recognition of the Aum as a religious organization in October 1995, but in 1997 a government panel decided not to invoke the Anti-Subversive law against the group, which would have outlawed it. A 1999 law continues to give the Japanese Government authorization to maintain police surveillance of the group due to concerns that the Aum might launch future terrorist attacks. Under the leadership of Fumihiro Joyu, the Aum changed its name to Aleph in January 2000 and tried to distance itself from the violent and apocalyptic teachings of its founder.[29] However, in late 2003, Joyu stepped down, pressured by members who wanted to return fully to the worship of Asahara. First designated in October 1997.

Key Leaders

- Asahara, Shoko (Aliases: Chizuo Matsumoto)
- Hayashi, Ikuo (No known aliases)
- Lida, Eriko (No known aliases)
- Lida, Eriko (No known aliases)
- Ouchi, Toshiyaso (No known aliases)

Asahara, Shoko

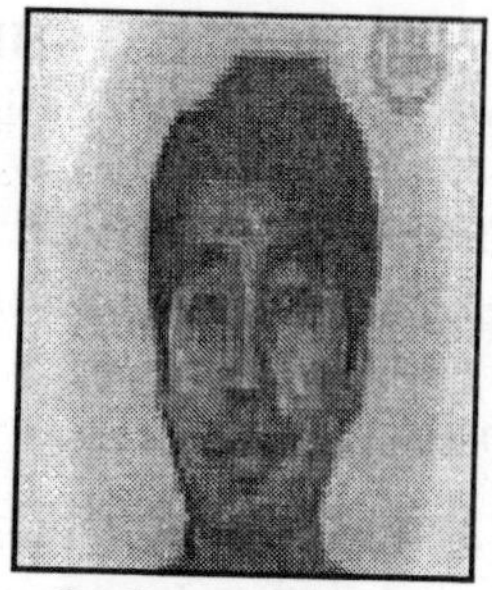

Ouchi, Toshiyaso

Activities

On March 20, 1995, Aum members simultaneously released the chemical nerve agent sarin on several Tokyo subway trains, killing 12 persons and injuring up to 1,500. The group was responsible for other mysterious events involving chemical indicents in Japan in 1994. Its efforts to conduct attacks using biological agents have been unsuccessful. Japanese police arrested Asahara in May 1995, and authorities sentenced him in February 2004 to death for his role in the attacks of 1995. Since 1997,

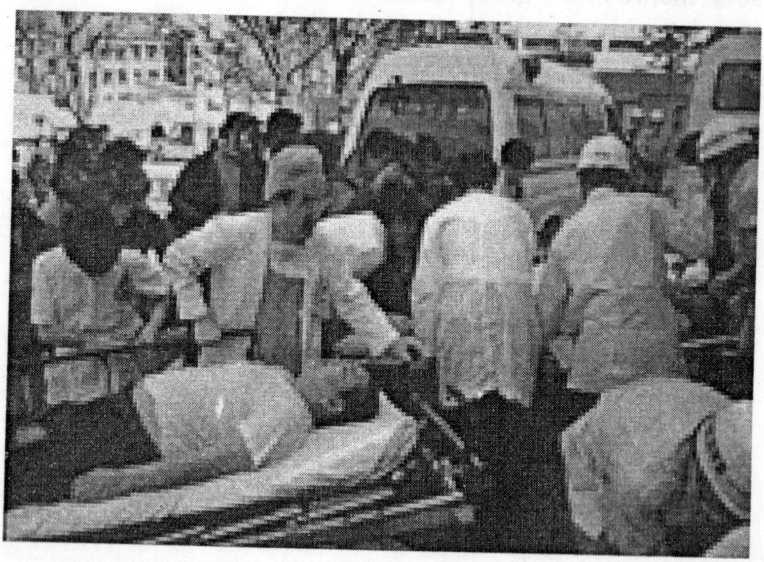

Victims of the Sarin Gas Attack

the cult has continued to recruit new members, engage in commercial enterprise, and acquire property, although it scaled back these activitise significantly in 2001 in response to public outcry. In July 2001, Russian authorities arrested a group Russian Aum followers who had planned to set off bombs near the Imperial Palace in Tokyo as part of an operation to free Asahara jail and smuggle him to Russia.[30]

Strength

The Aum's current membership in Japan is estimated to be about 1,650 persons. At the time of the Tokyo subway attack, the group claimed to have 9,000 members in Japan as many as 40,000 worldwide. [31]

Location/Area of Operation

The Aum's principal membership is located in Japan, but a residual branch comprising about 300 followers has surfaced in Russia.

External Aid: Unknown

3. HARAKAT UL-MUJAHIDIN (HUM)

(Designated as a Foreign Terrorist Organization)

Other Name: Harakat Ul-Ansar

Classification: Religious/Nationalist/Separatist.

Description

HUM is an Islamist militant group based in the Panjab district of Pakistan that operates primarily in Kashmir formed in 1985. It is politically aligned with the radical political party Jamiat Ulema-i-Islam's Fazlur Rehman faction (JUI-F). The long-time leader of the group, Fazlur Rehman Khalil, in mid-February 2000 stepped down as HUM emir, turning the reins over to the popular Kashmiri commander and his second-in-command, Farooqi Kashmiri.[32] It was believed to have close link with al-Qaeda and supported the position of Osama bin Laden in calling for attacks on western interests. Harakat Ul-Mujahidin is a radical Islamic Sunni Organization whose worldview is similar to that of the Taliban movement and the Pakistani Daavah Al-Irshad organization. This organization adopted the ascetic Islamic approaches of the Wahabian Stream and the Deoband School. A short time after its establishment, Harkat ul-Mujahidin began recruiting volunteers and sending them to the jihad in Afghanistan against the Soviet forces. In the framework of the American offensive in Afghanistan in 2001, facilities and camps of Harqwat ul-Mujahidin were also attacked due to its close links with Bin-Laden's organization.[33] The groups' main objective today is to continue the armed struggle against non-believer's and anti-Islamic forces.

Key Leaders

- Azhar, Maulana Masood (No known aliases)
- Khalil, Farooq Kashmiri.(Aliases: Farooq Kashmiri, Maulana Farooq Kashi)
- Khalil, Fazlur Rehman (Aliases: Maulana Farzul Ahmed Khalil)
- Khalil, Maulana Saadatullah (No known aliases)

Azhar, Maulana Masood

Khalil, Fazlur Rehman

Activities

Has conducted a number of operations against Indian troops and civilian targets in Kashmir. Linked to the Kashmiri militant group al-Faran that kidnapped five western tourists in Kashmir in July 1995, one was killed in August 1995, and the other four reportedly were killed in December of the same year. HUM was responsible for the hijacking of an Indian airlines on December 24, 1999, which resulted in the release of Masood Azhar. Azhar, an important leader in the former Harakat ul-Ansar, was imprisoned by the Indians in 1994 and founded Jaish-e-Muhammed after his release.[34] Also released in 1999 was Ahmed Omar Sheik, who was convicted of the abduction/murder in January-February 2002 of US journalist Daniel Pearls.

Strength

Has several hundred armed supporters located in Pakistan occupied Kashmir, Pakistan, India's Southern Kashmir, Doda regions and in the Kashmir valley. Supporters are mostly Pakistani's and a handful group of Kashmiris, and also include Afghans and Arab veterans of the Afghan war. Weapons in use are light and heavy machineguns assault rifles, mortars, explosives and rockets. HUM lost a significant shares of its membership in defections of the Jaish-e-Mohammed (JEM) in 2000. There are no exact figures as to the number of volunteers trained by the organization, but estimates place their total at about 5,000 fighters from Pakistan and some 6000 volunteers from other Islamic States.[35]

Location/Area of Operation

The bases are located at Muzaffarabad, Rawalpindi, and several other towns in Pakistan, but members conduct insurgent and terrorist activities primarily in Kashmir. HUM trained its militants in Afghanistan and also in Pakistan.

External Aid

This organization collects donation from Saudi Arabia,

other Gulf and Islamic States, Pakistanis and Kashmiris. HUM's financial collection methods also include soliciting donations in magazine ads and pamphlets. The sources and amount of HUM's Military funding are unknown. In anticipation of asset seizures in 2001 by the Pakistani government, the HUM withdrew funds from bank accounts and invested in legal businesses, such as commodity trading, real estate, and production of consumer goods. Its fundraising in Pakistan has been constrained since the government clampdown on extremist groups and freezing of terrorist assets.[36]

4. HIZB-I-ISLAMI GULBUDDIN (HIG)

Other Name: Unknown

Classification: Religious

Description

Gulbuddin Hikmatyar founded Hizb-I-Islami Gulbuddin (HIG) as a faction of the Hizb-I-Islami party in 1977, and it was one of the major mujahedin groups in the war against the Soviets. HIG has long-established links with Osama Bin Laden. In the early 1990s, Hikmatyar ran several terrorist training camps in Afghanistan and was a pioneer in sending mercenary fighters to other Islamic conflicts. Hikmatyar offered to shelter to Bin Laden after the latter fled Sudan in 1996. In a late 2004 press release, Hikmatyar reiterated his commitment to fight U.S and coalition forces.

Key Leaders

- Hikmatyar, Gulbuddin (Aliases: Gulbuddin Hikmatyar, Gulbuddin Khekmatiyar)

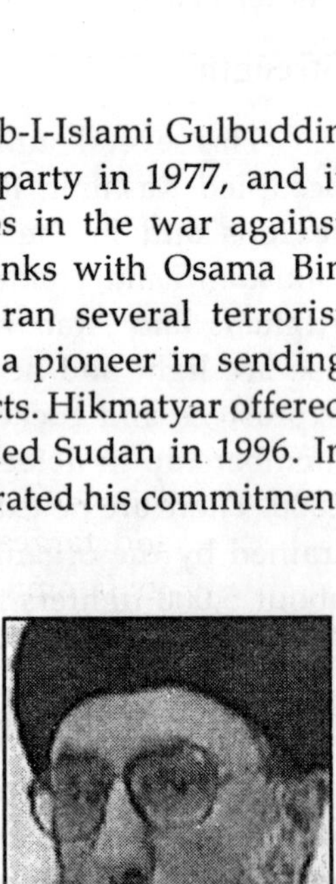

Gulbuddin Hikmatyar

Activities

HIG has staged small attacks in its attempt to force U.S troops to withdraw from Afghanistan, overthrow the Afghan Transitional Administration, and establish an Islamic fundamentalist state. In 2004, several U.S soldiers were killed in attacks in Konar, Afghanistan, the area in which HIG is most active.[37]

Strength

Unknown, but possibly could have hundreds of veteran fighters.

Location/Area of operation

Eastern Afghanistan (particularly Konar and Nurestan Provinces) and adjacent areas of Pakistan's tribal areas.

External Aid: Unknown.

5. HIZBUL-MUJAHEDIN (HM)

Other Name: HM of the Jamaat-e-Islami

Classification: Nationalist/Separatist

Description

Hizbul Mujahedin (HM), the largest kashmiri militant group, was founded in 1989 and officially supports the liberation of Jammu and Kashmir and its accession to Pakistan, although some cadres favour independence. The group is the militant wing of Pakistan's largest Islamic political party, the Jamaat-i-Islami, and targests Indian security forces, politicians and civilians in Jammu and Kashmir. It reportedly operated in Afghanistan in the mid 1990s and trained with the Afghan Hizb-I Islami Gulbudin (HIG) in Afghanistan until the Taliban takeover. The group, led by Syed Salahuddin, is comprised primarily of ethnic Kashmiris.[38]

Key Leaders

- Butt, Abdul Hameed (Aliases : Bombar Khan, Hameed Gada)
- Dar, Abdul Majeed (No known aliases)
- Dar, Master Ahsan (No known aliases)

- Shah, Ghulam Rasool (Aliases: Imran Rahi)
- Shah, Mohammed Yusuf (Aliases: Pir Sahib, Syed Salahuddin)

Abdul

Mohammed Yusuf

Activities

HM has conducted a number of operations against Indian Military targets in Jammu & Kashmir. The group also occasionally strikes at civilian targets, but has not engaged in terrorist acts outside India. HM claimed responsibility for numerous attacks within Kashmir in 2004.[39] HM also claimed responsibility for the suicide attack on May 23, 2006 in Kashmir near Hyderpora Airport road killed 1 & injured 25 BSF personnel.

Strength

Exact numbers are unknown, but estimates range from several hundred to possibly as many as 1,000 members in Jammu and Kashmir and Pakistan.

Location/Area of Operation

Jammu & Kashmir and Pakistan.

External Aid

Specific sources of external aid are unknown.

6. ISLAMIC JIHAD GROUP (IJG)

(Designated as a Foreign Terrorist Organization)

Other Name: IJU, Islamic Jihad Union

Classification: Religious / Nationalist / Separatist

Description

The Islamic Jihad Group (IJG), probably founded by former members of the Islamic Movement of Uzbekistan, made its appearance in early April 2004 when it claimed responsibility for a string of events-including shootouts and terrorists attacks—in Uzbekistan in late March and early April that killed approximately 47 people, including 33 terrorists. The claim of responsibility, which was posted to multiple militant Islamic Websites, raged against the leadership of Uzbekistan. In late July 2004, the group struck again with near-simultaneous suicide bombing of the U.S and Israeli Embassies and the Uzbek Prosecutor General's office in Tashkent.[40] The IJG again claimed responsibility via an Islamic website and stated that martyrdom operations by the group would continue. The statement also indicated the attacks were done in support of their Palestinian, Iraqi and Afghan brothers in the global jihad.

Key Leaders: Unknown

Activities

The IJG claimed responsibility for multiple attacks in 2004 against Uzbekistani, American, and Israeli entities. The attackers in the March and April 2004 attacks some of whom were female suicide bombers, targeted the local government offices of the Uzbekistani and Bukhara police, killed approx. 47 people, including 33 terrorists. On July 30, 2004, the group launched a set of same-day attacks against the US and Israeli Embassies and the Uzbek prosecutor General's office. These attacks left four Uzbekistanis and three suicide operatives dead. On May 25, 2005, the US State Department designated Islamic Jihad Group as a specially Designated Global Terrorist Group.

Strength: Unknown

Location/Area of Operation

Militants are scattered throughout Central Asia and probably parts of South-Asia.

External Aid: Unknown.

7. JAISH-E-MOHAMMED (JEM)

(Designated as a Foreign Terrorist Organization)

Other Name: Army of Mohammed Tehrik Ul-Furquaan, Khuddamul-Islam.

Classification: Nationalist/Separatist, Religious.

Description

Jaish-e-Mohammed is an Islamic extremist group based in Pakistan that rapidly expanded in size and capability in 2000 after Maulana Masood Azhar, a former ultrafundamentalist Harakat ul-Ansar (HUA) leader, announced its formation in February of the year. [41] The HUA, which had by this time known as Harakat Ul-Mujahideen (HUM) passed on to JEM its goal of uniting Kashmir with Pakistan. JEM is politically aligned with the radical, pro-Talipan political party Jamiat-i Ulema-i Islam (JUI-F). By 2003 JEM has splintered into Khuddam ul-Islam (KUI), headed by Azhar, and Jamaat ul-Furqan (JUF), led by Adbul Jabbar, who was released in August 2004 from Pakistani custody after being detained for suspected involvement in the December 2003 assassination attempt against President Musharraf.[42] Pakistan banned KUI and JUF in November 2003. Elements of JEM and Lashkar e-Tayyiba combined with other grops to mount attacks as "The Save Kashmir Movement."

Key-Leader

- Ahmed, Maulana Qari Mansoor (No known aliases)
- Azhar, Maulana Masood (No known aliases)
- Jabbar, C. Maulana Abdul (No known aliases)
- Saeed, Sheikh Omar (No known aliases)
- Usman, Maulana Sajjad (No known aliases)

Historical Evolution of Jaish-e-Mohammad (JEM)

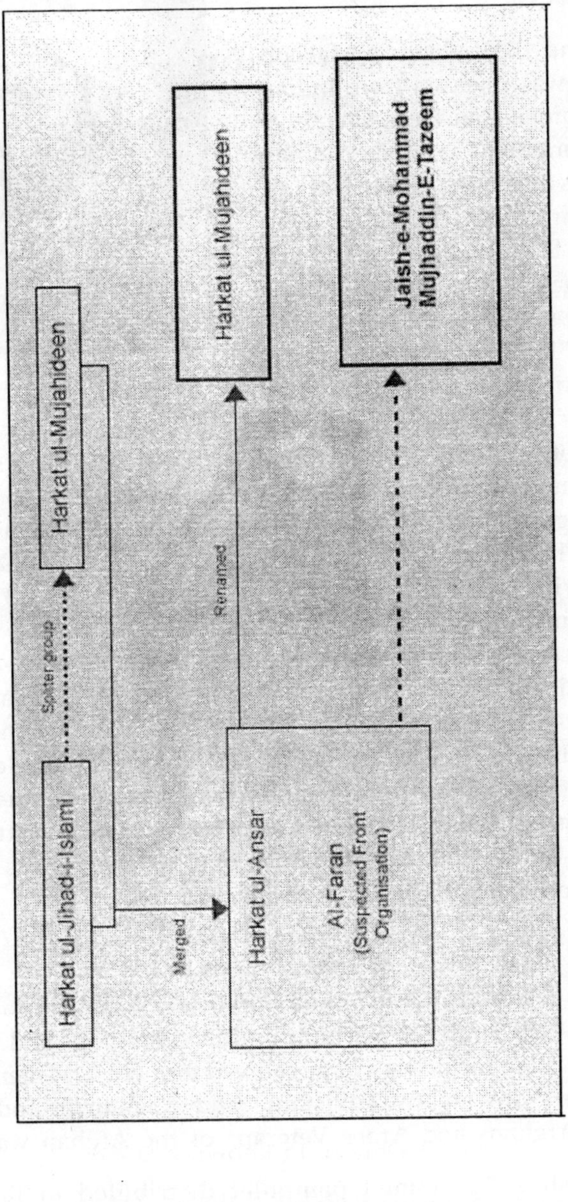

Activities

Sheikh Omar

The JEM's leader, Masood Azhar, was released from Indian imprisonment in December 1999 in exchange for 155 hijacked Indian Airlines hostages. The Harakat-ul-Ansar (HUA) kidnapping in 1994 of U.S and British nationals by Omar Sheik in New Delhi and the HUA / al-Faran kidnapping in July 1995 of Westerners in Kashmir were two of several previous HUA efforts to free Azhar. On October 1, 2001, JEM claimed responsibility for a suicide attack on the Jammu & Kashmir legislative assembly building in Srinagar that killed at least 31 persons but later denied the claim. The Indian Government has publicly implicated JEM, along with Lashkar e-Tayyiba, for the December 13, 2001, attack on the Indian Parliament that killed nine (in which 5 were terrorists and four were policemen) and injured 18.[43] Pakistani authorities suspect that perpetrators of fatal anti-Christian attacks in Islamabad, Muree and Taxida during 2002 were affiliated with JEM. The Pakistanis have implicated elements of JEM in the assassination attempts against President Musharraf in December 2003. JEM claimed responsibility for the attack in Srinagar on May 30, 2006 in which one policeman was killed and six other people were injured.

Strength

Has several hundred armed supporters located in Pakistan and in India's Southern Kashmir and Doda regions and in the Kashmir valley, including a large cadre of former HUM members. Supporters are mostly Pakistanis and Kashmiris and also include Afghans and Arabs Veterans of the Afghan war.

"Jaish-e-Mohammad pamphlet distributed in Rajouri warns that *the blood of the mujahideen will prove difficult to digest*

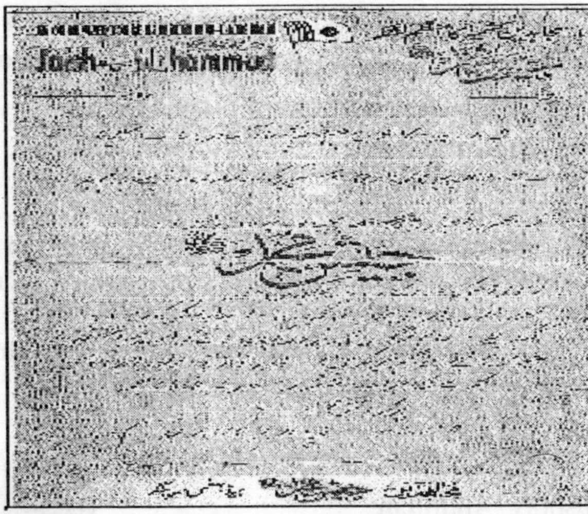

Jaish-e-Mohammad pamphlet distributed in Rajouri warns that the blood of the Mujahideen will prove difficult to digest and threatens to execute

and threatens to execute those who cooperate with the security forces."

Location/Area of Operation

Pakistan; JEM maintained training camps in Afghanistan until the fall of 2001.

External Aid

Most of JEM's cadre and material resources have been drawn from the militant groups Harakat Ul-Jihad-i-Islami (HUJI) and the Harakat ul-Mujahidin (HUM). JEM had close ties to Afghan Arabs and the Taliban. Osama bin Laden is suspected to giving funding to JEM. JEM also collects funds through donation requests in magazines and pamphlets.[44] In anticipation of asset seizures by the Pakistani Government, JEM withdrew funds from bank accounts and invested in legal businesses, such as commodity trading, real estate, and production of consumer goods.

8. JEMAAH ISLAMIYA ORGANISATION (JI)
(Designated as a Foreign Terrorist Organization)

Other Name: Islamic Community Islamic Group

Classification: Religious.

Description

Jemaah Islamiya is a Southeast Asian-based terrorist network with links to al-Qaeda. The network recruits and trained extremists in the late 1990s. Following the stated goal of creating on Islamic state comprising Brunei, Indonesia, Malaysia, Singapore, the Southern Philippines and Southern Thailand.

Keys Leaders

- Anshori, Abdullah
(Aliases: Abu Fatih, Abu Tayb)
- Bashir, Abu Bakar
(Aliases: Abu Bakar Ba' asyir)
- Bin Husin, Azahari
(No known aliases)
- Bin Isomoddin, Nurjaman
Riduan (Aliases: Hampali)
- Dujana, Abu (Aliases: Ainal Bahri)

Abu Bakar

Bin Husin, Azahari

Aftermath of Bombing of the J.W. Marriott Hotel
(Jakarta, Aug. 5, 2003)

Activities

Jemaah Islamiya organization is responsible for numerous high-profile bombings, including the bombing of the J.W. Marriot Hotel in Jakarta on August 5, 2003, and the Bali bombings on October ·12, 2002.[45] Members of the group have also been implicates in the September 9, 2004, attack outside the Australian Embassy in Jakarta. The Bali attack, which left more than 200 dead, was reportedly the final outcome of meetings in early 2002 in Thailand, where attacks in Singapore and against soft targets such as tourist spots were also considered. In June 2003, authorities disrupted a JI plan to attack several western embassies and tourist sites in Thailand. JI is also responsible for the coordinated bombings of numerous christian churches in Indonesia on Christmas Eve 2000 and was involved in the bombings of several targets in Manila on December 31, 2000.

A Couple Flees from the Bali Bombing

Strength

Exact numbers are unknown, but Southeast Asian authorities continue to uncover and arrest JI elements. Estimates of total JI members vary widely from the hundreds to the thousands.

Location/Area of Operation

JI is believed to have cells spanning Indonesia, Malaysia and the Philippines.

External Aid

JI is fully capable of its own fundraising although it also receives financial, ideological and logistical support from Middle Eastern and South Asian contacts, non-governmental organizations and other groups.

9. LASHKAR-e-TAYYIBA (LeT)

(Designated as a Foreign Terrorist Organization)

Other Name: Lashkar-e-Toiba, al Monsooreen, Army of Righteous, Army of the Pure, Army of Pure and Righteous.

Classification: Religious, Nationalist/Separatist.

LT LOGO

Description

Lashkar e-Tayyiba is the armed wing of the Pakistan-based religious organization, Markaz-ud-Dawa-wal-Irshad (MDI), an anti-U.S Sunni missionary organization formed in 1989. LT is led by Hafiz Muhammed Saeed and is one of the three largest and best trained groups fighting in Kashmir against India.[46] It is not connected to any political party. The pakistani Government banned the group and froze its assets in January 2002. Elements of LT and Jaish-e-Mohammed combined with other groups to mount attacks as "The save Kashmir Movement."

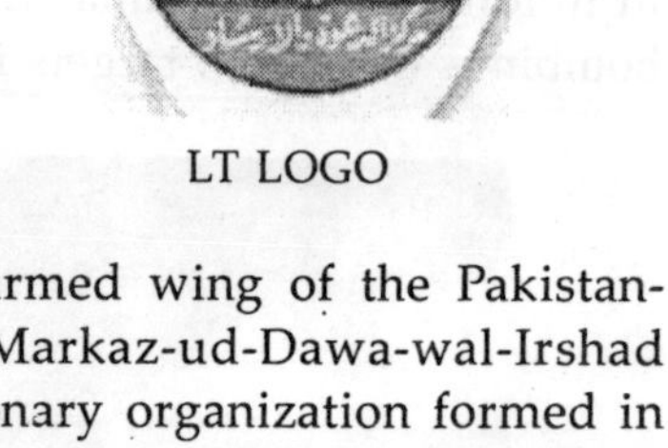

Saeed, Hafiz Mohammed

Key Leaders

- Iqbal, Zafar (No known aliases)
- Saeed, Hafiz Mohammed
- Kashmiri, Maulana Abdul Wahid (No known aliases)
- Saeed, Hafiz Mohammed Saifullah (No known aliases)

- Ul Rehman Lakhwi, Zaki (Aliases: Abdullah Azam, Zaki ur Rehman Lakhvi)

Activities

LT has conducted a number of operations against Indian troops and civilian targets in Jammu and Kashmir since 1993. LT claimed responsibility for numerous attacks in 2001, including an attack in January on Srinagar airport that killed at least eight officers and wounded several others; and an attack in April against Indian border security forces that left at least four dead. The Indian Government publicly implicated LT, along with JEM, for the attack on December 13, 2001 on the Indian Parliament building, although concrete evidence is lacking. LT is also suspected of involvement in the attack on May 14, 2002, on an Indian Army base in Kaluchak that left 36 dead. Senior al-Qaida lieutenant Abu Zubaydah was captured at an LT safe house in Faisalabad in March 2002, suggesting some members are facilitating the movement of al-Qaeda members in Pakistan.[47]

Strength

Has several thousand members in POK, Pakistan, in the Southern Jammu and Kashmir and Doda regions, and in the Kashmir valley. Almost all LT members are Pakistanis from Madrassas across Pakistan or Afghan veterans of the Afghan wars.

Location and Area of operation

Based in Muridke (near Lahore) and Muzaffarabad.

External Aid

Collects donations from the Pakistani community in the Persian Gulf and United Kingdom, Islamic NGOs, and Pakistani and other Kashmiri business people. LT also maintains a web site (under the name Jamaat ud-Daawa),[48] through which it solicits funds and provides information on the group's activities. The amount of LT funding is unknown. LT maintain ties to religious/militant groups around the world, ranging from the philippines to the Middle East and Chechnya through the fraternal network of its parent organization Jamat ud-Dawa (formerly Markaz Dawa ul-Irshad). In anticipation of asset seizures by the Pakistani Government, the LT withdrew funds from bank accounts and invested in legal businesses, such as commodity trading, real estate, and production of consumer goods.

10. LASHKAR-I-JHANGVI (LJ)

(Designated as Foreign Terrorist Organization)

Other Name: Army of Jhangvi; Lashkar E Jhangvi (LEJ)

Classification: Nationalist/Separatist

Description

Lashkar-i-Jhangvi (LJ) is the militant offshoot of the Sunni sectarian group Sipah-i-Sahaba Pakistan. LJ focuses primarily on anti-Shia attacks and was banned by Pakistani President Musharraf in August 2001 as part of an effort to rein in sectarian violence. Many of its members then sought refuges in Afghanistan with the Taliban, with whom they had existing ties. After the collapse of the Taliban, LJ members became active in aiding other terrorists wife safe houses, false identities and protection in Pakistani cities, including Karachi, Peshawar,

Asif, Choto

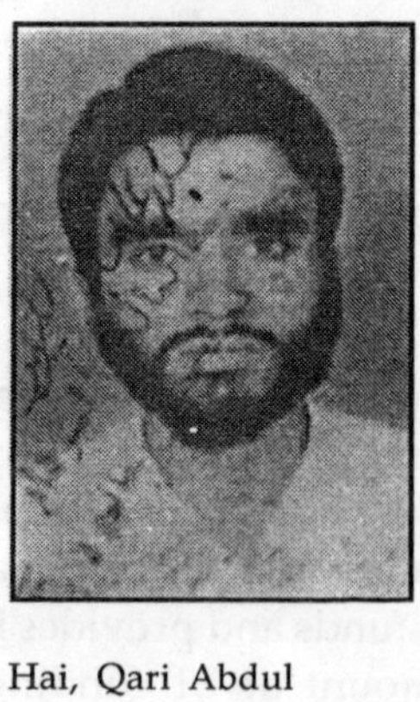

Hai, Qari Abdul

and Rawalpindi. In January 2003, the United States added LJ to the list of foreign Terrorist organization.[49]

Key Leaders

- Ajmal, Muhammad (Aliases: Akram Lahori)
- Asif, Choto (Aliases: Mohammed Rizwan)
- Basra, Riaz (No known aliases)
- Hai, Qari Abdul (Aliases: Qari Asadullah, Talha)
- Ishaque, Malik (No known aliases)

Activities

LJ specializes in armed attacks and bombings. The group attempted to assassinate former Prime Minister Nawaz Sharif and his brother Shabaz Sharif, Chief Minister of Punjab province, in January 1999. Pakistani authorities have publicly linked LJ members to the kidnap and murder of U.S journalist Daniel Pearl in early 2002. Police officials initially suspected LJ members were involved in the two suicide car bombings in Karachi in 2002 against a French shuttle bus in May and the U.S consulate in June, but their subsequent investigations have not led to any LJ members being charged in the attacks. Pakistani authorities believe LJ was responsible for the bombing in July 2003 of a Shiite mosque in Quetta, Pakistan. Authorities have also implicated LJ in several sectarian incidents in 2004, including the May and June bombings of two Shiite mosques in Karachi that killed over 40 peoples.[50]

Strength: Probably more than 100.

Location/Area of Operation

LJ is active primarily in Punjab and Karachi. Some members travel between Pakistan and Afghanistan.

External Aid: Unknown.

11. LIBERATION TIGERS OF TAMIL EELAM (LTTE)

(Designated as a Foreign Terrorist Organization)

Other Name: The Tamil Tigers; The Ellalan Force; World Tamil Association (WTA); World Tamil Movement (WTM); The Federation of Association of Canadian Tamils (FACT); The Ellalan Force, and the Sangilian Force.

Classification: Nationalist/Separatist.

LTTE LOGO

LTTE FLAG

Description

Sri Lanka is a state lacerated by two bitter conflicts. One is that of the state versus the People's Liberation Front (JVP, or Janatha Vimukthi Peramuna, the name of its founder), a Sinhalese extreme nationalist organization anxious to bring down the moderate Colombo government. The other is that of the Tamil Tigers, whose demand is for an altogether separate state. JVP has largely been contained by vigorous counter-terrorism; the Tamil Tigers

Prabakharan, Vellupillai

continue to rage unabated.[51] The so-called Tamil Tigers represent a terrorist faction whose activities have been a growing source of concern to thirty states over four continents. The Tamil Tigers had the highest rate of suicide mission in the world, with many hundreds of victims over the years. For an enterprising young Tamil, there seemed to be little to do but become a terrorist.[52] LTTE was founded in 1976, the LTTE is the most powerful Tamil group in Sri Lanka. It began its insurgency against the Sri Lankan Government in 1983 and has relied on a guerrilla strategy that includes the use of terrorist tatics.

Key Leaders

- Kausalyan, E (No known aliases)
- Prabakharan, Vellupillai (No known aliases)

Activities

It is calculated that 60,000 lives have been lost as well as thousands more people displaced by the struggle. Its attacks include suicide bombings. Since the 1980s the LTTE have conducted over 200 suicide bombings.[53] These suicide bombers are known as the 'Black Tigers' Among the targets include civilian, office buildings, Buddhist Shrines and a World Trade Center in Colombo, Sri Lanka's Capital. LTTE fighters have also been known to carry cyanide capsules in case they are caught.[54] Due to the vast number of suicide attacks carried out the Tamils have gained worldwide notoriety. In May 21, 1991 the LTTE murdered the Indian Prime Minister Rajiv Gandhi at an election campaign rally in India. In May 1993 it assassinated the Sri Lankan President Ranasinghe Premadasa.

Strength

Exact strength is unknown, but the LTTE is estimated to have 8,000 to 10,000 armed combatants in Sri Lanka with a core of 3000 to 6000, trained fighters.[55] With this strength, the Tigers control most of the northern and eastern coastal areas of Sri Lanka. From the Tigers headquarters in the Jaffina Peninsula, LTTE leader Velupillai

LTTE Checkpoint

Prabhakaran used the internal support network to establish a comprehensive pattern of checkpoints and informants to keep tabs on any outsiders who enter the LTTE's area of control.[56]

Location/Area of Operation

The LTTE controls most of the northern and eastern coastal areas of Sri Lanka but has conducted operations throughout the island.

External Aid

The LTTE's overt organizations support Tamil separatism by lobbying foreign governments and the United Nations. The LTTE also uses its international contacts and the Large Tamil diaspora in North America, Europe and Asia to procure weapons, communications, funding, and other needed supplies. As of now in a fierce battle the Sri Lankan Government has almost eliminated the LTTE. All top cadres are reportedly killed.

12. SIPAH-I-SAHABA/PAKISTAN (SSP)

Other Name: Unknown

Classification: Unknown

Description

The Sipah-i-Sahaba/Pakistan (SSP) is a Sunni sectarian group that follows the Deobandi School. Violently anti-Shia, the SSP emerged in Central Punjab in the mid 1980s as a response to the Iranian Revolution. Pakistani President Musharraf banned the SSP in January 2002. In August 2002, the SSP renamed itself Millat-i-Islami Pakistan, and Musharraf re-banned the group under its new name in November 2003. The SSP also has operated as a political party, winning seats in Pakistan National Assembly.

Key Leaders: Unknown

Activities

The group's activities range from organizing political rallies calling for Shia to be declared non-Muslims to assassinating prominent Shia leaders. The group was responsible for attacks on Shia worshippers in May 2004, When at least 50 people were killed.

Strength

The SSP may have approximately 3000, to 6000 trained activists who carry out various kinds of sectarian activities.

Location/Area of Operation

The SSP has influence in all four provinces of Pakistan. It is considered to be one of the most powerful sectarian groups in the country.

External Aid

The SSP reportedly receives significant funding from Saudi Arabia through wealthy private donors in Pakistan. Funds also are acquired from other sources, including other Sunni extremist groups, madrassas and contributions by political groups.[57]

European Terrorist Organizations

European Terrorist Organizations

S.No.	Location	Name	Other Name	Leaders	Classification
1	Northern Spain; South Western France	Basque Fatherland & Liberty (ETA)	Euzkadi To Askatasuna; Batasuna Basque Homeland	Aguirre, Harriet; Albizu Iriarte, Mikel; Alday, Gorka Palacios; Arregui, Jose Maria	Communist/ Socialist / Nationalist Separatist
2	Northern Ireland; Irish Republic; Great Britain & Europe	Irish Republican Army (IRA)	Provisional Irish Republican Army (PIRA); The Provos	Kelly, John; Murphy, Thomas; Regan, Michael; Sands, Bobby	Nationalist / Separatist
3	Italy	New Red Brigades (BR)	Communist Combatant Party (PCC); Brigate Rosse; Partito Comunista Combattents	Bortone, Nicholas; Galesi, Mario; Giorgieri, Sumonetta; Lioce, Desdemom	Communist / Socialist
4	Northern Ireland; Great Britain & Irish Republic	Real Irish Republican Army (RIRA)	32-Country Sovereignty Committee; True IRA	MC Kevitt, Michael; Murphy, Colm.	Nationalist / Separatist
5	West Germany	Red Army Faction	Baader-Meinhof Gang	Unknown	Unknown
6	Northern Ireland	Red Hand Defenders (RHD)		Unknown	Nationalist / Separatist
7	Athens	Revolutionary Nuclei (RN)	Revolutionary Cells; Revolutionary Poputar Struggle, ELA	Unknown	Anti Globalization Communist Socialist
8	Athens: Greece	Revolutionary Organization;17 November	Epanastatiki organosi 17 Noemvri; 17 November	Giotopoulos, Alexandros; Koufondinas, Dimitris; Serifis, Pavlos; Serifis, Yiannis	Communist, Socialist, Anti-Globalization Nationalist.

PROFILES OF INTERNATIONAL EUROPEAN TERRORIST GROUP

1. BASQUE FATHERLAND AND LIBERTY (ETA)

(Designated as a Foreign Terrorist Organization)

Other Name: Euzkadi Ta Askatasuna, Batasuna Basque Homeland and freedom.

Classfication: Communist/ Socialist/Nationalist/Separatist.

"Flag created to represent a theoretical Basque Homeland"

E.T.A. LOGO

Description

ETA was founded in 1959 with the aim of establishing an independent homeland based on Marxist principles and encompassing the Spanish Basque provinces of Vizcaya, Guipuzcoa, and Alava, as well as the autonomous region of Navarra and the Southwestern French Departments of Labourd, Basse-Navarra, and Soul. Spanish and French counter terrorism initiative since 2000 have hampered the group's operational capabilities.[58] Spanish police arrested scores of ETA members and accomplices in Spain in 2004, and dozens were apprehended in France, including two key group leaders. These arrests included the capture in October of two key ETA leaders in Southwestern France. ETA's political wing, Batasuna, remains banned in Spain. Spanish and French prisons are estimated to hold over 700 ETA members. First designated in October 1997.

Key Leaders

Aguirre, Harriet (No known aliases)

Aguirre, Harriet

Albizu Iriarte, Mikel

- Albizu Iriarte, Mikel (Aliases: Mikel Antza)
- Alday, Gorka Palacios (Aliases: Gorka Palacios)
- Arregui, Jose Maria (Aliases: Fiti)

Activities

Primarily involved in bombings and assassinations of Spanish Government officials, security and military forces, politicians, and judicial figures, but has also targeted journalists and tourists areas. Security service scrutiny and a public outcry after the Islamic extremist train bombing on March 11, 2004, in Madrid limited ETA's capabilities and willingness to inflict casualties.[59] ETA conducted no fatal attacks in 2004, but did mount several low-level bombings in Spanish tourist areas

during the summer and 11 bombings in early December, each preceded by a warning call. The group has killed more than 850 persons and injured hundreds of others since it began attacks in the 1960s. ETA finances its activities primarily through extortion and robbery.

Strength: Unknown; hundreds of members plus supporters.

Location/Area of operation

Operates primarily in the Basque autonomous regions of Northern Spain and South Western France, but also has attacked Spanish and French interests elsewhere.

External Aid

Has received training at various times in the past in Libya, Lebanon and Nicaragua. Some ETA members allegedly fled to Cuba and Mexico while others reside in South America.[60] ETA members have operated and been arrested in other European countries, including Belgium, The Netherlands and Germany.

2. IRISH REPUBLICAN ARMY (IRA)

Other Name: Provisional Irish Republican Army (PIRA), The Provos.

Classification: Nationalist/ Separatist

Description

Formed in 1969 as the clandestine armed wing of the political movement Sinn Fein, the IRA is devoted both to removing British forces from Northern Ireland and to unifying Ireland. The IRA conducted attacks until its cease fire in 1997 and agreed to disarm as a part of the 1998 Belfast Agreement. Which established the basis for peace in Northern Ireland. Dissension within the IRA over support for the Northern Ireland peace process resulted in the formation of two more radical splinter groups : continuity IRA (CIRA), and the Real IRA (RIRA) in mid to late 1990s.[61] The IRA, sometimes referred to as the PIRA to distinguish it from RIRA and CIRA, is organized into small, tightly-knit cell under the leadership of the Army Council.

Key Leaders

- Kelly, John (No known aliases)
- Murphy, Thomas (Aliases: Slab)
- Regan, Michael (No known aliases)
- Sands, Bobby (No known aliases)
- Stevenson, John (Aliases: Sean Mac Stiofain)

Logo of Sinn Fein, the IRA's political wing

Activities

Traditional IRA activities have included bombing, assassinations, kidnappings, punishment beatings, extortion, smuggling and robberies. Before the cease fire in 1997, the group had conducted bombing campaigns on various targets in Northern Ireland and Great Britain including Senior British Government officials, civilians, police and British Military "Logo of Sinn Fein, the IRA's political wing" targets. The group previously had disposed of light, medium and heavy weapons, ammunition and explosives in three rounds of decommissioning. However the IRA is believed to retain the ability to conduct paramilitary operations. The group's extensive criminal activities reportedly provide the IRA and the political party Sinn Fein with millions of dollars each year;[62] the IRA was implicated in two significant robberies in 2004, one involving almost $ 50 million.

Strength

Several hundred members and several thousand

sympathizers despite the defection of some members to RIRA and CIRA.

Location/Area of Operation

Northern Ireland, Irish Republic, Great Britain and Europe.

External Aid

In the past, the IRA has received aid from a variety of groups and countries and considerable training and arms from Libya and the PLO is suspected of receiving funds, arms, and other terrorist-related material from sympathizers in the United States. Similarities in operations suggest links to ETA and the FARC. In August 2002, three suspected IRA members were arrested in Colombia on charges of helping the FARC improve its explosives capabilities.

3. NEW RED BRIGADES (BR) [63]

Other Name: Communist Combatant Party (PCC), Brigate Rosse, Partito Comunista Combattente.

Classification: Communist/Socialist.

Description

The New Red Brigades is a Splinter group of the Red Brigades. This extreme left-wing secret organization formed in 1969 in Italy, in an effort to create a revolutionary state through armed struggle, based on Marxist-Leninist principles. It also sought to separate Italy from its Western alliance, NATO. The founder of the BR was Renato Curcio. The Red Brigades was officially declared to exist in November 1970 and 1980s.

Bortone, Nicholas

Key Leaders

- Bortone, Nicholas
  (Aliases: Vicenzo)

- Galesi, Mario (No known Aliases)
- Giorgieri, Simonetta (Aliases: Franc the Master)
- Lioce, Desdemona (No known Aliases)
- Luca, Antonio De (No known Aliases)

Lioce, Desdemona

Activities

In 2004, the BR/PCC continued to suffer setbacks, with their leadership in prison and other members under pressure from the Italian Government. The BR/PCC did not claim responsibility for a blast at an employment agency in Milan in late October, although the police suspect remnants of the group are responsible. In 2003, Italian authorities captured at least seven members of the BR/PCC, dealing the terrorist group a severe blow to its operational effectiveness. Some of those arrested are suspects in the assassination in 1999 of labor Ministary adviser Massimo D' Antona, and authorities are hoping to link them to the assassination in 2002 of Labor Ministery advisor Marco Biagi. The arrests in October came on the heels of a clash in March 2003 involving Italian Railway Police and two BR/PCC members, which resulted in the deaths of one of the operatives and an Italian security officer. The BR/PCC has financed its activities through armed robberies.[64]

Strength: Fewer the 20.

Location/Area of operation: Italy

External Aid: Unknown.

4. REAL IRISH REPUBLICAN ARMY (RIRA)

(Designated as a Foreign Terrorist Organization)

Other Name: 32-Country Sovereignty Committee, True IRA.

Classification: Nationalist/Separatist.

Description

RIRA was formed in the late 1990s as the clandestine armed wing of the 32 country Sovereignty Movement, a "political pressure Group" dedicated to removing British forces from Northern Ireland and unifying Ireland. The RIRA also seeks to disrupt the Northern Ireland peace process. The 32-County Sovereignty Movement opposed Sinn Fein's adoption in September 1997 of the Mitchell principles of democracy and non-violence; it also opposed the amendment in December 1999 of Articles 2 and 3 of the Irish Constitution, which had claimed the territory of Northern Ireland. Despite internal rifts and calls by some jailed members—including the group's founder Michael "Mickey" MC Kevitt for a ceasefire and disbandment, RIRA has pledged additional violence and continues to conduct attack.

MC Kevitt, Michael

Murphy, Colm

Key Leaders

- MC Kevitt, Michael
  (Aliases: Micky)
- Murphy, Colm
  (No known aliases)

Activities

Bombings, assassinations and robberies. Many real IRA members are former provisional Irish Republican Army members who left that organization after the Provisional IRA renewed its cease-fire in 1997. These members brought a wealth of experience in terrorists tactics and bomb making to RIRA. Targets have included civilians, British Security forces, police in Northern Ireland, and local Protestant communities. RI RA's most recent fatal attack was in August 2002 at a London army base that killed a construction worker. In 2004, RIRA conducted several postal bomb attacks and made threats against prison officers, people involved in the new policing arrangements, and senior politicians. RIRA also planted incendiary devices in Belfast shopping areas and conducted a serious shooting attack against a Police Service of Northern Ireland station in September.

The Organization reportedly wants to improve its intelligence-gathering ability, engineering capacity, and access to weaponry; it also trains members in the use of guns and explosives. RIRA continues to attract new members, and its senior members are committed to launching attacks on security forces. Arrests in the spring led to the discovery of incendiary and explosive devices at a RIRA bomb making facility in Limerick. The group also engaged in smuggling and other non-terrorist crime in Ireland.

Strength

The number of activists may have fallen to less than 100. The organization may receive limited support from IRA hardliners and Republican sympathizers dissatisfied with the IRA's continuing cease-fire and Sinn Fein's involvement in the peace process.

Location/Area of Operation

Northern Ireland, Great Britain and Irish Republic.

External Aid

Suspects of receiving funds from sympathizers in the United States and of and of attempting to buy weapons from US gun dealers. RIRA also is reported to have purchased sophisticated weapons from the Balkans, and to have taken materials from provisional IRA arms dumps in the later 1990s.

5. RED ARMY FACTION

Other Name: Baader-Meinhof Gang

Classification: Unknown

Description

The tightly knit and disciplined RAF is the successor to the Baader-Meinhof Gang, which originated in the student protest movement in the 1960s. Ideology is an obscure mix of Marxism and Maoism; committed to armed struggle. Organized into hardcore cadres that carry out terrorist attacks and a network of supporters who provide logistic and propaganda support.[65] Has survived despite numerous arrests of top leaders over the years.

Key Leaders: Unknown

Activities

Bombings, Kidnappings, assassinations and robberies. Targets Wests German Government and private sector and US interests. Among the latter, attempted to assassinated NATO Commander in Belgium in 1979; bombing of NATO Air Force headquarters at Ramstein (1981); rocket attack of USAREUR Commander in Heidelberg 1981;bombing, with AD, of Rhein-Main Air Force Base 1985; and assassination of Deutsche Bank Chairman Alfred Herrhausen in November 1989.[66]

Strength: **10 to 20, plus several hundred supporters.**

Location/Area of operation :- Mainly in West Germany.

External Aid

In Baader-Meinhof period, received support form Middle Eastern terrorist groups; some loose ties may still exist. Had close ties to the ADF in France and the CCC in Belgium before these groups were wrapped up by police.[67]

6. RED HAND DEFENDERS (RHD) [68]

Other Name: Unknown

Classification: Nationalist/Separatist

Description

The RHD is an extremist terrorist group formed in 1998

and composed largely of protestant hardliners from loyalist groups observing a cease-fire. RHD seeks to prevent a political settlement with Irish nationalists by attacking Catholic Civilian interests in Northern Ireland. In January 2002, the group announced all staff at Catholic Schools in Belfast and Catholic postal workers were legitimate targets. Despite calls in February 2002 by the Ulster Defense Association (UDA), Ulster Freedom Fighters (UFF), and Loyalist Volunteer Force (LVF) to announce its disbandment, RHD continued to make threats and issue claims of responsibility. RHD is a cover name often used by elements of the banned UDA and LVF. Designated under EO 13224 in December 2001.

Key Leaders: Unknown

Activities

In early 2003, the RHD claimed responsibility for killing two UDA members as a result of what is described as loyalist internecine warfare. It also claimed responsibility for a bomb that was left in the offices of Republican Sinn Fein in West Belfast, although the device was defused and no one was injured. In recent years, the group has carried out numerous pipe bombing and arson attack against "Soft" civilian targets such as homes, Churches, and private businesses. In January 2002, the group bombed the home of a prison official in North Belfast. Twice in 2002 the group claimed responsibility for attacks—the murder of a Catholic postman and a Catholic teenager-that were later claimed by the UDAUFF, further blurring distinctions between the groups. In 2001, RHD claimed responsibility for hoax bomb devices, and recently has set off petrol bombs and made death threats against local politicians.

Strength

Up to 20 members, some of whom have experience in terrorist tactics and bomb making. Police arrested one member in June 2001 for making a hoax bomb threat.

Location/Area of Operation: Northern Ireland.

External Aid: Unknown

7. REVOLUTIONARY NUCLEI (RN)

(Designated as a Foreign Terrorist Organization)

Other Name: Revolutionary Cells, Revolutionary Popular struggle, ELA.

Classification: Anti Globalization, Communist/Socialist.

Description

Revolutionary Nuclei (RN) emerged from a broad range of anti-establishment and anti-US/NATO/EU leftist grops active in Greece between 1995 and 1998. The group is believed to be the successor to or offshoot of Greece's most prolific terrorist group. Revolutionary people's struggle (ELA), which has not claimed an attack since January 1995. Indeed, RN appeared to fill the void left by ELA, particularly as lesser groups faded from the scene. RN's few communiqués show strong similarities in rhetoric, tone, and theme to ELA proclamations.

Key Leaders: Unknown.

Activities

Since it began operations in January 1995, the group has claimed responsibility for some two dozen arson attacks and low-level bombings against a range of U.S, Greek, and other European targets in Greece. In its most infamous and lethal attack to date, the group claimed responsibility for a bomb it detonated at the Intercontinental Hotel in April 1999 that resulted in the death of a Greek Women and injured a Greek man. Its modus operandi includes warning calls of impending attacks, attacks targeting property instead of individuals, use of rudimentary timing devices, and strikes during the late-evening to early-morning hours. RN may have been responsible for two attacks in July 2003 against a U.S insurance company and a local bank in Athens. RN's last confirmed attacks against US interests in Greece came in November 2000, with two separate bombings against the Athens office of Citigroup and the studio of a Greek-American Sculptor. The group did not conduct an attack in 2004.[69]

Strength

Group membership is believed to be small, probably drawing from the Greek militant leftist or anarchist milieu.

Location/Area of operation: Primary area of operation is in the Athens metropolitan area.

External Aid: Unknown but believed to be self-sustaining.

8. REVOLUTIONARY OGANIZATION 17 NOVEMBER

(Designated as a Foreign Terrorist Organisation)

Other Name: Epanastatiki Organosi 17 November, 17

Classification: Communist/Socialist/Anti Globalization/ Nationalist.

Description

17 November is a radical leftist group established in 1975 and named for the student uprising in Greece in November 1973 that protested the ruling military junta. For more than a quarter century, it has eluded authorities despite rewards for information that total $7 million. A Greek journalist has referred to November 17 as "Europe's Last Red Terrorists."[70] 17 November is an anti-Greek establishment, anti-united States, anti-Turkey, and anti-NATO group that seeks the ouster of US bases from Greece, the removal of Turkish Military forces from Cyprus, and the servering of Greece's ties to NATO and the European Union (EU). The group, which is still active, maintains its base of operation in Greece, primarily Athens. While it may have networked with other Greek terrorist groups and perhaps with other anti-establishment group outside of Greece.

"N17 Logo"

"N17 Flag"

Key Leaders

Giotopulos, Alexandros

Koufondinas, Dimitris

- Giotopulos, Alexandros (Aliases: Lambros, Michalis Economou, Mikhails Oikonomou)
- Koufondinas, Dimitris (Aliases: Loukas)
- Serifis, Paulos (Aliases: Nikitas, Vangelis)
- Serifis, Yiannis (No known aliases)

Activities

Initial attacks were assassinations of senior US officials and Greek public figures. They began using bombings in the 1980s. Since 1990, 17 November has expanded its targets to include EU facilities and foreign firms investing in Greece and has added improvised rocket attacks to its methods. It supported itself largely through bank robberies. A failed 17 November bombing attempt in June 2002 at the Port of Piraeus in Athens, coupled with robust detective work, led to the arrest of 19 members—the first 17 November operatives ever arrested. In December 2003, a Greek Court convicted 15 members—five of whom were given multiple life terms—of hundreds of crimes. Four other alleged members were acquitted for lack of evidence. In September 2004, several jailed members serving life sentences began hunger strikes to attain better prison conditions.[71]

Strength: Unknown but presumed to be small.

Location/Area of operation: Athens, Greece.

External Aid: Unknown

Middle East's Terrorist Organizations

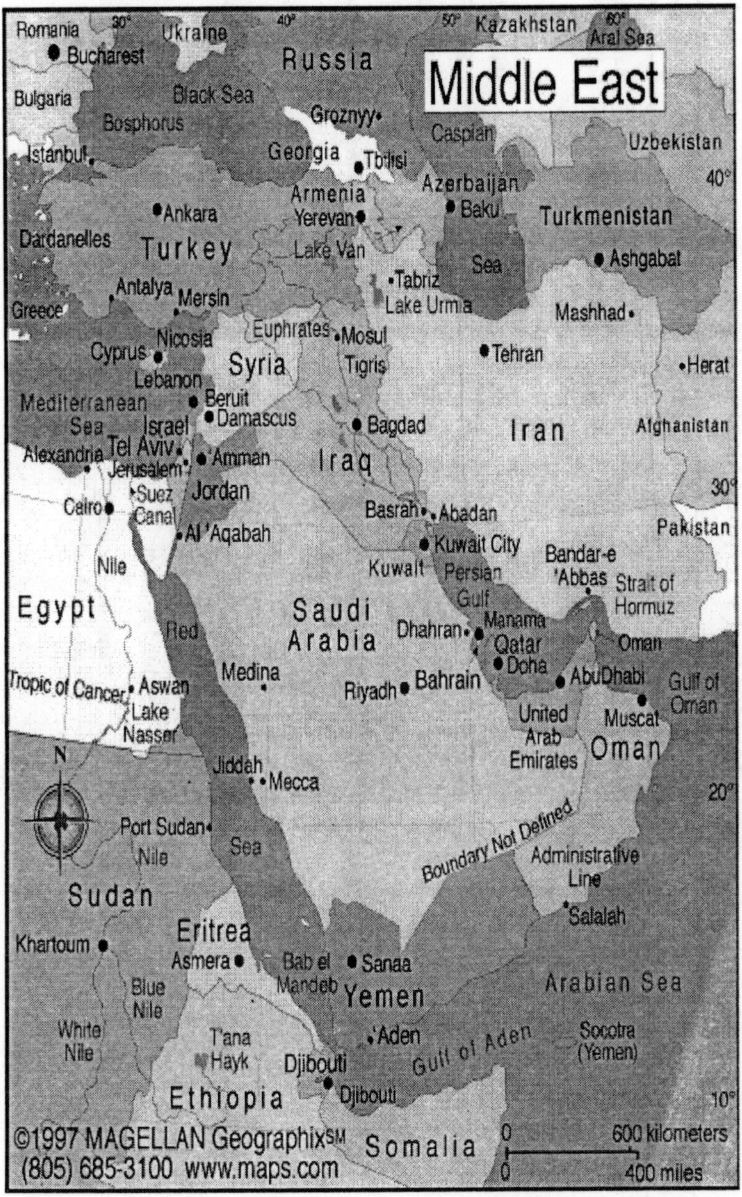

Middle East's Terrorist Organizations

S.No.	Location	Name	Other Name	Leaders	Classification
1	Iraq; Syria, Sudan	Abu Nidal Organization (ANO)	Fatah Revolutionary Council; Black September; Arab Revolutionary Brigades.	Al Banna, Sabri; Baker, Atef Abu; Issa, Abdel Rehman	Nationalist / Separatist
2	Israel; West Bank; Gaza Strip; Lebanon	Al-Aqsa Martyrs Brigades (al-Aqsa)	al-Aqisa Martyrs Abayat Battlion	Atef; al-Hamas, Alao; Barghouti, Marwan	Nationalist / Separatist
3	Afghanistan; Pakistan; Lebanon; Yemen.	Al-Jihad (AJ)	Jihad Group, Egyptian Islamic Jihad, EIJ.	al-Zumar, Abbud	Religious
4	Iraq, Israel, Jordan, Lebanon, Libya, Yemen etc	Al-Qaeda (The Base)	Qa'idat al-jihad; Maktab al khidamat; al Qadr.	Osama Bin Laden; Ahmed Taha, Rifai; al-Badawi, Jamal Mohammad; Bin Laden, Saad	Religious
5	Northern Iraq	Ansar al-Islam (Al)	Ansar al-Sunnah Partisans of Islam; Helpers of Islam; Jund al-Islam	Unknown	Religious
6	Sidon (Southern Lebanon)	Asbal al-Ansar	Band of Partisans; ·usbal al-Ansar	al Saadi, Ahmad Abd al Karim Shreidi, Abdullah; Shreidi, Hisham; Shreidi Mohammad	Religious

7	Israel; West Bank; Gaza Strip; Israel & Lebanon	HAMAS	Islamic Resistance Movement; Harakat al-Muqammah al-Islammiya.	al-Zahhar, Mahmud; Ghousheh, Ibrahim; Hanud, Mahmud Abu; Kahlil, Izz el-Deen-al-Sheikh;	Nationalist/ Separatist/ Religious
8	Southern Lebanon	Hizballah (Party of God)	Islamic jihad, Revolutionary Justice Organization, Hezbollah.	al-Mughassil, Ahmed Ibrahim; Atwa Ali; Musawi Abbas; Tufaili, Sobhi.	Nationalist/ Separatist/ Religious
9	Turkey; Iraq	Kurdistan Worker's Party (PKK)	Kongra Gel (KGK); Kurdistan Freedoms & Democracy Congress; Kurdistan People's Congress.	Bayik, Cemil; Kalkan Duran; Ocalan, Abdullah; Ocalan, Osman	Nationalist / Separatist/ Communist/ Socialist
10	Syria; Lebanon; Israel; West Bank; Gaza Strip	Popular Front for the Liberation of Palestine (PFLP)	al-Jabha ash-Sha'abiya Li-Tahrir Falastin.	al-Zibri, Mustafa; Habas, George; Mallouh, Abdel Rahim; Sa'dat, Ahmed	Nationalist / Separatist / Communist / Socialist
11	Iraq	Tanzim Qaidat al-Jihad fi Bilad al-Rafidayn (QJBR)	Al-Zarqawi Network; Al-Qaida in Iraq; Al-Qaida of Jihad organization in the land of the two Rivers.	al-Ja'af, Sami Mohammed Ali Said; al jayusi, Azmi; al- Juhaari, Abdallah Muhammed.	Religious / Nationalist/ Separatist

PROFILES OF INTERNATIONAL MIDDLE EAST'S TERRORIST GROUP

1. ABUD NIDAL ORGANIZATION (ANO)

(Designated as a Foreign Terrorist Organization)

Prior to the emergence of Al Qaida and Osama bin Laden perhaps the most famous of Islamic terrorist group was the Abu Nidal Organization (ANO). By some estimates this group has carried out attacks in 20 different countries.

Other Name

Fatah Revolutionary Council; Arab Revolutionary Brigades; Black September; Revolutionary Organization of Socialist Muslims.

Classification: Nationalist/Separatist.

Description

International terrorist organization founded by Sabri al-Banna and is located across parts of Middle East. It is linked to the Palestinian Struggle for a homeland and split from the Palestinian liberation organisation (PLO) in 1974. It has Camps in Lebanon's Bekaa valley and supporters among Palestinian refugee camps in the same country. In November 2002 Abud Nidal died in Baghdad the new leadership of the organization is unclear.[72]

Key Leaders

al, Banna, Sabri

- al, Banna, Sabri
  (Aliases: Abu Nidal)
- Baker, Atef Abu
  (Abu Bakr) (No known aliases)
- Issa, Abdel Rahman
  (No known aliases)

Activities

The ANO has carried out terrorist attacks in 20 countries, killing or injured almost 900 persons. Targets include the United States, the united kingdom, France, Israel, Moderate Palestinians, and various Arab Countries. Major attacks included the Rome and Vienna airports in 1985, the Neve Shalom Synagogue in Istanbul, the hijacking of Pan Am Flight 73 in Karachi in 1986, and the city of poros day excursion ship attack in Greece in 1988.[73] The ANO is suspected of assassinating PLO deputy Chief Abu Iyad and PLO security chief Abu Hul in Tinis in 1991. The ANO assassinated a Jordanian diplomat in Lebanon in 1994 and has been linked to the killing of the PLO representative there.

Strength

Few hundred plus limited overseas support.

Location/Area of Operation

Al-Banna relocated to Iraq in December 1998 where the group maintained a presence until operation Iraqi Freedom, but its current status in country is unknown. Sudan and Syria are thought to provide havens for ANO operatives and previously is also operated out of Libya. Training and financial assistance was given by Libya and Syria as well. Has demonstrated ability to operate over wide area, including the Middle East, Asia and Europe. Financial problems and internal disorganization have reduced the group's activities and capabilities.

External Aid

The ANO has received considerable support, including safehaven, training, logistic assistance and financial aid from Iraq, Libya and Syria (until 1987) in addition to close support for select operations.[74]

2. AL-AQSA MARTYRS BRIGADE (AL-AQSA)

(Designated as a Foreign Terrorist Organization)

Other Name: al-Aqsa Martyrs Battalion.

Classification: Nationalist Separatist.

Al-Aqsa Logo

Description

The al-Aqsa Martyrs Brigade Consists of an unknown number of small cells of terrorists associated with the Palestinian Fatah Organization. Al Aqsa emerged at the outset of the 2000 Palestinian intifadah to attack Israeli targets with the aim to driving the Israeli military and settlers from the West Bank, Gaza Strip and Jerusalem and to establish a Palestinian state. First Designated in March, 2002.

Key Leaders

- Abayat Atef (No known aliases)
- Al-Hamas, Alaa (No known aliases)
- Barghouti, Marwan (No known aliases)

Barghouti, Marwan

Activities

Al-Aqsa has carried out shootings and suicide operations against Israeli Civilians and military personnel in Israel and the Palestinian territories, rocket and mortar attacks against Israel and Israeli settlements from the Gaza Strip, and the killing of Palestinians suspected of collaborating with Israel. Al-Aqsa has killed a number of U.S citizens, the majority of them dual US-Israeli Citizens, in its attacks. In January 2002, al-Aqsa was the first Palestinian terrorist group to use a female suicide bomber in this region. On **June 30, 2006** Israel attacked private citizens and property target.

Strength: Unknown.

Location/Area of Operation

Al-Aqsa operates in Israel, the West Bank, and Gaza Strip, and has only claimed attacks inside these three areas. It may have followers in Palestinian refugee camps in Southern Lebanon.

External Aid

In the last year, numerous public accusations suggest Iran and Hizbullah are providing support to al-Aqsa elements, but the extent of external influence on al-Aqsa as a whole is not clear.

3. AL-JIHAD (AJ)

(Designated as a Foreign Terrorist Organization)

Other Name: Jihad Group, Egypitan Islamic Jihad, EIJ

Classification: Religious

Description

This Egyptian Islamic extremist group merged with Osama Bin Laden's al-Qaeda organization in 2001. Osama Bin Laden deputy, Ayman al-Zawahiri, was the former head of AJ. Active since the 1970s, AJ's primary goal has been the overthrow of the Egyptain Government and the establishment of an Islamic State. The group's primary targets, historically, have been high-level Egyptian Government officials as well as U.S. and Israeli interests in Egypt and abroad. Regular Egyptian crackdown on extremists, including on AJ, have greatly reduced AJ capabilities in Egypt. Al-Jihad's primary goal today have merged with al-Qaeda, to include attacks on U.S. and Israeli interests.

Key Leader

- al-Zumar, Abbud (No known aliases)

Activities

The Original AJ was responsible for the 1981 assassination of Egyptian President Anwar Sadat. It claimed responsibility for the attempted assassinations of Interior Minister Hassan al-Alfi in August 1993 and Prime Minister Atef Sedky in November 1993. AJ has not conducted an attack inside Egypt since 1993 and has never successfully targeted foreign tourists there. The group was responsible for the Egyptian Embassy bombing in Islamabad in 1995 and a disrupted plot against the U.S Embassy in Albania in 1998.

Strength

Unknown, but probably has several hundred hard-core members inside and outside of Egypt.

Location/Area of Operation

Historically AJ operated in the Cairo area. Most AJ members today are outside Egypt in countries such as Afghanistan, Pakistan, Lebanon, the United Kingdom and Yemen. AJ activities have been centered outside Egypt for several years under the auspices of al-Qaida.

External Aid

Unknown since 1998 AJ received most of its funding from al-Qaida, and these close ties culminated in the eventual merger of the groups. Some funding may come from various Islamic non-governmental organization, cover businesses, and criminal acts.

4. AL-QAEDA

(Designated as a Foreign Terrorist Organization)

Other Name: "The Base"; Qa'idat al-Jihad, Maktab al khidamat, Al-Jabhah al-Islamiyyah; Al Qaeda; al Qadr; Group for the preservation of the Holy Site; Usama Bin Laden Organization.

Al-Qaeda Logo

Classification: Religious

Description

Al-Qaeda was established by Osama Bin Laden in 1988 with Arabs who fought in Afghanistan against the Soviet union. Helped finance, recruit, transport, and train Sunni Islamic extremists for the Afghan resistance. Goal is to unite Muslims to fight the United States as a means of defeating Israel, overthrowing regimes it deems "non-islamic" , and expelling Westerners and non-Muslims from Muslim Countries.[75] Eventual goal would be establishment of a pan-Islamic caliphate throughout the world. Issued statement in February 1998 under the banner of "The World Islamic Front for Jihad Against the Jews and Crusaders"[76] saying it was the duty of all Muslims to kill U.S Citizens, Civilian and Military, and their allies everywhere. Merged with al-Jihad (Egyptian Islamic Jihad) in June 2001, renaming itself "Qa'idat al-Jihad". Merged with Abu Mus'ab al-Zàrqawi's organization in Iraq in late 2004, with al-Zarqawi's group changing its name to "Qa'idat al-jihad fi Bilad al-Rafidayns" [77]

Key Leaders

- Ahmed Taha, Rifai (Aliases: Abu-Yasir, Rifai Taha, Sheikh Rifai, Osama Bin Laden)
- Bin Laden, Saad (Soh of Osama bin Laden involved in 2001 attack.) (No known aliases)

- al-Bakri, Ali Sayyid Muhamed Mustafa (Aliases: Abd al-Aziz al-Masri, Abu Salsabil Hassan Omar.)
- al-Jag'iri, Abu Yasir (Aliases: Yasir al-Jazeeri)
- Ghul, Hassan (No known aliases)
- al-Badawi, Jamal Mohammad (Aliases: Abu Abdul Rahman Al-Adani, Jamal Mohammad Ahmed)

Osama Bin Laden (right) sitting with his son Saad Bin Laden (left)

al-Badawi, Jamal

Activities

Al Qaeda's tactics include bombing, hijacking, kidnapping, assassination, and suicide attacks. Reportedly, the group is actively seeking weapons of mass destruction (nuclear, chemical and biological weapons)[78] Al Qaeda has been linked to the production of the chemical VX in Sudan and the production of the biological agent ricin. On several occassions the group has tried to obtain enriched uranium. Targets tend to be prominent symbols like public buildings, embassy, historical monuments and military personnel etc. They had done many attacks, but the most horrified attack was on 11th September 2001 (9/11) on World Trade Center and Pentagon.

December 29, 1992

A bomb explodes in a hotel in Aden, Yemen. The bomb was intended to kill U.S. troops on route to Somalia, but the servicemen had already left the premises. Two Austrian tourists were killed in the blast. It is believed that this was the first attack involving al-Qaeda.

February 23, 1993

A large bomb exploded in the basement of the World Trade Center killing eight people and injuring more than 1,000. The spiritual leader behind the attack was Sheik Omar Abdel-Rahman. The bomb maker was Ramzi yousef who stayed in a Bin Laden "guest house" in Peshawar, Pakistan, both before and after the bombing.

November 13, 1995

Five Americans and two Indians were killed when a car bomb explodes outside of an American operated Saudi National Guard training center in Riyadh, Saudi Arabia.

August 17, 1998

On the anniversary of the ordering of U.S. troops in to the Gulf region, two large bombs detonates minutes apart outside U.S. embassies in Nairobi, Kenya, and Dares Salaam, Tanzania. The explosions killed 234, including 12 Americans and injuring more than 5000.

October 5, 2000

Suicide bombers attack the USS cole, killing 17 and wounding 39 Americans sailors in Yemen; al-Qaida suspected.[79]

September 11, 2001 (9/11)

On September 2001, 19 al-Qaeda suicide attackers hijacked and crashed four US commercial jets, two or World Trade Center (WTC) in New York City, one in to the Pentagon near Washington, leaving nearly 3,000 individuals dead or missing.

2002

Carried out bombing on November 28 of a hotel in Mombasa, Kenya, killing 15 and injured 40. Probably supported a night club bombing in Bali, Indonesia, on October 12 by Jamaah Islamiya that killed more than 200.[80]

2003

Carried out the assault and bombing on May 12 of three expatriate housing complexes in Riyadh, Saudi Arabia, that killed 30 and injured 216. Probably supported the bombing of the J.W. Marriot Hotel in Jakarta, Indonesia on August 5 that killed 12 and injured 149. Conducted two assassination attempt against Pakistani President Musharraf in December 2003. Was involved in some attacks in Afghanistan and Iraq.

Strength

Al-Qaida probably has several thousand extremist and associates worldwide inspired by the group's ideology. Al-Qaida also serves as a focal point or umbrella organization for a worldwide network that includes many Sunni Islamic extremist group including some members of Gama'a al-Islamiyya the Islamic Movement of Uzbekistan, and the Harakat ul-Mujahidin. The number of actual members pledging bayat (oath of allegiance) is unknown, but al-Qaeda has trained as many as 5000 militant in camps in Afghanistan and Indonesia.

Location/Area of Operation

Al Qaeda, being a truly international network with links in some 55 countries, is not limited to a specific area of operations. It has vowed to strike against its adversaries around the world. The following is a partial list of the areas of the networks operations: [81]

Middle East: Egypt, Iraq, Israel, Iran, Jordan, Kuwait, Lebanon, Libya, Morocco, Saudi Arabia, Sudan, Syria, Tunisia, Turkey, United Arab Emirates and Yemen.

Asia: Afghanistan, Bangladesh, China, India (Kashmir), Indonesia, Malaysia, Myanmar, Pakistan, and the Phillippines.

Europe: Albania, Belgium, Bosnia, Croatia, Denmark, France, Germany, Italy, Kosovo, Luxembourg, Netherland, Spain, Sweden, and the United Kingdom.

North America and South America: Canada, United States, Argentina, Brazil, Paraguay, Uruguay.[82]

External Aid

Al-Qaeda's activities are largely supported by Usama Bin Laden. He has long financed operation with his personal fortune, at one time estimated between $ 270 to $ 300 million, from the Bin Laden Group, his father's construction Company.[83] He also monopolized many export industries, such as seasame and corn products. However, al-Qaeda was able to use these companies to provide cover for the procurement of explosives, weapons, and chemicals, and to make large amounts of money. Other than Bin Laden, al-Qaeda continues to receive support throughout the world to continue it Jihad. The network has reportedly been receiving additional funds from various sources in the Middle East. It is believed that al-Qaeda has also received funds through the Dubai Islamic Bank in Dubai, which is controlled by the United Arab Emirates. The United States has traced several companies and Charitable aid organizations that are suspected of raising and laundering funds for al-

Qaeda. One of these charitable organization is the Mercy International Relief Agency.[84]

Headquarter

Al Qaeda's headquarters has subsequently moved with Osama Bin Laden throughout a number of camps in eastern Afghanistan, including the Zhawar kili camps.

5. ANSAR -AL-ISLAM (AL)[85]

(Designated as a Foreign Terrorist Organisation)

Other Name: Ansar al-Sunnah Partisans of Islam, Helpers of Islam, Jund al-Islam, Jaish Ansar al-Sunna, Kurdish Taliban.

Classification: Religious.

Description

Ansar al-Islam (AI) is a radical Islamist group of Iraqi kurds and Arabs who have vowed to establish an independent Islamic state in Iraq. The group was formed in December 2001. In the fall of 2003 a statement was issued calling all Jihadists in Iraq to united under the name Ansar al-Sunnah (AS). Since that time, it is likely that AL has posted all claims of attack under the name AS. AI is closely allied with al-Qadia and Abu Mus'ab al Zarqawi's group, Tanzim Qa'idata al-Jihad fi Bilad al-Rafidayn (QJBR) in Iraq. Some members of AI trained in al-Qaida camps in Afghanistan, and the group provided safe haven to al-Qaeda fighters before operation Iraqi Freedom (OIF). (Ansar al-Islam was designated on 20 February 2003, under E.O. 13224. The UNSCR 1267 Committee designated Ansar al-Islam pursuant to UNSCRs 1267, 1390 and 1455 on 27 February 2003) First designated in March 2004.

Key Leader: Unknown

Activities

AL continues to conduct attacks against coalition forces, Iraqi Government officials and security forces, and ethnic Iraqi groups and political parties. AI has also claimed responsibility for many high profile attacks, including the simultaneous suicide bombing of the PUK and Kurdistan Democratic Party (KDP) party offices in Ibril on February 1, 2004 and the bombing of the U.S military dining facility in Mosul on December 21, 2004. Before OIF, some Al members claimed to have produced cyanide-based toxins, ricin and alfatoxin.

Strength

Approximately 500 to 1,000 members.

Location/Area of operation

Primarily central and northern Iraq.

External Aid

The group receives funding, training, equipment, and combat support from al-Qaeda, QJBR, and other international jihadist backers throughout the world. AI also has operational and logistic support cells in Europe.

6. ASBAT -AL-ANSAR

(Designated as a Foreign Terrorist Organization)

Other Name: Band of Partisans, Usbal -al-Ansar.

Classification: Religious.

Description

Asbat al-Ansar, the League of the Followers or Partisans' League, is a Lebanon-based Sunni extremist group, composed primarily of Palestinians with links to Osama Bin Laden's al-Qaida organisation and other sunni extremist groups. The groups follows an extremist interpretation of Islam that justifies violence against civilian targets to achieve political ends. Some of the group's goals include overthrowing the Lebanese Government and thwarting perceived anti-Islamic and pro-Western influence in the country. First designated in March 2002.

Key Leaders

Abu Mohjen

- al-Saadi, Ahmad Abd al Karim (Aliases: Abu Mohjen)
- Shreidi, Abdullah (No known aliases)
- Shreidi, Hisham (No known aliases)
- Shreidi, Mohammed (No known aliases)

Activities

Asbat-al-Ansar has carried out multiple terrorist attacks in Lebanon since it first emerged in the early 1990s. The group assassinated Lebanese religious leaders and bombed nightclubs, theaters, and liquor stores in the mid 1990s. The group raised its operational profile in 2000 with two attacks against Lebanese and international targets. It was involved in clashes in northern Lebanon in December 1999 and carried out a rocket-propelled grenade attack on the Russian Embassy in Beirut in January 2000. Asbat al-Ansar's leader, Abu Muhjin, remains at large despite being sentenced to death in absentia for the 1994 murder of a Muslim cleric. Suspected Asbat al-Ansar elements were responsible for an attempt in April 2003 to use a car bomb against a McDonald's in a Beirut Suburb. By October, Lebanese security forces arrested Ibn al-Shahid, who is believed to be associated with Asbat al-Ansar, and charged him with masterminding the bombing of three fast food restaurant in 2002 and the attempted attack on a McDonald's in 2003. Asbat forces were involved in other violence in Lebanon in 2003, including clashes with members of Yasser Arafat's Fatah movement in the 'Ayn al-Hilwah refugee camp and a rocket attack in June on the future TV building in Beirut.

In 2004, no successful terrorist attack were attributed to Asbat al-Ansar. However, in September, operatives with links to the group were believed to be involved in a planned terrorist operation targeting the Italian Embassy, the Ukrainian Consulate General, and Lebanese Government offices.

Strength

The group commands about 300 fighters in Lebanon.

Location/Area of Operation

The group's primary base of operations is the Ayn al-Hilwah refugee camp near Sidon in Southern Lebanon.

External Aid

Probably receives money through international Sunni extremist network and possibly Usama Bin Laden's al Qaida network.

7. HAMAS

(Designated as a Foreign Terrorist Organization)

The Hamas group has gained international notoriety in its longstanding armed struggle to create an Islamic Palestinian state in the Middle East.

Other Name: Islamic Resistance Movement, Harakat al-Muqawammah al-Islammiya.

Classification: Religious/Nationalist/Separatist.

Description

Hamas was founded in 1987 in the West Bank of Gaza

Hamas Logo

Hamas Seal

Strip. But it is not confined to these contentious areas. It also has a strong religious base, as might be guessed from its name, and recruits members openly through mosques and also tries to raise funds by this method.[86] Various HAMAS elements have used both violent and political means, including terrorism, to pursue the goal of establishing an Islamic Palestinian state in Israel. HAMAS is also engaged in political activity, such as running candidates in West Bank Chamber of commerce elections. HAMAS and its armed militant using known as Iz el-Deen carried out continued bombing (including a large number of suicide bombings),[87] assassination, and kidnapping of those opposed to its existence.

Key Leaders

- al-Zahhar, Mahmud (No known aliases)
- Hanud, Mahmud Abu (No known aliases)
- Khalil, IZZ el-Deen al-Sheikh (No known aliases)
- Marzuq, Musa Abu (No known aliases)
- Ghousheh, Ibrahim (No known aliases)

al-Zahhar, Mahmud

Ghousheh, Ibrahim

Activities

It has carried out a number of especially those in the Iz el-Deen, al Qassam Brigades, have conducted many attacks, including large scale suicide bombings against Israeli civilian and military targets. In the early 1990s, they also targeted suspected Palestinian collaborators and Fatah rivals. In November 2002 claimed responsibility for a suicide attack on an Israeli bus in residential jerusalem, which killed at least 11 people with many of the victim being school children.[88] Hamas continues to confine its attacks to Israelis inside Israel and the occupied territories.

Strength

Unknown number of official members; tens of thousands of supporters and sympathizers.

Location/Area of Operation

HAMAS currently limits its terrorist operations to Israeli Military and Civilian targets in the West Bank, Gaza Strip and Israel. The group retains a cadre of Senior leaders spread throughout the Gaza Strip, Syria, Lebanon, Iran and the Gulf States.

External Aid

Receives some funding from Iran but primarily relies on donations from Palestinian expatriates around the world and private benefactors in Saudi Arabia and other Arab States. Some fundraising and propaganda activity take place in Western Europe and North America.[89]

8. HIZBALLAH (Party of God)

(Designated as a Foreign Terrorist Organisation)

Of the many Islamist groups that have emerged within the Muslim world since the mid 1980s, perhaps none had a great impact on Middle East and international affairs as HIZBALLAH, "The Party of God" is one of the most significant terrorist organization operating today.

Hizballah Logo

Other Name: Party of God, Islamic Jihad, Revolutionary Justice Organization, Hezbollah, Islamic jihad for the Liberation of Palestine.

Classification: Nationalist/Separatist/Religious.

Description

It was formed in June 1982 in Lebanon as the militant wing of a religious group, this Lebanon based radical Shi'a (also known as Shi'ite, Shi'ia or Shiite) group takes its ideological inspiration from the Iranian revolution and the teachings of the Late Ayatollah Khomeini. Hizbullah has had the ideological, Organizational and operational means to seize opportunities to get closer to its aim. Amir Taheri, in "Holy Terror" (1987), wrote that Hizbullah was motivated by two main concepts : a leadership seen to represent Allah's will on Earth and a very personal concept of MARTYRDOM.[90] According to the classical origins of the root of the word hizb means a community, sect or a group of followers. However, Hizballah ideology emphasizes the Quranic Origin of its political terminology. Almost all of the political terms that the party uses in its Political literature are derived from the Quran.[91] A Hizbullah leader Shaykh Ibrahim al-Amin, did not even reject the `terrorist' label of his party. He believes that the Quran `Ordered' them to engage in the fight against the USA and Israel. The group is vehemently anti American and anti-Israeli, and much of Hizbullah's terrorists activity has been directed against U.S and Israeli targets. It is widely supposed that the terrorists who have carried out the deadly mission of the shadowy Islamic Jihad have been tied to Hizbullah.

Hizbullah's official spokesman maintain that the Movement is a 'Mission' and 'way of life'. Other Hizbullah leader has insisted that Hizbullah 'is not an organization, for its members carry no cards and bear no specific responsibilities. It is a 'nation' of all who believes in the struggle against injustice and also who are loyal to Iran's Imam Khomeini.[92] Hizbullah is dedicated to liberating Jerusalem and eliminating Israel, and has formally advocated ultimate establishment of Islamic rule in Lebanon. Nonetheless, Hizballah has actively participated in Lebanon's political system since 1992.

Key Leaders

- al-Mughassil, Ahmed Ibrahim (Aliases: Abu Omran)
- al-Yacoub, Ibrahi, Salih Mohammed (No known aliases)
- Musawi, Abbas (No known aliases)
- Tufaili, Sabhi (No known aliases)
- Atwa Ali (Aliases: Ammar Mansour Bouslim, Hassan Rostom Salim)

al-Mughassil, Ahmed Ibrahim

Atwa Ali

Activities

Known or suspected to have been involved in numerous anti-U.S and anti-Israeli terrorist attacks, including the suicide truck bombings of the U.S Embassy and U.S Marine barracks in Beirut in October 1983 and the U.S Embassy annax in Beirut in September 1984. Three members of Hizbullah, 'Imad Mughniyah, Hasan Izz-al-Din, and Ali Atwa are on the FBI's list of 22 most wanted Terrorists for the hijacking in 1985 of TWA flight 847 during which a U.S Navy diver was murdered. Hizbullah also attacked the Israeli Embassy in Argentina in 1992 and the Israeli cultural center in Buenos Aires in 1994. In March 2004, Hizbullah and Hamas signed an agreement to increase joint efforts to perpetrate attacks against Israel.[93]

Strength

Several thousand supporters and a few hundred terrorist operatives.

Location/Area of Operation

Operates in the Southern suburbs of Beirut, the Beka's

Valley, and Southern Lebanon. Has established cells in Europe, Africa, South America, North America, and Asia.

External Aid

It is thought to have received finance, training, weapons, explosives, political, diplomatic and organizational aid from Iran and diplomatic, political and logistic support from Syria.[94]

9. KURDISTAN WORKERS' PARTY (PKK)

(Designated as a Foreign Terrorist Organization)

The Kurdistan workers party is one of the most active and well-organized terrorist organizations in the world. It is their goal to establish an independent nation for Kurds known as Kurdistan.

PKK OLD LOGO

PKK NEW LOGO

Other Name: Kongra-Gel (KGK), Kurdistan Freedom and Democracy Congress, Kurdistan People's Congress;

Classification: Nationalist/ Separatist/Communist/Socialist.

Description

Founded by Abdullah Ocalan in 1974 as a Marxist-Leninist Separatist organization and formally named the Kurdistan worker's party (PKK) in 1978. The group, composed primarily of Turkish Kurds, began its campaign of armed violence in 1984,[95] which has resulted in some 30,000 casualties. The PKK's goal has been to establish an independent, democratic Kurdish state in South East Turkey, Northern Iraq, and parts of Iran and Syria. In the early 1990,s the PKK moved beyond rural-based insurgent activities to include urban terrorism. Turkish authorities captured Ocalan in Kenya in early 1999, and the

Turkish State Security Court subsequently sentenced him to death. At a PKK Congress in January 2000, members supported Ocalan's initiative and claimed the group now would use only political means to achieve its public goal of improved rights for kurds in Turkey.[96] In April, 2002 at its 8th party congress, the PKK changed its name to the Kurdistan Freedom and Democracy Congress (KADEK) and proclaimed a commitment to non-violent activities in support of kurdishrights. After five years, the group's hard-line militant using the people's Defense force (HPG), renounced its self-imposed cease-fire on June 1, 2004. Over the course of the cease-fire, the group had divided into two factions—politically minded, reformists, and hardliners who advocated a return to violence. The hardliners took control of the group in February 2004.

Key Leaders

Bayik, Cemil

- Bayik, Cemil (Aliases: Cuma)
- Kalkan, Duran (Aliases: Abbas)
- Ocalan, Abdullah (Aliases: Apo)
- Ocalan, Osman (No known aliases)
- Pir, Kemal (No known aliases)

Kalkan, Duran

Activities

The PKK is not merciful when it comes to attacks on the government and its supporters, where casualties of their insurgency count scores of women and children amongst the dead and injured. This new wave of mayhem has lasted since for ten years and has resulted in an estimated 10,000 deaths during that time. In an attempt to damage Turkey's tourist industry, the then PKK bombed tourist sites and hotels and kidnapped foreign tourists in the early-to-mid-1990s. While most of the group's violence in 2004 was directed toward Turkish security forces, KGK was likely responsible for an unsuccessful July car bomb attack against the governor of Van Province,[97] although it publicly denied responsibility, and may have played a role in the August bombings of two Istanbul hotels and a gas complex in which two people died.

Strength

Approximately 4,000 to 5,000, most of who currently are located in Northern Iraq has thousands of sympathizers in Turkey and Europe.

Location/Area of operations

Operates primarily in Turkey. Other locations are Iraq, Europe and the Middle East.

External Aid

The PKK is financed in part through "revolutionary taxes" which it demands from the Kurdish population and also from its dealings in the worldwide heroin trade. Also received safehaven and modest aid from Syria, Iraq, and Iran. KGK uses Europe for fundraising and conducting political propaganda.

10. POPULAR FRONT FOR THE LIBERATION OF PALESTINE (PFLP)[98]

(Designated as a Foreign Terrorist Organization)

Other Name: al-Jabha ash-Sha'abiya Li-Tahrir Falastin

Classification: Nationalist/Separatist/ Communist/Socialist.

PFLP LOGO

Description

Formerly a part of the PLO, the Marxist-Leninist PFLP was founed by George Habash when it broke away from the Arab Nationalist Movement in 1967. The PFLP does not view the Palestinian struggle as religious, seeing it instead as a broader revolution against Western imperialism. The group earned a reputation for spectacular international attacks, including airline hijackings, that have killed at least 20 US citizens.

Key Leaders

al-Zibri, Mustafa

Habash, George

- al-Zibri, Mustafa (Aliases: Abu Ali Mustafa ; Mustafa Aki Kasam Zaberi)
- Mallouh, Abdel Kahmi (No known Aliases)
- Sa'dat, Ahmed (Aliases: Ahmed Saadat)
- Sanchez, Ilich Ramirez (Aliases: Carles the Jackal)
- Habash, George (Aliases: al Hakim)

Activities

The PFLP committed numerous international terrorist attacks during the 1970s. Since 1978 the group has conducted attacks against Israeli or moderate Arab targets, including killing a settler and her son in December 1996. The PFLP has stepped up its operational activity since the start of the current intifadah, highlighted by at least two suicide bombings since 2003, multiple joint operations with other Palestinian terrorist groups, and assassination of the Israeli Tourism Minister in 2001 to avenge Israel's killing of the PFLP Secretary General earlier that year.

Strength

Approximately 800 members.

Location/Area of Operation

Syria, Lebanon, Israel, the West Bank and the Gaza Strip.

External Aid

Receives safe haven and some logistical assistance from Syria.

11. TANZIM QA'IDAT AL-JIHAD FI BILAD AL-RAFIDAYN (QJBR)[99]

(Designated as a Foreign Terrorist Organisation)

Other Name: Al-Zarqawi Network, Al Qaeda in Iraq, Al-Qaeda of jihad organisation in the Land of The Two Rivers.

Classification: Religious, Nationalist/Separatist.

Description

The Jordanian Palestinian Abu Mus'ab al-Zarqawi (Ahmed Fadhil Nazzal al-khalaylah, or Abu Ahmad, Abu Azraq) established cells in Iraq soon after the commencement of operation Iraqi freedom (OIF), formalizing his group in April 2004 to bring together jihadists and other insurgents in Iraq fighting U.S and coalition forces. Zarqawi initially called his group "Unity and Jihad." Zarqawi and his group helped finance, recruit, transport and train Sunni Islamic extremists for the Iraqi resistance. The group adopted its current name after October 2004, when it merged with Osama Bin Ladin's al-Qaeda. The immediate goal of QJBR is to expel the coalition—through a campaign of bombings, kidnapping, assassinations and intimidation—and establish an Islamic state in Iraq. QJBR's longer-term goal is to proliferate jihad from Iraq into "Greater Syria", that is Syria, Lebanon, Israel and Jordan.

Key Leaders

- al Iraqi, Abu Maysarah (No known aliases)
- al-Ja' af, Sami Mohammed Ali Said (Aliases: Abu Yusef, Abu Omar Al-Kurdi.)
- al-Jayusi, Azmi (Aliases: Azmi Al-Jayousi)
- al-Juhaari, Abdallah Muhammed (Aliases: Abdallah Nahim, Abu Azzam, Abu Selwah, Emir of the Anbar.)

Activities

In August 2003, Zarqawi's group carried out a major international terrorist attack in Iraq when it bombed the Jordanian Embassy in Baghdad, followed 12 days later by a suicide vehicle-borne improvised explosive device (VBIED) attack against the UN Headquarters in Baghdad, killing 23, including the Secretary General's special representative for Iraq, Sergio Vieria de Mello. Also in August the group conducted a VBIED attack against Shi'a worshippers outside the Imam Ali Mosque in Al Najaf, killing 85 including the leader of the Supreme Council for the Islamic Revolution in Iraq (SCIRI). Zarqawi's group conducted VBIED attack against U.S Military personnel and Iraqi infrastructure throughout 2004, including suicide attacks inside the Green zone perimeter in Baghdad. The group successfully penetrated the Green Zone in the October bombing of a popular cafe and market. The group has claimed responsibility for the videotaped execution by beheading of Americans Nicholas Berg (May 8, 2004), Jack Armstrong (September 20, 2004), and Jack Hensley (September 21, 2004). The group may have been involved in other hostage incidents as well. Zarqawi's group has been active in the Levant since its involvement in the failed Millennium plot directed against U.S, Western and Jordanian targets in Jordan in late 1999. The group assassinated USAID official Laurence Foley in 2002, but the Jordanian Government has successfully disrupted further plots against U.S and western interests in Jordan, including a major arrest of Zarqawi associates in 2004 planning to attack Jordanian security targets.

Strength

QJBR's numerical strength is unknown, though the group has attracted new recruits to replace key leaders and other members killed or captured by coalition forces. Zarqawi's increased stature from his formal relationship with al-Qaeda could attract additional recruits to QJBR.

Location/Area of Operation

QJBR's operations are predominately Iraq-based, but the

group maintains an extensive logistical network throughout the Middle East, North Africa and Europe.

External Aid

QJBR probably receives funds from donors in the Middle East and Europe, local sympathizers in Iraq, and a variety of businesses and criminal activities. In many cases, QJBR's donors are probably motivated by support for jihad rather than affiliation with any specific terrorist group.

SOUTH AMERICAN TERRORIST ORGANIZATIONS

South American Terrorist Organisations

S.No.	*Location*	*Name*	*Other Name*	*Leaders*	*Classification*
1	Chile	Manuel Rodriquez Patriotic front (FPMR)	Unknown	Unknown	Unknown
2	Colombia & Venezuela	National Liberation Army (ELN)	Unknown	Canas Serrano, Pedro Elias; Chamorro, Herlintong Javier; Galan, Francisco.	Communist / Socialist
3	Colombia; Brazil; Peru; Venezuela; Panama & Ecuador.	Revolutionary Armed Forces of Colombia (FARC)	Unknown	Arango, Luciano Marin; Granda, Rodrigo; Guzman, Noel Mata Mata.	Communist / Socialist
4	Peru	Shining Path	Sendero Luminoso people's Liberation Army (SL)	Comrade Artemio; Gugman, Abimael Reynoso; Ramirez Durand, Oscar	Communist / Socialist

PROFILES OF INTERNATIONAL SOUTH AMERICAN TERRORIST GROUPS

1. MANUEL RODRIQUEZ PATRIOTIC FRONT (FPMR)

Other Name: Unknown

Classification: Unknown

Description:

Founded in 1983 as the armed wing of the Chilean Communist Party and named for the hero of Chile's war of independence against Spain. Splintered into two factions in the late 1980s and one faction became a political party in 1991. The dissident wing FPMR/D is Chile's only remaining active terrorist group.[100]

Key Leaders: Unknown

Activities

FPMR attacks civilians and international targets including U.S businesses and Mormon Churches. In 1993, FPMR bombed two MC Donald's restaurants and attempted to bomb a Kentucky Fried Chicken (KFC) restaurant. Successful government counter terrorist operations have undercut the organizations significantly. Four FPMR members escaped from prison using a helicopter in December 1996.

Strength: Estimated 50 to 100 members

Location/Area of Operation: Chile

External Aid: Unknown

2. NATIONAL LIBERATION ARMY (ELN)

(Designated as a Foreign Terrorist Organisation)

Other Name: Unknown

Classification: Communist/Socialist.

ELN Flag

ELN Logo

Description

The ELN is a Colombian Marxist insurgent group formed in 1965 by Urban intellectuals inspired by fidel castro and Che Guevara. It is primarily rural-based, although it possesses several urban units. In May 2004, Colombian President Uribe proposed a renewal of peace talks but by the ends of the year talks had not commenced.[101]

Key Leaders

From left to right, ELN member Francisco Galan

- Canas Serrano, Pedro Elias (Aliases: Lucas El Mono)
- Galan, Francisco (Aliases: Gerardo Bermudez)
- Chamorro, Herlintong Javier (Aliases: Antonio Garcia)
- Lamus, Arcesio (No known aliases)

Activities

Kidnapping, hijacking, bombing and extortion. Minimal

conventional military capability. Annually conducts hundreds of kidnappings for ransom, often targeting foreign employees of large corporations, especially in the petroleum industry. Derives some revenue from taxation of the illegal narcotics industry. Frequently assaults energy infrastructure and has inflicted major damage on pipelines and the electric distribution network. [102]

Strength

Approximately 3,000 armed combatants and an unknown number of active supporters.

Location/Area of Operation

Mostly in rural and mountainous areas of northern, north-eastern, and south western colombia, and venezuelam border regions.

External Aid

Cuba provides some medical care and political consultation. Venezuela continues to provide a hospitable environment.

3. REVOLUTIONARY ARMED FORCES OF COLOMBIA (FARC)

(Designated as a Foreign Terrorist Organisation)

Other Name: Unknown

Classification: Communist/Socialist.

Description

FARC Flag

FARC Logo

Established in 1964 as the military wing of the Colombian Communist Party, the FARC is Latin America's oldest, most capable, and best-equipped insurgency of Marxist origin. Although only nominally fighting in support of Marxist goals today, the FARC is governed by a general secretariat led by long-time leader Manuel Marulanda ("Tirofijo") and six others, including senior military commander Jorge Briceno ("Mono Jojoy".) Organized along military lines but includes some specialized urban fighting units. A Colombian military offensive targeting FARC fighters in their former safe haven in Southern Colombia has experienced some success, with several FARC mid-level leaders killed or captured. On December 31, 2004 FARC leader Simon Trinidad, the highest ranking FARC leader ever captured, was extradited to the United States on drug charges.

Key Leaders

- Arango, Luciano Marin (Aliases: Ivan Marquez)
- Granda, Rodrigo (Aliases: Granda)
- Guzman, Noel Mata Mata (Aliases: Efrain Guzman, El Cucho, El Viejo Efrain, Mecato).

Arango, Luciano Marin

Guzman, Noel Mata Mata

Activities

Bombings, murder, mortar attacks, kidnapping, extortion and hijacking, as well as guerrilla and conventional military action against Colombian political, military, and economic targets. In March 1999, the FARC executed three U.S indegenous rights activists on Venezuelan territory after it kidnapped them in Colombia. In February 2003 the FARC captured and continues to hold three U.S contractors and killed one another American when their plane crashed in Florencia. Foreign citizens often are targets of FARC kidnapping for ransom. The FARC has well documented ties to the full range of narcotics trafficking activities, including taxation, cultivation, and distribution.

Strength

Approximately 9,000 to 12,000 armed combatants and several thousand more supporters mostly in rural areas.

Location/Area of Operation

Primarily in Colombia with some activities-extortion, kidnapping, weapons sourcing and logistics suspected in neighbouring Brazil, Venezuela, Panama, Peru and Ecuador.

External Aid

Cuba provides some medical care, safe heaven, and political consultation. The FARC often uses the Colombia/Venezuela border area for cross-border incursions and considers venezuela territory as a safe heaven.

4. SHINING PATH (SL)

(Designated as a Foreign Terrorist Organization)

Other Name: Sendero Luminoso
People's Liberation
Army.

Classification: Communist/
Socialist.

PCP Logo

Description

Former university professor Abimael Guzman formed SL in Peru in the late 1960s, and his teachings created the foundation of SL's militant Maoist doctrine. In the 1980s, SL became one of the most ruthless terrorist groups in the Western Hemisphere. The Peruvian Government made dramatic gains against SL during the 1990s, but report of recent SL involvement in narco-trafficking and kidnapping for ransom indicate it may be developing new sources of support.[103] In 2001, the Peruvian National Police thwarted an SL attack against "an

American objective", possibly the U.S Embassy, when they arrested two Lima SL cell members. Additionally, Government authorities continued to arrest and prosecute active SL members, including Ruller Mazombite ("Camarada Cayo"), Chief of the protection team of SL leader Macario Ala ("Artemio"), and Evorcio Ascencios ("Camarada Canale") logistics chief of the Huallaga Regional Committee.[104] Counter terrorist operations targeted pockets of terrorist activity in the upper Huallaga River valley and the Apurimac / Ene River Valley, where SL Columns continued to conduct periodic attacks. SL's stated goal is to destroy existing peruvian institution and replace them with a communist peasent revolutionary regime.

Key Leaders

- Comrade Artemio (Aliases: Ciro Chamorro, Gobriel Macario Ala)
- Guzman, Abimael Reynoso (Aliases: Puka inti, Presidents Gonzalo)
- Tparraguirre, Elena (Aliases: Miriam, Noemi)
- Ramirez Durand, Oscar (Aliases: Angel, Feliciano)

Comrade Artemio

Guzman, Abimael Reynoso

Activities

Conducted indiscriminate bombings campaigns and selective assassinations. Approximately 30,000 persons have died since Shining Path took up arms in 1980.[105]

Strength

Unknown but estimated to be some 300 armed militants.

Location/Area of Operation

Peru, with most activity in rural areas.

External Aid

Unknown. Cocaine trafficking their own financial sources.

MOST WANTED TERRORISTs
FBI Update:10/10/01

Osama bin Laden | Ayman Al-Zawahiri | Abdelkarim Hussein Mohamed Al-Nasser | Abdullah Ahmed Abdullah | Muhsin Musa Matwalli Atwah

Ali Atwa | Anas Al-Liby | Ahmed Khalfan Ghailani | Hasan Izz-Al-Din | Ahmed Mohammed Hamed Ali

Fazul Abdullah Mohammed | Imad Fayez Mugniyah | Mustafa Mohamed Fadhil | Sheikh Ahmed Salim Swedan | Abdul Rahman Yasin | Saif Al-Adel

Fahid Mohammed Ally Msalam | Ahmad Ibrahim Al-Mughassil | Khalid Shaikh Mohammed | Muhammad Atef | Ali Saed Bin Ali El-Hoorie | Ibrahim Salih Mohammed Al-Yacoub

REFERENCES

1. Gus Martin, *Understanding Terrorism,* Sage Publication London; 2003; p. 33.
2. R.C. Mishra, *Terrorism Implications of Tactics & Technology,* Authorspress Publication, New Delhi, 2004, p. 37.
3. Ranjit K. Pachnanda, *Terrorism and Response to Terrorist Threat,* UBS, New Delhi, 2002, p. 36.
4. Vijai K. Nair; *AAKROSH* (Volume 4) Number 10; January 2001; Forum for Strategic and Security Studies Publication, p. 23.
5. Gus Martin; Understanding Terrorism; Sage publications London; 2003; Pg 33.
6. B.P. Singh Sehgal, *Global Terrorism Socio-Politico and Legal Dimensions,* Deep & Deep Publication, New Delhi, 1995; p. 331.
7. R.C. Mishra, *op. cit,* p. 37.
8. David J. Whittaker, *The Terrorism Reader,*Second Edition; Routledge Taylor & Francis Group, New York, 2003, pp. 35-36.
9. www. Patterns of Global Terrorism.com.
10. Jay M. Shafritz, E.F. Gibbons; *Almanac of Modern Terrorism;* Facts on File Publishers, New York, Sydney, 1991, p. 68.
11. Anna Sabasteanski, *Patterns of Global Terrorism,* Vol. 1 1985-2005; Berkshire Publishing Group U.S.A., 2005; p. 164.
12. *Ibid,* p. 166.
13. http://www.tkb. org/FTO.Jsp.
14. Cindy C. Combs and Martin Slann, *Encyclopedia of Terrorism;* Facts on File, Inc. New York, 2002, p. 15.
15. Anna Sabasteanski, *Patterns of Global Terrorism 1985-2005* U.S. Department of State Report With Supplementary Documents And Statistics; Berkshire Publishing Group, U.S.A., 2005; p. 171.
16. *Ibid,* p 172.
17. K.R. Gupta, *International Terrorism,* Volume II; Atlantic Publishers & Distributers New Delhi, 2002, p. 433.
18. LLoyd Pettiford and Harding; *Terrorism The New World War;* Arcturus Publishing, London, 2003; p. 130-131.

    Luxor : 3,500 year old temple of Hatshepsut, Luxor, one of the greatest archaeological attraction of Egypt. Luxor attack is an attack in which 58 tourist were killed and four Egyptians and wounded dozens more. 35 of the dead came from Switzerland and another victim lived there.

19. Jay M. Shafritz, E.F. Gibbons, *op. cit.*, p. 154.
20. http://www. trb. org/FTO.JSP
21. Amna Sabasteanski, *Patterns of Global Terrorism 1985-2005*; Vol. I, Berkshire, U.S.A., 2005, p. 185.
22. *Patterns of Global Terrorism,* (Ibid) p. 188.
23. *Ibid,* p. 189.
24. K.R. Gupta, *International Terrorism,* Volume II; Atlantic Publishers & Distributor, New Delhi, 2002, p. 429.
25. Cindy C. Combs and Martin Slann; *Encyclopedia of Terrorism,* Facts on File, Inc. New York, 2002, p. 2.
26. Lloyd Pettiford and David Harding, *op. cit.*, p. 78.
27. www.tkb. org/FTO.JSP
28. Anna Sabasteanski, *op.cit.*, p. 167.
29. http://www. tkb. org/FTO.JSP
30. Cindy C. Combs and Martin Shann, *op. cit.*, p. 25.
31. Anna Sabasteanski, *op. cit.*, p. 168.
32. Lloyd Pettiford, and David Harding, *Terrorism, The New World War*; Arcturus Publishers, London, 2003; p. 77.
33. Yoram Schweitzer & Shaul Shay, *The Globalization of Terror;* Transaction Publishers, New Brunswick, USA; 2003; p. 85.
34. K.P.S. Gill, Harinder Baweja, *Most Wanted Profiles of Terror,* Lotus Collection, New Delhi, 2002, p. 40.
35. Yoarm Schweitzer, Shaul Shay, *The Globalization of Terror, The Challenge of Al Qaeda and the Response of the International Community,* Transaction Publication, U.S.A, U.K., 2003; p. 84.
36. K.R. Gupta, *International Terrorism,* Vol. II, Atlantic Publishers and Distributors, New Delhi, 2002; p. 447.
37. Anna Sabasteanski, *op. cit.*, p. 176.
38. David J. Whittaker; *Terrorism Understanding the Global Threat;* Longman Publishers, London, New York, 2002, p. 43.
39. http://www.mipt.org
40. Anna Sabasteanski, *op.cit.*, p. 178.

41. Cindy C. Combs and Martin Slann, *op.cit.,* p. 101.
42. www. Ict. Org (Internet Site of SATP)
43. http://www. Kashmir herald. Com/Profiles/Jaishe Mohammad/ htm/.
44. LLoyd Pettiford and David Harding, *op.cit.,* p. 78.
45. www. Patterns of Global Terrorism.com

    MDI is a prominent Pakistani madrassa based in a sprawing acre campus at Muridke, with some 130-satellite institutions under its auspices.
46. Jane's Intelligence Review November 2002, p. 14; Jir. Janes.com.
47. K.P.S. Gill; Amir Mir; *Most Wanted Profiles of Terror,* Lotus Collection, New Delhi, 2003, p. 67.
48. Jay M. Shafritz, E.F. Gibbons, *op.cit.,* p. 154.
49. Anna Sabasteanski, *op.cit.,* p. 183.
50. *Ibid.,* p. 184.
51. David J. Whittaker, *The Terrorism Reader-Second Edition*; Routledge Taylor and Fracis Group, London and New York; 2003, p. 83.
52. *Ibid.,* p. 85.
53. Adluri Subramanyam Raju; *Terrorism in South Asia,* Indian Research Press, New Delhi, Year 2004, p. 219.
54. Swamy Narayan, *Tigers of Sri Lanka,* Boys to Guerrillas; Konark Publishers New Delhi, 1994, p. 223.
55. K.R. Gupta, *op.cit.,* p. 456.
56. Maj. Genl. Ashok K. Mehta, *AAKROSH,* July 2002, Vol. 5, Number 16; Forum for Strategic and Security Studies Publishers; p, 44.
57. www.tkb.org/FTO.JSP
58. David J. Whittaker, *op.cit.,* pp. 52-53.
59. Times of India New Delhi; March 14 2004; p. 11.
60. David J. Whittaker, *op.cit.,* p. 145.
61. LLoyd Pettiford and David Harding, *op.cit.,* p. 89.

    Sinn Fein, "We Alone," is a nationalist political party in the Republic of Ireland, which professes a socialist, anticapitalist ideology. Part of its strength lies in its relationship with the IRISH Republican Army (IRA), and later the provisional IRISH Republican Army (PIRA), of which Sinn Fein is sometimes describes as the political wing.

62. David J. Whittaker, *op.cit.*, p. 55.
63. www. Patterns of Global Terrorism.com
64. Anna Sabasteanski, *op.cit.*, p. 188.
65. LLOYD Pettiford, *op.cit.*, p. 85.
66. K.R. Gupta, *International Terrorism*, Vol. II, Atlantic Publishers New Delhi, 2002, p. 467.
67. Cindy C. Combs and Martin Slann, *op.cit.*, p. 171.
68. *Ibid.*, pp. 172-173.
69. www. tkb. org/FTO.JSP.
70. Yonah Alexander, and Dennis A. Plunchinsky, *European Terrorism Today & Tomorrow*, Brassey's (US), Inc. Washington, 1992, p. 99.
71. Anna Sabasteanski, *op.cit.*, p. 160.
72. Prof. Ramesh Chandra,*Global Terrorism*, Vol-1, *Potential of World Terrorism*, Kalpaz, New Delhi, 2003, p. 151.
73. *Ibid.*
74. Verinder Grover, *Encyclopedia of International Terrorism*, Deep & Deep Publishers, New Delhi, 2002, p. 58.
75. Rohan Gunaratha, *Inside Al Qaeda Global Network of Terror*, Lotus Collection Roli Books New Delhi, 2002, p. 17.
76. Rohan Gunaratna; *AAKROSH*, April 2003, Vol. 6, Number 19, p. 74.
77. *Ibid.*
78. Central Intelligence Agency, Statement by Director of Central Intelligence George J. Tenet before the Senate Select Committee on Intelligence on "The Worldwide Threat in 2000 : Global Realities of our National Security", February 2, 2000, also available at: www. odci.gov/cia/PUBLIC_affairs htm.
79. Yonah Alexander and Michael S. Suletnam; *Usama Bin Laden's al Qaida : Profile of a Terrorist Network;* Transnational Publishers Inc., U.S.A.; 2001; p. 32.
80. Shaul Mishal, Maoz Rosenthal, *Studies in Conflict and Terrorism;* Vol. 28, Number & July-August 2005; Routledge Taylor & Francis Group London and New York, p. 277.
81. Yonah Alexander and Michaels Suletnam, *op.cit.*, p. 31
82. http://www.cnn.com/2001/US/09/12/binladen profile/
83. Luis S.R. Vas; Osama Bin Laden, King of Terror; Pustak Mahal Delhi, 2001, p. 14.

84. http://www.cnn.com/SPECIALS/2001/tradeCenter/binLaden.Section. Html
85. Anna Sabasteanski, *op.cit.,* p. 165.
86. Cindy C. Combs and Martin Slann; *Encyclopedia of Terrorism,* Facts on File, Inc. New York, 2002, p. 84.
87. LLoyd Pettiford and David Harding, *op.cit.,* pp. 70-71.
88. *Ibid,* p. 73.
89. K.R. Gupta, *op.cit.,* p. 448.
90. Jay M. Shafritz, Gregury, E.J. Scott, *op.cit.,* p. 145.
91. David J. Whittaker, *op.cit.,* p. 55.
92. David J. Whittaker, *op.cit.,* pp. 57-58.
93. *Pattern of Global Terrorism,* United States Department of state; April 2003. www. zmag.org.
94. Ahmad Nizar Hamzeh, *In Path of Hizbullah,* Syracuse University Press New York, 2004, p. 139.
95. Jay M. Shafritz, E.F. Gibbons, *op.cit.,* p. 220.
96. Cindy C. Combs And Martin Slann, *op.cit.,* p. 109.
97. K.R. Gupta, *op.cit.,* p. 465.
98. www. tkb. arg/FTO.Jsp.
99. www. Patterns of Global Terrorism.com.
100. K.R. Gupta, *op.cit.,* p. 460.
101. Lloyd Pettiford and David Harding, *op.cit.,* p. 100.
102. "Colombians Search for Peace," 07/24/2000, BBC news.
103. David J. Whittaker, *op.cit.,* p. 163.
104. *Ibid,* p. 168.
105. *Ibid.,* p. 58.

3

Motives of Terrorism and Its Impact on World Peace

What motivates people to strap plastic explosives to their bodies, go to a public place, and detonate? Are they soulless criminals? Are they insane fanatics? Or is something else going on? Understanding the motivation of terrorist individuals and terrorist groups is important because it helps us to understand why terrorist are doing what they are doing, their modus operandi, and whether they are prepared to die for the cause.

For many years, small groups of people are willing to die for a cause have managed to sow terror in the hearts of thousands, even millions. Terrorism has existed for a long time, and it arises not only out of the Middle East. Nor does it attack only the great cities of Europe. It is a plague that has struck many countries for many decades, in periods of war and in period of peace.[1]

Terrorism is now in full-bloom around the world specially in Afghanistan and Pakistan, a strategic centre of the Islamic World. Nowadays terrorism has become a worldwide phenomenon. During the last two decades the world has witnessed an increasing number of terrorist attacks. Terrorism poses a real threat to the very survival of humanity and is set to deprive humankind of its most highly prized treasures of peace, security and understanding among nations. Which are the key underpinnings of sustainable human progress. Terrorism is a direct and serious threat to social and economic development democracy and human rights. There is a general impression that terrorism is on the rise and rampant worldwide as it has never been before. No society is safe from individuals to groups to international network, and thus poses a challenge to the internal intelligence systems of governments round the world. It can cause disruption in all sectors of national life and become a major problem for government.[2] Terrorists have many different reasons or motives for their acts. Many politically motivated terrorists, whether they are of the left or the right, want to bring down an existing government or regime. Many religious terrorists want to attack those that they see as attacking their religion. Others want publicity for their cause. Suicide terrorists have almost always had at least one relative or close friend who has been killed, maimed or abused by an enemy. There is also no single psychological profile of terrorists. Most but not all suicide terrorists are aged between 16 and 28. Most are male, but 15 percent are female and the proportion is rising.[3] Most come from poor backgrounds and have limited education, but some have university degree and come from wealthy families.

The personal, social, cultural and religious motivations of the terrorists are a complex field of psychological work. Psychological motivation for terrorism derives from the terrorists personal dissatisfaction with his/her life and accomplishment. Terrorists do not even consider that they may be wrong and that others views may have some merit.

Who is a "Terrorist" ?/ Why they become "Terrorist"

"Terrorist", what sort of mental images come to mind when you think of a terrorist? Most persons would likely think of men with assault rifles and bombs, men who feel so betrayed by anyone, even the innocent, to get the territory or the recognition they believes is due to them. They are motivated by bitter heart and it breeds bitterness and hatred.

No one wakes up one morning and decides that today is the day to become a terrorist the trajectory by which normal people become capable of doing terrible things is usually gradual, perhaps, imperceptible to the individual. This chapter addresses the question: Why do some men and women resort to terrorism? And what are their motives?

Terrorism occurs in waves; it has its ups and downs. It appears whenever people have grievances; that grievances cause frustration and frustration may lead people to terrorism. Policymakers, journalists, and laypersons often ask psychologists to answer such questions as: what developmental factors make a person a terrorist? Why does he hate his victim so much that he will sacrifice his own life in order to kill him? What motivates a young person to join such a hard life and remain away from his or her own families and society? As terrorists are also aware of the hard fact that he has to face death at any time and any where during the terrorist activities.[4]

An individual becomes terrorist in many different ways and for many different reasons. Walter Laqueur says that no one can develop a composite picture of a terrorist because no such picture exists. Terrorism fluctuates over times and the profile of terrorism changes with circumstances. There can be no terrorist mosaic because there are different types of terrorism. In terrorist groups most terrorists are young but their action and psychological make-up vary according to social and cultural conditions. [5] Today it has been noted that the environment shapes the actions of many terrorists.

It seems important to ask what makes a terrorist different from the average person who commits crimes. What makes terrorists different from those people who raised in similar environment and don't act in violent ways to accomplish a goal?

Facts are scarce but some rather hypothetical sketch of personality has frequently been possible; peer pressure, chance encounter, perhaps imitative behaviour, appear to draw in adolescents. Sometimes from broken families, whose live hitherto have lacked success? They may feel alienated, distance from opportunity, perhaps exploited, and altogether marginalised in the community. Adolescence for many is a time of rebellion against established values and authority in home and society. Deeper difficulties with self-confidence and self-image trouble many young people.

The circle of revenge and retaliation is one of the most noticeable elements in terrorism. In many cases, the terrorists want to retaliate against real or imaginary enemies who did something bad to the people, to their culture, to their religion or to their social group. [6]

The terrorist, one could say is action-orientated, aggressive, keen to find excitement, with a fair measure of intolerance and readiness to find fault with others but not necessarily violent by nature. Those coming from the margins of society realise for the first time in life that they really belong to something. 'What matter is what you feel called upon to do now'. The others, after all, are doing the same. Nor is there any compunction to search within yourself for the explanation of earlier failures. Unwilling or unable to face up to self-scrutiny, the terrorist easily blames others in the establishment. Evidently, the members of a terrorist group are liable to changes in behaviour once they join. Many people join terrorist groups in their youth, and indeed it is the interests of groups to "get them when they're young" as that is when they are most impressionable and most vulnerable to group manipulation and indoctrination.[7] The young minds get psychologically influenced very soon and their journey begins towards terrorism.

Terrorists are usually young men (in very few women) faceless enemy at all costs. They are well trained, educated and blindly obedient to authority, living in a time zone of fatalism and totally dedicated to a religious-cultural ideology. Their attacks are not senseless violence; they require extensive planning, training, professional expertise, financial resources and network of co-conspirators.

No member is likely to show disloyalty, risking their membership and the disapproval of the leader. Committed to certain goals and methods, the leader, the recruit and the rest must show iron-bound consensus. In this light violence is easy enough to accept even by those who would never have chosen it by themselves. Before long, no member of a group will dare to cut the strings of attachment withdrawal becomes quite impossible.

Some educated youth are motivated through literatures, films, documentaries and fiery speeches. Like, Maulana Masood Azhar who specialize in indoctrinating the young mind.[8] Money, Name, and fame remain prime motivating factors. It has also become a way of gaining employment and supporting the families. Some of the boys who have joined militancy belong to poor families with a disturbed childhood and a bleak future. The more fundamentalist a village is, the more vulnerable its youth are towards terrorism. There have been a few well-educated youth who have taken up militancy but their numbers are still marginal. Educated terrorists indulge more in indoctrinating the youth through propaganda and provide basis to the movement. They work mostly behind the scenes. Many join terrorist organization to secure their life after death. They are under the illusion that they will be embraced by 72 houries (fairies) in heaven if they embrace martyrdom while fighting for jihad. This seems to be a great motivating factor for most of them. For a few others money is important.

Terrorism now have become a career as much as passion. What start out as moral fervour becomes a sophisticated organization. Grievance can end up as greed for status, attention, political power or money. Terrorist offer a "basket of emotional, spiritual and financial rewards to potential recruits, designed to appeal to a variety of followers whose needs and desire change over time." They have a feel for what the newcomers want, what they are thinking and what is missing. [9]

Leaders, who have been true believers in their youth, cynically take advantage of zealous recruits, manipulating them and ultimately using them as weapons.

In thinking about how to respond to terrorism it is important to realise how unlikely it is that terrorism can be persuaded to change their approach. Terrorist, now have become professionals and after some time on the job, it can be hard for them to imagine another life.

Their is another point which is important to address is the psychological need behind religion as many of the terrorists today act in the name of religion. The social scientist Durkeim concludes that a number of goals and functions that are associated with religion: the promotion of life meaning, emotional comfort, impulse control, intimacy, social solidarity physical health, a sense of control and a better world. Often religion proves to be an effective method for coping. But the problem occurs when religion turns to violence. Religiously motivated terrorists, such as Osama Bin Laden's Al Qaeda, representing a growing trend towards hatred of the west, have few goals other than to "punish" their enemies and to killing as many of them as possible.

Types of Terrorists

Many different types of terrorist are there. Some terrorist act based on religious beliefs whereas others act based on political motives and some terrorists believes in the life after death.

According to Ted G. Gortzel terrorists can be divided into three categories: the political strategist, the radical theorist and the militant activist.[10] Other categorize terrorist in either international or domestic terms. Visible terrorism seems to have changed over time. The change occurred at the turn of the twentieth century, when people stopped focusing on attacking political leaders and instead began to attack random people. Maxwell, Taylor categorize this as a shift from personal terrorism to impersonal terrorism.[11]

Terrorist are not born but created by circumstances. Nevertheless, if everyone takes it upon himself to settle scores in this way, there will not be any escape from this vicious circle. The problem has to be cut from the root itself; therefore, a sincere effort should be made to eliminate the cause, which force these youngsters in to taking up arms against society.

To defuse the terrorist, we must understand the "mind" of the terrorist. To understand the mind of the "terrorist", we must understand their psychology.

Terrorists have been discussed from every angle but no attention has been paid to understand their psychology.

Psychology of Terrorist

The word psychology is derived from the Greek word 'Psyche' meaning 'soul' or 'mind'.

The word "psychology" is the combination of two terms—Study (*Ology*) and Soul (*Psyche*), or mind. The derivation of the word from Latin gives it this clear and obvious meaning: "The Study of the Soul or mind".

Let's see what a few dictionaries have to say and how a word could alter and lose its true and actual meaning.

"Psyche" is defined as:

1. The spirit or soul
2. The human mind
3. In psychoanalysis, the mind functioning as the center of thought, emotion and behaviour.

And defining "Soul" we have:

1. The spiritual or immortal elements in a person.
2. A person's mental or moral or emotional nature.

In other words, 'Psychology' is the study of the human mind.[12]

Many of the problems faced by modern world are rooted in human behaviour, so psychological knowledge can help us to find solutions. There is increasing recognition that mental health has an impact on physical health and that psychological insights can help us in our personal and professional relationships and activities.

The terrorists are crazy nuts. But can psychology 'the

study of the mind', tells us what motivates terrorists and how they differ from us?

This analysis is not to support the terrorists and the extreme measures they often utilize to convey their beliefs, but to understand the oppression that exists and that likely is a cause for the practice of these destructive measures. Many people in today's society commit heinous crimes, but it seems essential to understand what allows for the terrorist to attack many innocent bystanders in comparison to a person who commits other crimes against smaller groups of people.

Albert Bandura, a well-known social psychologist, studied individuals who participate in activities that prove harmful to others but further their own personal interests. He named the process moral disengagement. In general, people do not engage in destructive behaviour unless they have created a way in which to morally justify their actions. In essence, people need to experience a cognitive reconstruction, which allows them to view certain concepts previously thought of as immoral as justifiable. Terrorist organizations recognize this process, thus, through extensive training, recruits are desensitized and morally disengaged in small does so as not to fully recognize his/her personal transformation. At the same time part of this process of moral disengagement is recognizing that it is much easier to hurt others when suffering is not evident (i.e. setting off a bomb from a distance) or they have created a way in their own mind to dehumanize the victim.[13] The psychological study of terrorism is a relatively new field of scientific investigation. Psychology has shown that terrorists have been carefully shaped as they programmed to destroy the enemy at any expense, even with their own lives.

They practise blind obedience to authority and are completely involved in a political or religious ideology. They are fatalistic and educated, have few material possessions, and the certainty that they have nothing to lose except their lives for the achievement of a superior and very important cause. They can destroy, damage, kill or harm themselves. Psychologists assert that terrorist introduce "Creative evil" in its extreme form.[14]

Psychologists recognize two kinds of aggression, Emotional and Instrumental.

1. Emotional Aggression is associated with anger and does not calculate long-term consequences. The reward of emotional aggression is hurting someone who has hurt you.

2. Instrumental Aggression is more calculating-the use of aggression as a means to other ends. The balance is important to determining how to respond to terrorism: As argued above, emotional aggression should be less sensitive to objective rewards and punishments, while instrumental aggression should be more sensitive.

Urban areas produce the greatest potential for unrest and the greatest availability of weapons. When government fails to address social pressures in such areas, the likelihood of terrorism increase. Jeffrey Iran Ross believes structural factors interact with the psychological make-up of potentially violent people to produce terrorism. As a result, he identifies five psychological factors involved in the development of terrorism.

They are:

1. *Facilitating Traits*: Terrorism research has identified a variety of prominent characterists in individual terrorist. He calls these facilitating traits. Terrorists exhibit fear, anger, depression, guilt, anti social behaviour, a strong ego, the need for excitement, and a feeling of being lost. He says the more of these traits a person exhibits, the more likely that the person will engage in terrorism.

2. *Frustration-Narcissism Aggression*: Narcissism-Aggression means that a person has suffered a blow to the ego and reacts hostility. Frustration refers to aggression channelled toward another person or symbol. The high frustration may result in terrorist acts. This, in turn, interacts with structural factors to cause more violence.

3. *Associational Drives*: Most terrorist act are committed by groups and when potential terrorists perceives benefits

from particular groups, they tend to join those groups. Once inside, acts of terror are likely to increase because the group reinforces violent behaviour.

4. *Learning Opportunities*: The existence of groups and engaging in acts of terrorism create an environment for teaching terrorism to other. As learning opportunities increase, the amount of terrorism increases.

5. *Cost benefit calculations:* The decision to engage in terrorism depends on the benefits to terrorist violence. If individual feels they will get gains from terrorist actions, terrorism will increase.[15]

Most terrorists feel that they are doing nothing wrong when they kill and injure people, or damage property. Most seems to share a features of a psychological conditions known as anti-social personality disorder or psychopathic personality disorder, which is an absence people's pain. However, they do not appear unstable or mentally ill. Psychopaths can be intelligent and very much in contact with reality; their problem is that they are socially and morally deficient. They are law-breakers, deceitful, aggressive, and reckless in disregarding the safety of self and others. They do not feel remorse for hurting others. As some individual cannot see colors, psychopaths cannot feel empathy or affection for others.

Like, the behaviour of Nezar Hindawi a freelance Jordanian terrorist, is very similar to that of those diagnosed with psychopathic personality disorder. Nezar Hindawi was born in Jordan in 1954, he sent his pregnant fiancee with, Unbeknownst to her, a parcel of Semtex hidden in a computer to board Israeli plane from London to Tel Aviv, saying that 'they would be married when he joined her there'. The planned explosion would have taken place over Southern Europe, killing all 375 passengers, including his finance and unborn child. Owing to the vigilance of the airport guards, the plot was foiled. Had Hindawi been a true martyr, he would have taken the suicide mission himself, but according to all the evidence he was not particularly religious, and he had been promised $ 250,000 for his part in the operation. Western Commentators denounced Hindawi as a particularly brutal criminal devoid of any shred of conscience, and during his trial he made it clear that he could not have cared less about the fate of his finance and unborn child. But it is also true that this behaviour was not thought to be particularly loathsome in the part of the world where he came from partly because his wife was not muslim. But even if she had been Muslim, would the reaction have been different? Hindawi was a psychopath and there are many like him. The culture they live in, the combination of nationalism and religion, gives them the legitimating for acting out their cruelty.[16] Hindawi's willingness to sacrifice his fiancée and unborn child displays an exceptional lack of empathy.

A closed-minded certainty is also a commonly observed feature of much terrorist thinking. A document left behind by Mohammad Atta, one of the 11 September attackers, illustrates this:

"Everybody hates death, fear death, but only those, the believers who know the life after death and the reward after death, would be the one who will be seeking death". Also, "Check your weapons, say morning prayer together and if you take a taxi to the airport, when you arrive, smile and rest assured, for Allah is with the believers and the angels are protecting you." Again, however, this mode of thinking is not different from terrorists and suicide cults.

The following behavioural models will help us to study the psychopathology in detail.

(1) Developmental models

Terrorists, particularly political terrorists, may come from upper rather than lower class background, as in the vigilante group that make up right-wing, pro government "death squads" in Latin America and Asia. Terrorists are often the products of overly permissive, wealthy families with whom they were in conflict, had inconsistent mothering, or were isolate from. According to the famous psychologists, A. Kalpan terrorists have a pathological behaviour. He differentiates between the reasons and causes of terrorism by proposing that reasons are the social variable that facilitate terrorism or help rationalise terrorist behaviour. However, he says that the causes of terrorist behaviour "must be sought in the psychopathology of the assassin." He proposes that terrorists have a pathological need to pursue absolute ends. He proposed that this is an overreaction to childhood experiences of humiliation at the hands of an aggressor, which result in a sense of failure and lack of self-esteem. Thus, their personality is defective and cannot cope with life stress through socially appropriate means. It is also noted that suicide bombers often come from broken families and they suffer from low self-esteem.

(2) Social Learning Models

Many terrorists come from places where peace is not the norm; place like the Middle East or Northern Ireland, where all the present generation of young people have known is regular, extreme, well publicised violence. Violence could be the norm for such young people, whether it is on a wide scale or within a smaller community or family. It may come to be considered the normal response to achieve objectives. Exposure to terrorism as a child can produce a tendency to terrorism as an adult. This cannot be the only factor because relatively few children exposed to terrorist violence grow up to become terrorists.

(3) Group Dynamics

Group dynamics are much more significant in the latter case. For these people, the group becomes the sole source of support and friendship. Their sense of belonging, sense of purpose, perhaps even their sense of identity, is derived from the relationship within the group. For such people, providing an alternative support structure may be a way of preventing involvement in a terror group.

(4) Behaviourist Model

According to this model, most terrorists are heroes to someone and such reinforcement increases the likelihood of terrorist behaviour.

(5) Economic Model

Some groups choose the terror option because it is relatively inexpensive and yet can have huge effects. It does not require large amount of money (although some terrorist like Bin Laden are very wealthy). It does not require large number of people or equipment. It is the warfare of the poor and disaffected. [17]

Other psychologists links frustration to terrorism by naming this phenomenon the frustration-anger theory. Anger is the emotional reaction to pain, particularly the pain of frustration. For terrorists, the frustration with regards to social inequality is substituted with violence.

Defense mechanism and hidden feelings are another commonly referred to in the field of psychotherapy. Defense mechanism protect us, making life more bearable. These unconscious strategies distort with the reality with the intention of reducing anxiety and depression. Some psychologists view defense as normal methods for coping, adaptations, whereas other see them as pathology.[18] Behind these defenses lie one's true feelings, also known as hidden feelings, which one cannot be fully aware of as they cause too much pain and anxiety. Common hidden feelings include anger, sadness, the desire for affection and love, fear of death, grief etc. The result is what noted psychologist Karl Menninger diagrammed as a triangle of conflict.

Anxiety, hidden feelings and defense mechanism make up the three corner of the triangle. In order for the anxiety to disminish, one needs to learn to deal with the hidden feelings by breaking down the existing defense mechanisms. In essence, terrorists act is specific ways in efforts to distance themselves from their hidden feelings.[19]

After thoroughly researching this point, the analysis seems to point in the direction of environment as the main cause of terrorism. Many people grow up in difficult situation that include hidden feelings, childhood trauma, and moral disengagement. However, many of these people do not look to terrorism as a means do fulfill personal needs. Thus, it remain if a person grows up or find his/herself in a certain place at a fragile time in one's life, this person has the potential to be swept up in a terrorist group that practices violence as a means to achieve psychological safety and personal needs. As humans, we all experience much of what was described above, yet so many people do not resort to terrorist behaviour.

Considering the psychology of the terrorist from a behavioural perspective allows us to present a coherent picture- even though it is neither a complete nor sufficiently integrated picture of the cycle of terrorism.

Terrorists create terror, and terror creates fear and anger. Fear and anger creates aggression, and aggression against people of different culture and religion creates discrimination, this in turn leads to new form of terrorism. This is the vicious circle that social psychological research should try to understand it and break it.

Motives of Terrorists

After the horrific bombing in New York and Washington on September 11th 2001, there were questions in everybody's minds. Why did those terrorists do what they did? What possible motives could they have had? The Pentagon in Washington a military target and tempting one for those who wanted to weaken the United States militarily and politically. The World Trade Center, though how is it that those innocent workers there from many lands were victims of some dreadful plot? It is understandable that such questions are a predictable response to grief and anger.

Terrorists are insane and inhuman. Can their motives be thought of as rational or calculated? And if it is possible to work out their likely motives are not so inexcusable the retaliation must be our prime consideration? It is always important to stress that our attempt to understand terrorist motives are mainly based on assumptions. Where methods of terror are acknowledged to be the last resort, say, of these fighting for freedom the question as to motives answers itself and there may be but be thought inevitable. The definition of terrorism and the psychology of terrorist has been amplified, let us now see what are the motives of terrorists.

Terrorism is designed to bring about political or social changes. It erodes the authority of state by creating chaos, fomenting political uncertainty and promoting economic discord. It fosters law and order problem with a view to weakening the fabric of society.

Motivation has long been studied by sociologists and psychologists in great detail. Motives can be said to be forces, which impel action to realise desire, wants and goals. They may also seek to repel unwanted, threatening or damaging conditions. Motives initiate, direct and sustain behaviour.[20]

For leaders of a group or a movement, motives must be proclaimed to make intentions clear to acolytes and to a wider audience, even to those who will contest intention and goals.

Thus, the first and foremost objective of the terrorist is to draw worldwide attention and sympathy for their cause. The new international terrorism has grasped that a high drama coupled with horror needs to be stayed to interest the media and reach the masses through the press, radio and television. It proves to be relatively inexpensive and efficient way of publicity. Terrorist motives are essentially two-headed. There is the initial destructive impulse of he who would create a paralysing sense of fear in a target community. There is another impulse quite different from that behind the launching of a conventional military attack. The terrorist's arsenal is one of the psychological warfare. Motives use the imagination of others either directly or through the media. Anxiety and uncertainty are manipulated so that a victim or an onlooker helps the terrorist to achieve his ends.[21] The terrified, pressuring the establishment, are the helpmates of the terrorist.

Terrorism inflicts immediate damage in destroying lives and property, but terrorists hope that the long-term costs will be much greater. They want to create fear and uncertainty far beyond the victims and those close to them. They want their enemy to spend time and money on security. In effect, the terrorists aim to lay an enormous tax on very aspect of the enemy's society, a tax that transfer resources from productive purposes to anti-productive security measures. The cost of increased security are likely to be particularly high for a country like the United States and Europe, where an open society is the foundation of economic success and high tech military. They are already paying enormous taxes of this kind.[22]

Another main motive of terrorists is to cripple normal functioning of the government by undermines the faith of the people in the government and in the role of law. Their main targets of attack are the visible symbol of government authority, centres of communication business establishment, airport, media personnel, policemen and their informers. Terrorists may create public fear in order to influence their negotiation with targeted government authority.

The main motive of terrorism is to terrorise and paralyse a population or a government in to submission.

At one level, the terrorist must try to disorient the population by showing functions for its subjects that are the provision of safety and order. On deeper level, however the object is, to isolate the citizens from his or her social context.[23]

Another internal function served by terrorism is that of building morale amongst members of the movement and their supporters. If terrorists can penetrate in to a security ring and explode a bomb, kill a highly protect target on force concessions out of a target organization, their power and credibility will be enhanced.

A terrorist act is not impulsive, without premeditation, or the fruit of an instant rage. It usually implies planning, premeditation, a careful study for months or even years, specific skills and training, and economic and human resources.

Like in the case of September 11, 2001, terrorist trained for long time to pilot aircraft, spent a lot of money, participated in international network and planned each detail carefully.

We should not demonize the terrorist as an alien breed. Instead we should focus on their motivations and the dispositional determinants of their behaviour.

The motivation of terrorists can be categorised as follows:

(1) Ideological Motivation

Terrorist of this type usually have extreme political, racist, ethnical or religious orientation. Their attack might be a demonstration of political protest, it might be aimed at exterminating political, ideological and racial opponents, and it may have symbolic purpose (to become known) or to change public opinion. The attacks are usually carried out by professionally trained persons (specialists).

(2) Experimental Motivation

Terrorists of this type are curious to see how their equipment or method (invented by them) works, they enjoy the effects, the response or the panic they cause. It is more a criminal act, than an act of terrorism pursing objectives.

(3) Vandalistic (destructive) Motivation

The basis of the activities of these terrorists is Idiosyncratic. They may suffer from mental diseases, or be influenced by narcotics. In this case, it is usually a criminal act. It might be however, also a motive for terrorists pursuing ideological, religious or political objectives in the form of attacks on symbolic things like, monuments, historical buildings, state symbols etc.

(4) Profit-driven Motivation

Such terrorist carry out their attacks with the aim of ganing financial, material or other profit (including confidential and secret information, elimination of competitors, gaining a more advantageous position, etc.), necessary for further terrorist operations. The attacks are usually carried out by professionally trained persons (specialists).

(5) Passionate Motivation

Such terrorist carries out their attack under the influence of a strong disappointment in social relationship (refusal by a loved person, jealousy of the success by sibling, friend, etc). The act has more a criminal context, although it might be carried out by professionals-the so-called terror ordered by the organised crime.[24]

Indeed, long claims that terrorism is essentially a psychological phenomenon, "fear and publicity two of its most important elements."

Motivations know no bounds. "How far can you hold back our plans by shackling us? Our amirs (leaders) are very determined. They won't rest till they give shape to their designs. Allah will show them the way". This is what one of the 11th Indian Muslim youth, all Pakistan-trained followers of Deoband-Tableegh Jamaat, now in judicial custody in the state told his interrogator.[25]

In the Middle East a range of motives can be discerned operating at a number of distinct levels. Fundamentally, the mainspring for the Palestinian Arab living under Israeli. Subjection is to work for its overthrow. He will do this by means of active resistance to any Jewish occupation or edict. The savage demands of the crusading jihad recognise no limits to motives and methods—they are apocalyptic in western eyes.

The suicide bomber, the car bomber, the sniper, wrench lives out of opposers, and of anyone who gets in the way. Here the main urge is primitive. In recent years, evident splits have been visible between more moderate Arab leadership and opinion and fedayeen commandos such as Hizbullah, Hamas and the Democratic Front for Palestine. The moderate wing fears that continued suicide bombing by the Palestinian religious fanatics only plays into the hands of Ariel Sharon and his militarists. Motives are misdirected.[26] Political urgency has been accompanied by religious imperatives, which assert that the blessed state of martyrdom is a matchless motive.

Most of the terrorist came from white-collar families. Half of them were from broken families and, one among the group of three was female. These conflicts ridden youths do appear to have had difficulty with their perspectives and rationality. In their verbal conflicts (usually when arrested) they struck their interviewers as excessively dogmatic and hyper-emotional. Their political judgements were black and white, crude and ill informed. Motives were impulsive and inconsistent.

Europe has to take account of terrorists motivated by deeply felt saparatist intentions as is illustrated in Northern Ireland, Chechnya, Bosnia, Geogia, Nagorno-Karabakh and Basque ETA movement. Campaigning is low cost, sometimes spasmodic and public sympathies cannot always be assured.[27]

African terrorism has been most pronounced in the Central Republic of Rwanda. Armed militias from rival tribes, the Tutsi and the Hutu, have set out systematically to hunt down and eleiminate others on a vast scale. Typically, this terror warring is savage and without compromise. Whole sector of a civilian population are often terrorised in to fleeing their homes to escape genocidal massacre, rape and torture as in 'ethnic cleansing'.

South-East Asia, is so dependent upon capitalist intervention from outside, longs to throw it off. This struggle is a mix of neo-marxist notions and Islamic faith. Indonesia has its 'dark forces' of rogue ex-soldiers and other, almost certainly with al-Qaeda mercenaries, who are willing to wreck the economy and bring down the government. In nearby Pakistan, still a sanctuary for al-Qaeda and the defeated Taliban, the mainsprings of terrorism are more overtly political, stimulated with a murderous urge to destroy any trace of United States influence. Pakistan looks nervously at Afghanistan where warlords enrol their own bands of desperate tribesmen, armed to the teeth and ready to kill by order. Motives here are raw-Mercenary, political, religious and on the whole entirely destructive.

In Kashmir, for so many years the contest ring between India and Pakistan, each of the major states accuses the other of sponsoring terrorists to fight the cause of separatism. There is a more complex set of motives in Central and South America. In Argentina, Peru, Guatemala and Honduras there are elements of the extreme left dedicated to Marxist diffusion and to the toppling of any regime they deem capitalist and repressive. Frustration drives many into violence, sometimes that of the urban guerrilla. Colombia has the added scourge of virulent gang warfare occasioned by rivalry over narcotics trading, where competitive urge may lead to a cut throat.

An intriguing example of motivational change in South America is the case of Peru. Nobody could ever have thought that a group of young professors in a rural university would ever launch a vicious reign of terror. By the mid-1970s the government in Lima had grown understandably fearful. Their tentative control measures only emboldened the professors. The educational programme, the Shining Path to the future, the way of peace, now became the shining path (sendero Luminoso), the way of terrorism and a people's war. Motives and Methods are now completely and ominously different. Now motives are turning rigid and sour. Regional Committees recruited almost 10,000 people, dispersing them across the countryside in guerilla cells. Shining path had turned itself in to a terrorist group with their original leader, Professor Guzman, as a Megalomaniac Messiah. Motives had swerved sideways in to eliminating anyone who was not a party member. Power for the people had hideously become power for the party.[28] Once again, terrorist motives lie in suspense.

The Rationality of the Terrorist

Trauma usually breeds prompt decision. Those who have carved out a path of violence are thought to be inhuman and insane. Can their motives be calculated and rational? If it is possible to workout their possible motives are these not so inexcusable that retaliation seems an appropriate response? However, terrorists these days are generally considered to be rational in beliefs and behaviour. They certainly claim to be so. From time to time random and impulsive acts of destruction hit the headlines but the evidence reveals that individuals, generally members of groups, estimate carefully the risks involved in carrying out their strategies. They think carefully about objectives, perhaps compiling a list of them.

Feasible targets are selected and option taken in to account. Detailed planning goes into tactics. Where and when will it be best to act? How many people will be needed? What methods are to be used? How do we set about the business? Who will be chosen for particular tasks? What about the security of the place we intend to attack? And wear do we get away afterwards, that is, unless we have a suicide mission in mind?[29]

It came as a shock to many people to realise that the 19 well educated terrorists responsible for 9/11 had been training for three years with the hijacking and crashing of four aircraft in mind. Their plans were meticulously drafted. Yet how rational were these men? One might argue that terrorists of this kind associates political calculations with destructive and symbolic expressions of contempt and hatred and that in so doing their rational decisions have more to do with their thinking out, point by point, appropriate means to secure particular goals.

Motives originating as political or ideological or religious are soon translated in to compulsive ideas and behaviour.[30] Terrorists groups now have different motivations, organizations, structures, and tools. Changes in motives have produced changes in the organization and structure of terrorist groups.

The new terrorist groups may be willing to inflict mass causalities for a variety of motives others than political goal. The emergence of a new breed of terrorist less constrained by traditional ethics or political pressures, coupled with the diffusion of know-how about nuclear, biological and chemical weapons. May result into increase the probability of many major incidents of terrorist activities?

Impact of Terrorism on World Peace

(1) Morale of the people: -

An explosion too loud for your eardrums to hear,
and young children squealing like pigs in the square,
and all faces chalk-white and streaked with bright red,
and the glass and the dust and the terrible dead.
For an old lady's legs are ripped off,
and the head of a man's hanging open,
and still he's not dead. He is screaming for mercy,
and his son stand and stares and then suddenly, quick,
disappears.
And Christ, little Katherine Aiken is dead,
and Mrs. Mc Laughlin is pierced through the head.
Meanwhile to Dungiven the killers have gone,
and they're finding it hard to get through on the Phone.[31]

–Jessica Weisbach

The purpose of sharing above poem is to help clearly through poetry the devastation and destruction caused by terrorism. It helps us to form the impression of a terrorist bombing attack in a way that picture or abstract accounts can never convey.

Terrorism is the illegal use or threatened use of violence by groups with political or ideological motives. Their goal is to coerce societies or governments by inducing fear in their population. The Central goal of terrorism, in other words, is to create a climate of fear, uncertainty and vulnerability.

Terrorism intentionally hits emotional "hot buttons." It has several features that magnify the average person's perception of its risks : terrorist acts are both vivid and catastrophic ; they are unfamiliar and difficult to avoid; and they are caused by human malevolence.

Terrorists believe that their struggle is just because every one in the communal of the world is unjust in their eyes, therefore killing of even a child is justful for the cause of the terrorist movement.

Every person in the eyes of terrorist can be a target and thus is an expendable material, a wasteful commodity, which can conveniently be dispensed with, when required. For the terrorists every human being represents a government or social order, which is corrupt and requires modification. Thus every person can be a victim of terrorism. The victims are however, always regarded as a commodity, a symbol of state authority without personality or individual value. Once the terrorist incident has taken place, helping effort must concentrate on reducing the harm in causes. These efforts include the attempt to defuse the situation itself as early as possible with minimum loss of life. While concern for the victim's safety plays a major role in resolving the situation, many other political and situational factors influence decision makers. After the incident is over it is also essential to have a programme design, specific techniques and psychological primers that may be helpful in the care and rehabilitation of the victims.

All victims of terrorism share certain common features, both physical and psychological including loss or limitation of freedom of action and loos of power over one's fate. While the different people involved may react differently, both physically and psychologically, certain patterned forces react against the victim's will to resist which produces anxiety leading to panic with little or no possibility for free movement or action. Victims correctly perceive that they are in danger of losing their lives.[32] In the case of hostage taking, the victim, stunned with sock and exhaustion, loses all sense of time as if time has come to a standstill. Mental faculties cease working. He refuses to believe what is happening. Some count hours, others are in trace looking everywhere, nowhere. Fear prevails and manifests itself in profuse sweating, shivering, shaking and cramp in the stomach. Victims sit and stare apathetically. The nights are endless and days restless. Occasionally somebody moans or cries quietly. In state of shock as per the medical scientists, the heartbeats get faster and more strongly, blood is diverted from the skin to the muscles.

Psychologically, a victim under forced detention starts with the feeling of fear and anxiety. As time passes the victim becomes hopeful of getting released. He gains some confidence. When nothing happens he gets frustrated, impatient and intolerant. This is the most serious and dangerous stage because in a state of frustration a victim may start behaving irrationally.

Victims of terrorism more often that not, do not even known who the terrorists are, what their demand are and whether it will be possible to appease them at all. Lack of information creates a syndrome of uncertainty. Victims experience a peculiar sense of insecurity, which is often painful and intolerable.

The effect of captivity on the mind or attitude or outlook is far more damaging. It destroys the morale of the people, the will to live, shatters faith in the living beings, in the surroundings and in humanity in general. When the initial shock and refusal to accept the reality is over the victim becomes frightened and the emotional shock and fear persist for a considerable period.

The basic process of terrorisation involves an unpredictable, powerful force, threatening the victim with annihilation. The experience is immensely stressfully and generates in the victim feelings of total helplessness and powerlessness. Terrorisation denies the victim's ability to control his behaviour. Psychological and physical shock, characteristic of any severe trauma follows. Such feelings of importance shatter the self image, dissolve the self-confidence and set in motion a sequel of complex and interrelated social psychological and physiological response mechanism.[33]

Psychological studies highlights three key consequences of fear and anxiety. First, fear tends to elevate risk perceptions. This is consistent with the more general finding that events, which arouse negative feelings, lead to an overestimation of risk.

Lerner, Gonzalez, Small and Fischoff (2003) examined the effects of 9/11 in an experimental setting by showing research participants video clips that either heightened fear or anger in response to the attack. They found that individuals with experimentally elevated fear level judged the risk of future terrorism more highly than individual in the anger condition. In other words, anxiety and fear promote a heightened sensitivity to threat.

Second, fear leads to risk aversion. That involve the potential for physical harm such as crime, natural disaster, and violent conflicts provide evidence that personal threat and fear leads to a change in personal behaviour designed to minimize risk (and presumably fear). Queens and long Island who felt they could personally be victimized by a terrorist after 9/11 were more likely to have stopped using public transportation in Manhattan and had traveled less often by air.[34]

Reaction to other terrorist event highlight "the transformation of reasonable fear in to a kind of irrational hysteria", as exemplified by American tourists avoidance of Europe in response to a spate of terrorist incidents in 1985 and 1986, the deep reluctance of Americans to fly after 9/11, or the precipitous decline in tourism in Kashmir due to serial terrorist attacks.

Third, fear can have a deleterious effect on the rational processing of information because it leads to worsened cognitive functioning. This fits with research findings on the quality of elite and group decision-making process deteriorate under conditions of threat perception and stress. Most of these findings suggest some degree of cognitive "Shutdown" under threatening conditions, which has also been a central theme in work or fear emotions. [35]

A minority of respondents also reported symptoms linked to depression a distinct but related psychological response to the event. The survey includes three indicators of depression: having trouble concentrating, feeling depressed, and having trouble sleeping.

Like after 9/11 attack, a small number (21%) reported that it had been somewhat or very difficult to concentrate on their job and other normal activities in the past week, and an even smaller number (13%) reported having had difficulty sleeping in the previous week because of the terrorist attacks.[36]

These reactions are strongly tied to the experience of fear and anxiety. This suggests the reported feelings of fear and anxiety may have real behavioural manifestation. In subsequent analyses, we treat depression as an outcome of fear and anxiety and do not consider its separate political effects. The determinants of depression and fear are analyzed in tandem to reinforce their affinity.

Individuals with poor health reported more psychological and emotional stress symptoms (e.g. Lack of appetite, increased smoking, increased headaches, difficult sleeping, crying, loss of temper, dizziness, rapid heart beat etc.) and were having greater difficult recovering from such symptoms following the terrorist attacks.[37] Like after September 11 attack a majority of Americans reported difficulty paying attention at work or school, depression feelings, distrupted sleep, distress and anger. Many also changed their behaviour by altering travel patterns and by increasing cigarette smoking, and alcohol consumption.

The more directly a person is affected by a terrorist act, the greater is the risk of developing Post-Traumatic Stress Disorder (PTSD)* and other disorder. After September 11 it is found that a sizable number of residents in and outside of New York City had developed PTSD symptoms even though they were not directly affected by the attack.

Children reactions to trauma are similar to those of adults. Children are directly and indirectly involved, they are particularly vulnerable to the far-reaching impact of terrorism and disasters. Children at risk for experiencing mental health.

---

* Psychopathic-severe mental disorder resulting in violent behavior.
PTSD : Symptoms that typically occur after exposure to a stressful situation. It is a condition that develops in response to witnessing or experiencing a threatening or harmful event that elicits fear, helplessness or horror.

Difficulties after a disaster or act of terrorism include those who are near to or actually witness the event, those who lose loved ones as a result, and even those children who merely live in the affected community or watch coverage of the event on television.[38]

Risk factors that may increase adjustment problems for children includes:

- Intense or prolonged exposure to the event, including geographic proximity.
- Witnessing or sustaining an injury.
- Perceiving a threat to themselves or loved ones.
- Death of parents, siblings, or close friends.
- Television exposure following the event, even if the child was not directly affected.

Post-traumatic stress disorder is the most common response to disastrous events in children, occurring in up to 40% of children exposed to disasters and typically within three months after the event. It can still be present more than 15 years after a terrorist event.

Almost one year after the Oklahoma City bombing, 50% of local elementary school children reported clinical level of PTSD, and one half reported being concerned about the safety of their family. A recent study found that six months after September 11, 2001, approximately 75,000 New York City Public school children in grades 4th through 12th were suffering from PTSD, including children who were not directly affected by the event.[39]

Disrupted consciousness, uncontrollable intense grief, change in sleeping or eating patterns and extreme cognitive impairments may appear in severely affected children.

Other symptoms include depression, anxiety, increased startle response and arousal level, safety and security concerns, restlessness, aggression, a decline in academic performance, and a decreased interest in previously enjoyed activities.

The psychological impact has been very significant. We all felt and still feel to some extent the shock and grief that came in the immediate after any terrorist attack. In addition, there are continuing fear resulting from the spate of anthrax incident and the specter of biological and chemical terrorism.[40] The fear generated by terrorism and by the possibility of victimization in an ever-widening arena is raising the social cost of the problem, in addition to the economic costs. They do so by weakening the social and political fabric of affected countries and by diverting scare economic and criminal justice resources from other vital areas.

Impact of Terrorist Attack on the Economy

The world we live in underwent a big change on the morning of September 11, 2001 when a group of young men destroyed the twin towers of the World Trade Center in New York and a portion of the Pentagon in Washington DC, which symbolized American economic and military might respectively. The terrorist attack on World Trade Center affected both the American and the global economy. The economic consequences can largely be broken down in to short-term direct effect; medium-term confidence effect and longer-term productivity effects.

The direct economic costs of terrorism, including the destruction of life and property, responses to the systems and the infrastructure affected, and the provision of temporary living assistance, are most pronounced in the immediate aftermath of the attacks and thus matter more in short run.

Direct economic costs are likely to be proportionate to the intensity of the attacks and the size and the characteristics of the economy affected. The indirect cost of terrorism can be significant and have the potential to affect the economy in the medium term by undermining consumer and investor confidence. Deterioration of confidence associated with an attack can reduce the incentive to spend opposed to save, a process that can spread through normal business cycle and trade channels. Likewise, falling investor confidence may trigger a generalised drop in asset price and a flight to quality that increases the borrowing costs for riskier borrowers. The size and distribution of the effects over countries, sector, and time would depend on a range of factors, including the nature of the attacks, the multiplier effects, the type of policies adopted in response to the attacks, and the resilience of the markets.

The September 11 attacks primarily affected the major industrial countries through a fall in demand generated by the loss in confidence about the economy and its impact on output.

Despite having been the direct target of terrorism, which materially affected the market infrastructure and operations, following the September 11 attacks, the financial markets demonstrated resilience and a capacity to return to normalcy quickly. This allowed the financial markets to perform one of their key functions: that of digesting the information on the economic and financial impact of the terrorist attack after an initial shock and efficiently incorporating the information into asset prices so that it could be integrated into decisions about the future. Financial instruments involve commitments over time and, therefore, prices provide a hedge against uncertainty.

While the initial effect of any major crisis may involve a financial market overreaction because of higher level of uncertainty, as the new information is being assessed and absorbed, once the long-term impact of the crisis is assessed, markets return to their pre-crisis condition. Thereafter, financial markets shift up or down according to investors perceptions of how the crisis will be resolved. Finally, over the longer term, there is a question of whether the attacks can have a negative impact on productivity by raising the costs of transactions through increased costs of financial and other counter terrorism regulations.[41]

As noted above, financial markets have been directly and indirectly the victims of terrorist attack. Striking at the core of the world's main financial centre, the terrorist attacks of 9/11 aimed at undermining the stability of the U.S. and international financial system. In the aftermath of the attacks, the financial markets were not only confronted with major activity disruptions caused by the massive damage to property and communication systems, but also with soaring levels of uncertainty and market volatility. Numerous key market players had substantial operations in or around the world Trade Center that were destroyed or damaged in the attacks, causing a widespread closure of the New York financial markets. The impact of the September 11 attacks was visible worldwide on the major equity markets, which experienced sharp and rapid declines, demonstrating that market participants perceived the event as a global shock.[42]

Other Factors also Influenced Economic Pessimism

- The perceived risk of a future attack increases the perceived impact of the attack on the national economy and one's personal finances. Younger peoples, women and others are also more pessimistic about the immediate future trajectory of the economy.

- The impact of terrorism on oil as well as the tourism industries were repeatedly projected as vulnerable, but resilient.

- The terrorist bombings in Madrid on March 11, 2004 immediately affected the Capital's hotel industry as Spaniards reduced their travel in the subsequent months. An incidents at one airport has a tremendous impact on others around the world. After the 9/11 attack on the United States, all flights from Europe was stop within four minutes.[43]

- The impact of terrorism on the financial institutions also covered its likely impact on the stock market and on the "feel good" feeling in the economy as a whole. The overall view was that the stock markets had got used to periodic news of terrorist strikes in some part of the world or the other and do not exhibit enduring nervousness or panic. The negative effects have generally been of short duration.

Impact of Terrorism on Social Life

Terrorist acts produce devastating injuries, destruction, and death. But their ultimate goal is psychological: to create a climate of fear, uncertainty, and vulnerability. Through psychological means, the perpetrators hope to attain what they cannot accomplish militarily.

After attack populations, such as women, radical/ethnic group, and people with prior health and mental health problems, are at increased risk for psychological problems, such as depression, anxiety, and post-traumatic stress disorder. After terrorist attacks rates of PTSD and symptoms of stress were found to substantially increase in adults and children across the country and not only in areas where the terrorist attacks occurred.[44]

The terrorist attacks had a powerful psychological impact on social life. Terrorism destroys the solidarity, cooperation and interdependence on which social functioning is based, and substitutes insecurity and distrust. The breakdown of social trust and cooperation could have serious effects on how society functions. If trust is essential to the accumulation of social capital, mistrust is likely to undermine a society's social resources. An erosion of trust could diminish political involvement is electoral politics to activity in local educational and community groups. In this sense, a decline in social capital furthers terrorist aims because it distances citizens from their government and each other, emphasizing personal security over the collective good.

The obvious result of terrorism is the tragic loss of human life and property. But there are other detrimental effects.

As terrorist expert Brain Jenkins has written: "Terrorist acts cause crisis, provoke outrage, fray community ties, and undermine faith in our democratic institutions." [45]

Broadly speaking, there are three main ways in which physical danger has affected urbanisation.

First, Cities are no more safe harbour against modern terrorism.

Second, there in the target effect-cities have historically been rich targets for looting bandits of terrorists seeking to maximize damage. The impact of an explosion is increasing in the density of the surrounding area, so higher density areas make more attractive targets.

Third, impact of danger is on the costs of transportation.[46]

In early 2002, air travel and hotel booking were significantly below levels recorded in the months after the terrorist attacks. Beyond fear of flying, there is evidence that not only Americans, but the whole world became generally more anxious and insecure. It was noted that their was a big decrease in air travel as evidence of a big increase in fear, but it may be that even a small increase in fear can produce a large decrease in willingness to fly.

Fear of flying is not the only fear to emerge for September 11, 2001. Survivors of the attacks on the World Trade Center (WTC), those who fled for their lives on September 11, are fearful of working in a high rise building and afraid of even all the parts of lower Manhattan that were associated with community to and from the World Trade Center.[47]

Thus, modern terrorism is a means of instilling in every individual the feeling that the next terror attack may have his name on it. Terrorism work to undermine the sense of security and to disrupt everyday life so as to harm the target country's ability to function.

Impact on National Security

Terrorism is now seen as a threat to the security of the whole international community, including the United States, which was the only remaining superpower in the global arena. Terrorism now have become the main strategic threat in 21st century.

The lives of many people are in continual danger often in real time during the very work of the intelligence agencies. The rules of the game are cruel, for the security personnel and for the terrorists themselves.

Overall, fear and anxiety lead to less clear information processing, the overestimation of risk, and greater risk aversion. These reactions hold important implications for support of anti-terrorism policies. National security policies that have potentially violent consequences should be less popular among fearful individuals than policies that address the threat of terrorism without increasing the prospect of further retaliatory action. In other words fear should decrease support for risky overseas military action, but should not diminish support for homeland security policies, such as domestic surveillance, identity checks, and other forms of internal security that do not exacerbate threat. It could lead to an overestimation of the negative consequences of both terrorist action and government retaliation and reduce the absorption of important information about national security because it diminishes cognitive processing capabilities. We explore one additional consequences of fear suggested by the terrorism literature is social dislocation. As noted earlier, It is believe that fear leads to a greater mistrust of one's fellow citizens and thus, weakens social bonds.

Terrorism is a real threat to security on many levels. Human security is a term that acknowledges the individual level of security. If people are insecure, then the insecurity can quickly spread throughout a state, the region, and the globe. In other words, human security is really a bottom-up approach towards national and international security.

Human insecurities are derived from those threats that target the survival of human being and which states cannot, will not, or are unable to deter or prevent. Such threats includes disease, famine, poverty, political oppression, lack of housing etc.[48]

It is an indication that despite all the efforts deployed by the security and intelligence services, they have failed to find answers to all the challenges posed by the new terrorist actors.

Experts suggest that terrorism has several central aims, but in all scenario the public is used as a pawn in a game played with governments. Terrorist groups aim their actions at ordinary people, although their ultimate target remains the political authorities, which terrorists hope to force in to meeting their demands. Fear plays an important role in this process. Terrorists hope to sow public disaffection with government, weaken public support for tough antiterrorism policies, and disrupt social ties through the creation of fear and anxiety.

Terrorism is a cancer, and if it is not curbed, it will spread through the body politik and destroys democracies. It is not a marginal threat to democratic societies. It undermine the faith of the people in the government and in the role of law.

REFERENCES

1. Chris E. Stout, *Psychology of Terrorism,* Vol. I, Prager Publishers, U.S.A, 2004, p. 45.
2. Maxwell Taylor, *The Fanatics: A Behavioral Approach to Oolitical Violence;* Brassey's Publishers, London, 1991, p. 25.
3. R.C. Mishra, *Terrorism Implication of Tactics and Technology;* Authorspress Delhi, 2004, p. 170.
4. N. S. Jamwal, "Terrorist's Modus operandi in Jammu & Kashmir," *Strategic Analysis,* Vol. 27, No. 3; Jul-Sep 2003, p. 383, Institute for Defence Studies and Analysis, New Delhi.
5. R.C. Mishra, *Terrorism Implications of Tactics and Technology;* AuthorsPress Delhi, 2004, p. 167.
6. David J. Whittaker, *Terrorist and Terrorism in the Contemporary World;* Routledge Taylor and Francis Group, New York and London, 2004; p. 60.
7. Chris E. Stout, *Psychology of Terrorism,* Condensed edition coping with the Continuing Threat; Prager Publishers, U.S.A, 2004, p. 45.
8. N.S. Jamwal, "Terrorist's Modus operandi in Jammu and Kashmir" *Strategic Analysis,* Vol. 27, No. 3/Jul-Sep. 2003, p. 384; Institute for Defence Studies and Analyses (IDSA) New Delhi.
9. Jessica Stern, *Financial Times Weekend,* Saturday June 12/Sunday June 13 2004, "How Terrorist Think," London, p W1.
10. Stout, Chris E., Goertzel, Ted G., "Terrorist Beliefs and Terrorist

lives" *The Psychology of Terrorism: A Public Understanding,* Praegar Publishers London, 2002; pp. 97-98.

11. Maxwell Taylor, *The Terrorist,* Brassey's Defence Publishers London, 1988; p. 58.
12. http://www.sntp.net/psychology-definition.htm
13. http://harvard.edu/~t656-web/peace/Articles-spring 2004/ Weisbach _ Jessica-terrorist_mind.htm; Pg 3
14. Chris E. Stout, *The Psychology of Terrorism,* Vol.I, Westport Connecticut, London, 2002, p. 10.
15. R.C. Mishra, *op.cit.,* p. 169.
16. Rajpal Kaur, *Bio-Terrorism Threat and Challenges,* Deep & Deep Publications, New Delhi, 2006; p. 213.
17. R.C. Mishra, *op.cit.,* pp. 173-174.
18. Vaillant, George E, The wisdom of the Ego, Cambridge; Harved University Press, 1993, p. 43.
19. http://gseweb.harvard.edu_web/peace/Articles-2004/weisbach _Jessica_terrorist_mind.htm; p. 3.
20. David J. Whittaker, *op.cit.,* p. 50.
21. *Ibid,* p. 61.
22. Chris E. Stout, *op.cit.,* p. 49.
23. Maxwell Taylor, *The Terrorist;* Brassey's Defence, Publishers, London, 1988, p. 143.
24. R.C. Mishra, *op.cit.,* pp. 42, 43.
25. Uday Mahurkar, *Learning to Kill; India Today,* September 29, 2003, p. 44.
26. Amitav Acharya, *Age of Fear, Power Versus Principles in the War on Terror;* Rupa, New Delhi, 2004, p. 55.
27. Pippa Norris, Monlague Kern and Marion just; *Framing Terrorism, The News Media, the Government and the Public,* Routledge New York & London, 2003, p. 255.
28. *Ibid.,* p. 258.
29. David J. Whittaker; *Terrorism : Understanding The Global Threat;* Longmen Publishers, London; 2002, p. 73.
30. *Ibid.,* p. 78.
31. Maxwell Taylor, *The Terrorist;* Brassey's Defence publishers London; Year 1988, p. 43.

32. R.C. Mishra, *op.cit.*, p. 184.
33. David J. Whittaker; *op.cit.*, p. 138.
34. Pippa Norrius, Montague Kern and Marion Just, *op.cit.*, pp. 257-258.
35. *Ibid.*, p. 258.
36. http://gseweb.harvard.edu_web/peace./Articles_2004/weisbach_Jessica_terrorist_mind.htm p. 4.
37. Maqbool Hasan, *International Terrorism*; Maxford Publishers, Delhi, 2006, p. 251.
38. http://www. apa.org/ppo/issues/pterrochild.html.
39. *Ibid.*
40. Fathali M. Moghaddam & Anthony J. Marsella, *Understanding Terrorism*; American Psychological Association Washington, DC, 2004, p. 265.
41. Maqbool Hasan, *op.cit.*, p. 296.
42. *Ibid.*, p. 298.
43. *Ibid.*, p. 324.
44. Pippa Norris, Montague Kern and Marion Just; *op.cit.*, p. 143.
45. http://www.brook.edu/comm/transcripts/200 00210a. htm.
46. *Ibid*
47. Pippa Norris, Montague Kern and Marion just; *op.cit.*, p. 256.
48. James J.F. Forest; *The Making of a Terrorist Recruitment, Training and Root Causes*. Vol. III. Praeger Security International Publishers, London, 2006; p. 220.

4

Terrorist Methods and Possibilities of New Adventures

On May 21st 1991, India's former Prime Minister Rajiv Gandhi stood smiling among a throng of supporters and well-wishers in the peaceful village of Sriperumbudur (in the province of Tamil Nadu, India) when a young Tamil woman named Dhanu stepped forward, bent down to touch his feet in a customary sign of reverence, and detonated the explosive belt she was wearing (a harness of six grenades). Prime Minister Rajiv Gandhi and seventeen others were killed instantly, while other were injured or maimed for life. On August 15th, 1998, a car bomb packed with 5000 pounds of explosives detonated in the popular shopping district of Omagh, a small town in country Tyrone, Northern Ireland. The entire front wall of SD kells clothes shop was blasted in to the building, and the roof collapsed on to the top floor. At the pine Emporium, a furniture could latter be seen sticking out the windows at the back of the building. A water main under the road was exposed by the blast, and this began pouring gallons of water over the wreckage, washing bodies down the hill. All in all, twenty eight people were killed by the blast, and hundreds more were injured.[1]

On September 11th, 2001, terrorists dealt a devastating blow to the United States of American Airlines at roughly the same time. Two of them were used to hit and destroy the twin towers of the World Trade Center in New York, the symbol of American capitalist power. One was used to hit and destroy the Pentagon in Washington, a symbol of American Military Might. The fourth one apparently aimed at the white house but field to reach their destination and crashed in a field in Pennsylvania. More then 3,000 people were killed and many were injured. This attack has been almost unanimously characterized as the worst in this century.

Additionally, in the September 11 (9/11) attack the perpetrators identity was not immediately clear. The suicide terrorist who carried out the attack had been trained as pilots in aviation school within the U.S. so that they could take over from the pilot of the aircrafts, which they had hijacked. The operation was carried out with meticulous precision but relatively cheaply since they used American resources, including aircraft as their weapons.[2]

On October 28, 2001, six members of the Islamist Sipah-e-Sihaba group entered St. Dominic's Church in Behawalpur, Pakistan, during protestant services and opened fire on the congregation, sixteen people were killed, including the minister and a Muslim guard posted outside the church.

On October 12, 2002, On the Indonesian island of Bali the two bomb explosions took place in two bars at Kuta Beach. One was in Paddy's Bar and the second was in Sari Club late on a Saturday evening when the bars were almost packed to capacity with tourists. The explosions took place within six seconds of each other. As well as those who died, around 200 and another 132 people were injured. The first bomb was triggered by a mobile phone while the second and much larger bomb was in a minibus parked outside the Sari Club. Those killed or injured in the blasts were mostly Australian tourists.[3]

And on January 7, 2005 a group of suspected Islamic Militants was arrested in Manila, the capital of the Philippines. The group was discovered in the process of assembling bombs for what was intended to be an attack on the Christian festival of the Black Nazarene, an annual event, which attracts tens of thousands of devotes. When police examined the improvised explosive device and bomb components, including timing gadgets and cables, they realized that the death toll of the explosions, had they occurred would have been considerable.

New stories similar to these can be found today and tomorrow, somewhere in the world a group or individual with the motivation to kill innocent need only act upon that motivation, and the world bears witness to yet another terrorist attack.

There is a remarkable variety of means of destruction and pin pointed targets. These are among some of the methods that terrorist have used: arson, assassination or targeted murders, bombing, chemical substance, commercial and industrial sabotage, hijacking, kidnapping, grenades, gun, letter bombs, human bombs, mortar and rocket launchers. And these are some of the targets: airports, historical monuments, diplomats, embassies, hotels, markets, railways, roadways, religious places and etc.

The use of remote controller and delayed action devices and superior means of communication have made hit and run action a little easier and prompt detection and prevention rather more difficult. For those whose responsibility is security and counter-terrorism there will always be a problem with accurate prediction, despite the terrorists use, now and then, of coded warnings. The terrorist incident, which is most difficult to anticipate, is the one, which leads to mass murder and widespread damages. The destruction of New York's International Trade Center on September 11, 2001 was a new method in that using jet aircraft and all their passengers as suicide bombers had never been tried before.

Every day there was a fresh incident, usually that of a car bomb or suicide bomber decimating civilians and triggering the hardest of response from a government feeling itself beleaguered. Each of the terrorist events described thus required specialized knowledge of explosives, covert movement and communication, and automatic weapons. It is known that successful terrorist attack require careful recruitment, planning and training, in addition to intense personal motivation on the part of the attackers. However, the type of knowledge required for such activities is not typically found in local library, public school, or in other traditional place where formal learning takes place. Thus the question arises, where and how does learning take place in the terrorist world?

Recruitment

In terrorism recruitment plays a very important role because without recruitment terrorism cannot survive and develop. Recruitment provides the killers, the suicide bombers, the kidnappers, the executions, the engineers and the soldiers—the armies of modern terrorism.

Theorists have long argued that poverty, lack of education, and unemployment produce terrorist recruits and supporters. However, Osama bin Laden comes from the richest non-royal Saudi family, and his principal strategist Dr. Ayman Al Zawahiri, is from one of the most educated families in Egypt. Although, those who live in poverty or unemployed or underemployed are most vulnerable to ideological indoctrination, it also generates recruits and support for terrorism in developed countries, as well as among wealthy and educated classes.

However, because the socio economic and political conditions in Asia, Africa, the middle East, Latin America and the former USSR are conducive to inculcating of terrorist ideologies, the bulk of the terrorist groups are located in the poorer regions of the world. However, casual factors of terrorism can be very diverse, as they often depend on various, sometimes-interrelated factors—individual circumstances external environment, psychology, upbringing and so on. It is necessary to know how groups recruit members and the often very sophisticated manipulative process that group utilize.

The oldest example of recruitment by a terrorist organization comes from a thousand years ago, and carried out by those who gave the word assassin.[4] They were members of a secret Islamic order active in Persia, Iraq and Syria about 1090-1272, who believed that it was a religious duty to harass and murder their enemies. The most important members of the order were those who actually did the killing. Having been promised paradise in return for dying in action, the killers it is said were made to yearn for paradise by being given a life of pleasure that included the use of the hashish. From this came the name for the secret order as a whole, "ashishin" or "hashish users". In the thirteenth century, Mongol and Arab armies went after the "ashishin", destroying their castle and killing their leaders.

At the beginning, religion and drugs were used to persuade young men to join the group of the "Assassins". Indeed, both then and now, it takes a combination of factors to recruit new terrorists. First, one needs a cause to attract and motivate recruits. Very often the target population is poverty stricken feeling oppressed, deprived, and hopeless. Religion is another recruitment tool and motivational dimension, but not a necessary condition. For example, the Tamil terrorists in Sri Lanka rely more on patriotic and social motives. However, oppression and a well-run organization which a channel the resentment into action are essential.

Sometimes the attractions to join a terrorist group are material—for example, the family of the terrorist may be rewarded with money and public praise after the family member successfully conducts an attack. This factor is most important among the poor, the young, and the economically dispossessed. Thus poverty, anger, resentment, religious and nationalistic zeal, and even the desire to the take revenge for a relative killed by the enemy are all used to successfully attract and recruit new terrorists.

More important to note are "social bonds" among the young volunteers, the sense of clandestine belonging the develop, and their ability to make reinforcing contact with Al Qaeda leaders or trainers. Group of young men become effective terrorist cells "through mutual emotional and social support, development of a common identity, and encouragement to adopt a new faith." Personal problems are also exploited by recruiters; often, people with mental problems are targeted, as long as their disability does not make them incapable of terrorist operations. Widows or unmarried women who have lost their parents or partners are another source of recruits. People who have been condemned to death by religious courts may be given the option of becoming a suicide bomber to atone for their crime, and some are provided cash for their families.

Al Qaeda uses the most advanced headhunting methods to recruits terrorist agents. It advertises by using recorded videos on Internet websites CD-ROMs, recorded cassettes, and blast faxes. They also use Internet for terrorist recruitment and mobilization "The Internet has become the new Afghanistan for terrorist training, recruitment, and fundraising. ... Terrorist groups are exploiting the accessibility, vast audience and anonymity of the Internet to raise money and recruit new members."[5]

Abdullah Azzam, Bin laden's mentor, inspired many al-Qaeda volunteers with his fiery preaching. Bin laden and his al-Qaeda aides emulate him by persuading Muslim preachers around the world to help with recruiting. The many thousands of Afghan Arabs whom he trained and fought with against the Soviets in Afghanistan still take their lead from al-Qaeda. The network recurits terrorist world-wide, including from immigrant communities in the United States and western Europe as well as Australia, the Philippines, Indonesia and Malaysia. Its agents seek new human talent in all six inhabited continents.

Modern Recruitment Method

Adam Gadahn was an average American boy who loved watching television and listening to music, rose by parents who farmed goats in riverside country, California. However, at the age of seventeen he discovered Islam on the web and soon started a conversion process that led to his joining al-Qaeda. In 2003, U.S. Federal authorities labeled him an enemy, saying he was one of seven individual suspected of being al-Qaeda operatives who may be working to mount a terrorist attack in the United States. Gadahn, now twenty-five, has attended Al-Qaeda training camps and worked as a translator for the terrorist group, the FBI said. Authorities said he might be using the name Adam Pearlman or Abu Suhayb al-Amriki. In his own words, Gadahn described how the Internet was the gate for his recruitment:

"The turning point, perhaps, was when I moved in with my grandparents here in Santa Ana, the country seat of Orange, California. My grandmother, a computer whiz, is hooked up to America online and I have been scooting the information superhighway since January. But when I moved in, with intent of finding a job, I began to visit the religion folders on AOL and the use net newsgroups, where I found discussions on Islam to be the most intriguing.[6]

The recruitment application was translated from Farsi as follows:

In The Name of God

Preliminary Registration for Martyrdom Operation

I... child of ...., born 13 .... [Islamic calendar], the city of: Proclaim my preparedness for carrying out Martydom operations .... against the occupiers of the holy sites [referring to Najaf, Karbala, and other place in Iraq]. .... against the occupiers of [Jerusalem]. .... for carrying out the death sentence of the infidel salman Rushdie.

Also, I would like to become an active member of the Army of Martyrs of the International Islamic Movement.

Yes ...., No ....

Contact telephone:

Applicants address:

Applicants Signature:

Many other modern recruitment operations have emerged on the web. For example, in June 2004, the magazine Insight Online obtained a recruitment appeal seeking Iranians who would commit suicide in deadly attack on American and coalition forces in Iraq, on Israel and on U.S. citizens around the world. It was posted on the Internet by an Iranian recruiting group.[7] Reuters news agency reported on June 5th 2004 that the group is known as the committee for the commemoration of Martyrs of Global Islamic campaign. It quoted the group's spokesman, Mohammad Ali Samadi, as saying, "some 10,000 people have registered their names to carry out martyrdom operations on our defined targets."

In October 2004, Intelwire presented an al-Qaeda recruiting video showing young boys training in terrorist techniques.[8] The video includes a statement read in Arabic by a young son of Osama bin Laden. The video was hosted on an Arabic language website connected to Tawhid Wal Jihad, the terror organization led by Abu Musab al-zarquawi. The Video, titled "Hamza Laden", appears to show young boys between the age of ten and fourteen engaged in commando training, including marching in information, running a military-style obstacle course, rappelling, and reading written statements in Arabic. All these example show how modern terrorists are using advanced communication technologies to attract and seduce potential (followers, recruits, supporters and would be terrorists. potential audience, fast flow of the great virtues of the internet-ease of access, lack of regulations, vast information, and so forth—have been turned to the advantage of groups committed to terrorizing societies in order to achieve their goals. Today, as recent studies have revealed, almost all active terrorist group have established their presence on the internet.[9]

Scan of the internet revealed thousand of websites (serving terrorists and their supporters websites) are only one of the Internet's services used by modern terrorism: There are other facilities in the Net—e-mail, chat rooms, e-groups, forums, virtual message boards—that are used more and more by terrorists. Terrorism on the Internet is a very dynamic phenomenon; websites suddenly emerge, frequently modify their formats, and then swiftly disappear—or, in many cases, seem to disappear by changing their online address but retaining much the same content. To locate the terrorists' sites, numerous systematic scans of the Internet were conducted, feeding an enormous variety of names and terms into search engines, entering chat rooms and forums of supporters and sympathizers, and surveying the links on other organizations' websites to create and update a comprehensive set of lists. This is often a herculean effort, especially because in some cases (e.g. Al Qaeda's websites) the locations and contents of websites change almost daily.

The Internet can be used to recruit and mobilize supporters to play a more active role in support of terrorist activities or causes. In addition to seeking converts by using the full range of website technologies (audio, digital, video etc) to enhance the presentation of their message, terrorist organizations capture information about the users who browse their website. Users who seem most interested in the organization's cause or well suited to carrying out its work are then contacted. Sophisticated methods are used by terrorists to refine or customize recruiting techniques on the Net: "Using some of the same marketing techniques employed by commercial enterprises, terrorist servers could capture information about the users who browse their websites, and then later contact those who seem most interested. Recruiters may also use more interactive Internet technology to roam online chat room and cyber cafes, looking for receptive members of the public—particularly young people. Interested computer users around the world engaged in long-term 'cyber relationships' that could lead to friendship and eventual membership."

However, it should be noted that modern terrorist do not recruit direct online; they use the Net only to identify, profile, and select potential candidates for recruitment. Afraid of having their group infiltrated by security agencies and counter terrorism forces, they will use the Internet only for the early stage of the recruitment process.

The Internet is very popular among children and youth. Terrorist (know this, and are increasingly) using the Internet to target children. One of the Hama's websites, al-Fateh (The conqueror), appears every other week and is clearly meant for children, with its cartoon-style design and colorful children stories. The websites title promises "pages discussing jihad, scientific pages, the best stories not be found elsewhere, and unequalled tales of heroism." The al-Fateh sites has a link to the official Hamas site, www.Palestine—info.com.[10]

Hizballah also targets children and adolescents use of the Internet. In 2003, Hizballah began online marketing of a computer game simulating terrorist attacks on Israeli targets. The computer game, called "Special Force", was developed by the Hizballah central Internet Bureau, and its development according to a report in Lebanon's Daily Star—took two years. The game places the player in different Hizballah operations against Israelis. The producers of "Special Force" argue that it is based on actual Hizballah battles with Israeli forces. "Special Force" can be played in Arabic, English, French and Farsi, and is available one of the Hizballah websites.

"I will make my body a bomb that will blast the flesh of Zionists., the sons of the pigs and monkeys. I will tear bodies in to little pieces and cause them more pain than they will ever know." [11]

Thus, while it may be disturbing, it should be no surprise that children are also present in the dark terrorist domain of modern global conflict. As on the world's battlefields, children are increasingly present in terrorist groups. Many of these group have long had "youth wings" to provide broader support in the populace, but now growth are increasingly being used in actual operations to strike at targets behind the battle line. This occurs for the same fundamental reasons that children are now on the battlefield: Children offer terrorist group leaders cheap and easy recruits, who provide new options to strike at their foes.

Perhaps the most disturbing aspect of contemporary

terrorism is the growth in suicide bombing, particularly emanating from the Middle East. Here, too, children are present. Radical Islamic group like Palestinian Islamic jihad and Hamas have recruited children as young as thirteen to be suicide bombers and children as young as eleven to smuggle explosives and weapons. The recruitment mechanism of potential suicide bombers varies among the different organizations. However, recruitment methods can generally be classified in to three main types. The first is when a person approaches the organization and offers him or herself for a suicide mission. The second is the grass-roots mobilization of a group of people who are committed to a certain cause and who are willing to die for it. These people sometimes approach the organization for specific guidelines regarding the suicide mission. The third method, which is the most common, is active recruitment. This is when the organizations 'enlistment officers' are sent to recruit new members. In the majority of cases, new members are first given the offer of becoming fighters, and only after the training process are some singled out for suicide acts.[12]

However, the most common recruitment method is still by means of 'enlistment officers'. One of the most explicit manifestations of this recruitment method is evident in the case of the LTTE. Suicide Bombers are willing to die on behalf of his/her community group. The LTTE is the first and the only group that killed two prominent national leaders in the world. They are responsible for the assassination of the former Indian Prime Minister, Rajiv Gandhi in May 1991 and another one assassinated the incumbent Sri Lankan President Ranasinghe Premadasa in May 1993. LTTE women warriors refused to use red kum kum on their foreheads and thali/jewellery around their necks. Their desire to transform their biological and cultural marked body to that of 'heroic' masculinity can be seen in the following poem:

The ideal women of Tamil Eelam
Her forehead shall be adorned not with
Red Kum Kum but with blood
All that is seen in her eyes is not the

Of youth but the tombs of the dead
on her neck will lay no tali
but a cyanide capsule
she has embraced not men
but weapons ?[13]

Women are actively involved in the LTTE operations. The LTTE has a separate wing for women's forces. It focused its recruitment on women to fill losses of it cadres. By joining the movement, women achieved a social status equal to men. Women wanted to become 'Black Tigers'. They worship Prabakarn, the leader of the LTTE. They felt grievances and fight against oppression and exploitation exercised on them.

The recruitment process to the PKK was rather similar. Many PKK fighters who were recruited from the Kurdish Diaspora in Europe were approached by organization 'enlistment officers' in Kurdish cultural centers where many youths spent their time. There is evidence that, at these centers, young men went through a process of indoctrination, the aim of which was to build up their Kurdish identity and introduce them to the PKK.[14] A similar process took place in Kurdish summer camps. Children were approached in their schools by representative of the PKK and were invited to cultural camps all over Europe where they learned about the Kurdish struggle. Some of these children never returned home but rather were sent directly to the battle zone in the southeast Turkey.

The PKK's method of recruiting specifically for suicide mission was slightly different. Women carried out most suicide attacks mounted by the organization, and organization activities usually approached younger, under educated potentials from large, poor families residing in Turkey. Some of these women were lost their close family in combat with the Turkish forces. It is hard to find evidence indicating that financial incentives were offered to the women during the recruitment phase and religious rhetoric was also not visible. The most prominent incentives evidently were the urge for vengeance, Commitment to the Kurdish cause and devotion to the leader of PKK, Abdullah

Ocalan. Terrorist recruit children because they are relatively low cost way to build out there forces, whose youth also brings certain distinct advantage in operation.

This same rationale also holds for why groups recruit children for suicide bombing suicide bombing is an efficient method for weaker forces to strike at an otherwise well-prepared opposition. Even if they lack the technology for guided missiles or other "smart bombs", the inclusions of the human element allows groups to create a thinking bomb that can adjust to changing circumstances. As one leader of Hamas commented, "we do not have tanks or rockets, but we have something superior our exploding Islamic human bombs. In place of a nuclear arsenal, we are proud of our arsenal of believes."[15]

By the standards of typical cost of guided weaponry, the human bomb is stunningly cheap. All that is needed to make an effective bomb suit for the terrorist is a nine-volt battery, a light switch, a short cable, mercury (readily obtainable from thermometers), acetone, gun powder and some from of homemade shrapnel such as nail or screws. Experts note that the total cost of a typical operation is about $150, with the most expensive part often being the bus fare to transport the bomber to his/her target. Add in a young terrorist, and the bomb is then able to kill or wound all individuals within a 25-50 meter area.[16] While there are multiple reasons for children to become involved in terrorist groups, none are simply coincidental or beyond the control of the groups themselves. Instead, they are usually the result of the combination of a harsh environment that leaves children with no good choices and a deliberate mobilizations strategy by the group itself to pull children in to terrorism or suicide terrorism.

In order to discuss suicide terrorism, it is extremely important to explain what exactly is meant by this term. There are several difficulties with defining the phenomenon. The first such difficulty concerns the difference between the readiness to die and the desire to die. For this reason it is useful to define a suicide operation on the basis of the perpetrators death as a precondition of a successful attack. In other words: if the perpetrator does not die the attack cannot take place. From such a definition, high-risk operations in which the perpetrator has the smallest chance of surviving are excluded. Another problem is represented by the difficulty in making a distinction between cases in which he or she is unaware of his her death being a part of the plan. There have been several cases in which the terrorist were fooled into believing that they were only transporting the explosive that was latter remotely detonated while in their possession by organizers of the attack. Even though such cases should not be considered, the difficulty of determining the suicide bomber's intentions after their death inevitably results in the misclassification of many such attacks as suicide bombings.

A suicide terror attack is defined as a premeditated as of ideologically or religiously motivated violence, in which the success of the operation is contingent on self-inflicted death by the perpetrators, during the attack.'[17]

According to Boaz Ganor* suicide terrorism is defined as "the operational method in which act of the attack is dependent upon the death of perpetrator." Even more importantly he says, suicide terrorism is aimed at "Striking a blow to public moral."

The terrorist organization benefits from the success of the suicide attack in several ways. First, the terrorists fulfill their aim of slaughtering human beings, and, Second, they grab the attention of the media, focusing on a nationalistic or religious causes.[18]

The first modern suicide bombing by a terror group occurred in 1951, when a young communist suicide volunteer assassinated French Brigadier General Charles, Marie Chanson in Sadec, Indonesia.[19]

Suicide, terrorism is nothing new in human history, it first appeared long before modern times. This phenomenon

---

* Boaz Ganor a director of the International Policy Institute for Counter Terrorism (ICT)

was already seen among the Jewish Sicaris as early as the first century, among the Muslim Hashishiyun in the eleventh century and among the Asians in the eighteen century.[20] However, in the late twentieth century, and especially during the last two decades, suicide terrorism has become one of the most prominent type of terrorism, globally widespread, and especially dominant in countries such as Lebanon, Egypt, Israel, Turkey and Sri Lanka.

The first organization in Modern times that used suicide terrorism consistently was Hizballah in Lebanon conducting several attacks during the 1980, mostly against the Israeli army in South Lebanon.[21] This was followed by LTTE (Liberation Tigers of Tamil Eelam) an organization that was formed in Sri Lanka as part of the struggle for the independence of the Tamil minority on the island. During the 1990s, the Kurds in Turkey (the Kurdistan workers Party or PKK), the Palestinians in Israel (Hamas, Fateh and Palestinian Islamic Jihad), and of course al Qaeda and other terrorist organization world wide also adopted suicide tactics in their terrorist campaigns. In contract to other terrorist attacks, even the most dangerous ones, the suicide attack is an "operational method in which the very act of the attack is dependent upon the death of the perpetrator." The terrorist is fully aware that if he does not kill himself, the planned attack will not be successful. Hence, because suicide terrorism obligates the perpetrator to make the biggest sacrifice of all-his life—Understanding and exploring how such an individual has been recruited, trained and convinced to undertake such an act, has become one of the most intriguing features of the phenomenon as well as key to understanding its growing prominence all over the world.

How does a terrorist recruit transform into a live bomb?

To begin with the story of Zarema Muzhakhoeva is instructive. Muzhakhoeva was a twenty-three years old single parent when she was recruited for a suicide attack by a group of Chechen rebels. Her main incentive to join the "black widows"* was financial. Shortly after her husband was killed during the course of a business dispute, the dead husbands family took away Muzhakhoeva's newborn baby girl, and she was prevented from seeing her child. Spurred on by her disasters, Muzhakhoeva stole her grandmother's jewels, sold them for $600, and made her way to her mother-in-law's house. She asked her permission to spend some time with her daughter, yet her real plan was to run away with the baby to Moscow. Members of her late husband's family kept a close watch on her the whole time and when Muzhakhoeva tried boarding an aircraft, they took her child away. Muzhakhoeva was heartbroken; not only had she stolen her grandmothers jewels, she had also lost her daughter. After that she joined the Shamil Basayeu faction of the Chechen rebel movement her only incentive in doing so was financial. She learned that the family of a suicide bomber received $1,000 for carrying out a mission for this faction. Muzhakhoeva, who did not see much point in continuing life without her daughter, thought that with her death, at least her grandmother would be compensated for the stolen jewels. After she joined the "black widows" group, she was trained for two weeks in a training camp and was then sent to carry and detonate a bomb inside a military bus at a Russian military base. However, as revealed later in her statement after she was caught, Muzhakhoeva did not really want to sacrifice her life, so she told her operators that she had missed the bus. Shortly thereafter, she was sent to Moscow and taken on her tour of the city, where she was introduced to various potential targets. The next day she was dressed in black and given a text to read in front of a video camera. She was told that the tape would be sent to her family. Two days later, on July 9th 2003, she was given an explosive belt to wear, and sent to Red Square; from there, she took a taxi to the coffee shop where she was supposed to detonate her explosives. However, she panicked again, told a guard in the area that she had been sent to blow herself up, and was immediately arrested.[22]

Economic deprivation, however, is just one of the various motives used by terrorist organizations to recruit suicide bombers. Another example is Hanadi Jaradat a twenty-nine year old female Palestinian suicide bomber who exploded on

October 2003 in a restaurant in the city of Haifa, killing nineteen people and injuring more than sixty was recruited in to the Palestinian Islamic Jihad (PIJ) organization after her Fiance and her brother were killed by Israeli security force. In this case, the PIJ activists who recruited her used her strong urge for revenge.

Such examples illuminate the intriguing process of recruiting and training these human bombs. The recruitment and training process of suicide bombers, argue that this phenomenon is a result of encouraging environmental and personal motivation, both of which are being used by terrorist organization implementing suicide attack.

The ability to locate the right candidate for a suicide attack is the most important element in the preparations stage of the attack, since all the success of the attack is virtually dependent on the abilities, skills and loyalty of the suicide bomber. Moreover, the recruiting process demands that the organization overcomes a basic contradiction. On one hand, there is a need to verify that the candidate has the skills, ability and loyalty to execute a successful suicide attack, and on the other hand, in most cases the organization cannot afford to use suicide bombers who are well trained. Hence, there is a need to recruit a candidate that the organization can spare, but still demonstrate the appropriate skills and loyalty for the organization.

In general, recruitment procedures can be classified in two main categories. The first category includes cases in which the candidates, approaches the organization on their own initiative, volunteering to participate in suicide attack, while the second category encompasses these individuals who are recruited directly by an organization that feels they could be persuaded to become suicide bombers because they show great identification with its goals.

Another method of suicide mission recruitment involves instances where an organization constants certain individuals who show great potential for identification with its goals. In such cases, the movement's leaders feel that they can convince, this new recruit to sacrifice his or her life for the organizations goals. Al Qaeda is a good example of this aggressive method of recruitment. Its leaders have been especially in enlisting young people in the west or Arab countries. The organization finds its candidates mainly among lonely, rootless young men who congregate in the mosques for company. Al Qaeda also has a network or experienced fighters, who were trained in camps through Afghanistan.

Once again the unemployed young persons were the most vulnerable group for recruitment. The main incentive for joining the rebel forces was the salary offered by recruiters. In sum, terrorist recruitment involves many dimensions, some of which are unique to suicide attack.

Training for new recruitments is also a unique subcategory within the broader discussion of terrorist organization.

Training

Once selected, the terrorist often goes through an intense period of mental preparation. The training process begins with the selection of children. The training of children in terrorist action varies as much as the techniques for recruitment. Indeed, it is a process that is undergoing constant refinement. In addition to their intelligence and enthusiasm, appearance, in relation to potential target is highly important.

The training often includes study of text that reinforces the notion of sacrifice, as well as tasks memorization and visualization. A focus is also made on the ease of death. It pleasures are extolled in contrast to a future life of sadness, sickness, and continued humiliation. Hamas, for example, has its recruits rest in empty graves, in order to see how "peaceful" death will be.[23] In turn, LTTE survivors tell of training drill in which they would rehearse what they would do if captured or wounded. Their coaches would instruct them how to bite into the cyanide capsule* that they would wear in necklace during operations.

---

* Cyanide capsule is a capsule, which mixes with blood, and within one second they die.

The LTTE, known to have connections with Hezbollah, imitated and improved Hezbollah suicide techniques and also adopted their training methods. Every new recruit to the LTTE, most of the whom were children, had to go through a basic training period of four months. Basic training included indoctrination to military tactics and of course indoctrination in the organizations ideology.

A typical daily routine at LTTE camps began with an early wake-up call at 5 a.m. The children then underwent two hours of physical training in jungle, followed by lessons in the martial arts. In the afternoon, they attended classes, where they were introduced to the history of the organization and the Tamil people. In order to toughen them up and take the edge off their doubts about killing, instructors showed them war movies and later sent them to attack designated targets, applying the knowledge acquired from the movies. Evenings were mostly devoted to classes in intelligence gathering and the handling of explosive devices.

Throughout the training period, children were isolated from their families and subject to the draconian rulers of the camp. For example, there are testimonies about trainees who were caught drinking alcohol being punish by death. At the same time, in order to keep families happy while their children were going through the training period, the organization provided them with financial support.[24]

Only after the basic training period did the selection process for the suicide squad, the Black Tigers begin. Prospective suicide bombers were selected according to their achievement in the initial training period. Specific training for suicide missions lasted for a few more weeks during which trainees learned the suicide tactic in great detail.

The training process of suicide bomber differs considerably depending on the given cultural, regional, and ideological context. Those who are volunteer for the operation from the outside as non-members requires a different training approach than experienced operatives who are recruited from within the group's ranks.

In first stage, they are asked to give three reasons for why they want to carry out a Martyrdom operation. After their motives are analyzed and confirmed; the bombers are asked to prepare a videotape of their last will, which serves as a propaganda and a recruiting tool for the future, as well as an insurance policy against the bombers possible change of mind. The actual training then begins with a period of crystallization, in which the candidate is deliberately placed in surprising and even life-threatening situations in order to test his or her reactions and susceptibility to panic. This period is followed by a segment of ideological and religious preparation, in which candidates watch films depicting the life before the occupation, as well as propaganda videos showing the brutality of enemy soldiers and the glory of past martyrs. During this period, the recruit also commonly undergoes religious indoctrination by spending time with clerics and reading certain passages from known over and over again.[25]

In Sri Lanka, by contrast, most of the perpetrator of suicide bombing attacks are not outside volunteers but rather experienced members of the group who have already established their credibility. The LTTE even has a permanently attached suicide squared called the 'Black Tigers', comprised of the most devoted and able volunteer selected out of the group's toughest combat unit.[26]

However, in the vein of Hizbullah, mental preparation was more important. The instructor's objective was to get the recruit to commit fully to the mission and make sure he or she would not have second thoughts.

Not surprisingly, the training process of the PKK was not much different. One striking resemblance to the LTTE was the nature of the program in which the suicide bomber underwent during the training process. Again, the organization did everything possible to prevent the person from having second thoughts.

A comparative analysis of different terrorist organizations reveals that the training process is conducted in two separate dimensions. The first dimension of the training process is focused on giving the suicide bomber the basic operational skills for executing his attack. This includes an introduction to basic military techniques and knowledge on how to penetrate security, approach the target, operate the explosive, and avoid being detected, as well as protocols of operation for specific situation that might be encountered during the attack.

The second dimension of the training process is focused on developing the appropriate mental mindset of the perpetrator—an ideological perspective that guarantees that at the right moment he or she will not hesitate to die for the success of the attack. The organizations main concern is to make sure that the potential bomber does not back down, a move that would not only jeopardize the specific mission but could also disclose organization members and tactics.

However, although all the organizations employ this two—dimensional training process, two types of implementation can be detected. The first is a rapid one, when the entire process takes place in a matter of weeks, while the second one consists of months and sometimes years of preparation. In most cases, these differences are due to the specific operational capabilities and character of an organization.

Whether the organization uses a short and suicide—oriented training process or a military type long-term training process, a comparative examination reveals important similarities, which is divided in to three phases. In the first phase, the potential suicide bombers go through long sessions with recruits who talk to them about the religious importance of their acts and also try to remove the fear of dying. In some cases, this includes taking the recruits to a cemetery and placing them inside a grave. The second stage includes technical and operational preparations. The final stage includes a public demonstration of the potential suicide bombers, most of the time through videotape, in which the bomber reads a prepared testament, declaring that the decision to go in the suicide mission was made willingly and no compulsion was involved. A day before the mission, the candidate will be shown the tape over and over again, will ask for mercy for all his or her sins, and will check that all the equipment is ready. All these stages of this process take only a matter of days to complete.[27]

Stages in the Perpetration of Suicide Attack

Recruitment of the Suicide Attacker

Physical and emotional training of the attacker for the mission

Preparation for the attack

Gathering Intelligence

Formulation of the operation plan

Preparation of combat means

Preparation of collaborators infrastructure

Farewell ceremony for the suicide attacker and his send off too execute the mission

Perpetration of the suicide attack

Tapping the media potential of the attack

Another most important part in terrorist training is the psychological phase. The organization put most of the emphasis on bringing the recruits to a mental state in which they were fully committed to the organization and its goals were willing to sacrifice everything, including their own lives, for its sake.

In training they also offer tips on various ways to make, "suitable preparation for battle"—physical training, martial arts, survival and outdoor training, firearms training and military training. Terrorists get training to carry out their activities in their camps. The training camps are provided with facilities equal to that of a military camp. They get instructions from well-educated cadres in all aspects: to assassinate, to murder, to kidnap, to carry out nuclear, bio and cyber attack.[28] The typical training camp requires a combination of resources, geographic isolation, and individual with specific abilities. Throughout history, they have served as perhaps the most important place where the transformation from individual to terrorist has taken place.

Al Qaeda's training camps in the places like Afghanistan and Bosnia are perhaps the most commonly cited locations where terrorist training is known to have taken place. However, terrorist training camps have existed in a wide variety of locations throughout the world—indeed, the geography of former and current centers of terrorist learning includes dictatorship and advanced industrial democracies.

In the Middle East, groups like the Palestinian Liberation Organization and Hizballah have established training camp in the Bekaa Valley of eastern Lebanon. During the 1970s, Libya began providing a safe heaven for a variety of terrorist training camps, and particularly for groups committed to the spread of Islam. During 1990s, Islamic separatist groups in Algeria built and used training camps both within their country and across the border in Tunisia, where new recruits were taught combat tactics, explosives production, and weapons handling.

In South East Asia, Jemaah Islamiyah-a religious extremist organization which seeks to create a pan-Islamic state writing Indonesia, Brunei, Malaysia, Singapore and the Southern Philippines developed and operated several training facilities such as camp Jabal Quba on Mount Kararao, where courses in weapons and explosives have been provided. In Sri Lanka, the guerilla/ terrorist group Liberation Tiger of Tamil Eelam

(LTTE) operates in areas in the northern part of the country.

In February 2003, French police discovered a training area in the Secluded Landes forest in South Western France, which had been used to teach members of the Spanish separatist group Euzkadi Ta A Skatasuna (ETA) how to the use homemade grenade-launchers capable of piercing armored cars.

Terrorist groups like Sendero Luminoso (the Shining Path) and Tupac Amaru in Peru have operated training facilities on various remote regions of the country, where new recruits are taught terrorist strategy and the use of firearms and explosives.

Even the United States has played host to terrorist training camps in recent decades. In Northern Idaho, the Aryan Nations Church's 20 Acre, gated fortress with guard towers provided a sanctuary in which Christian identify adherents received weapons training, combat tactics and indoctrination.

Finally, another important "place" where terrorist training occurs is the Internet. Madeleine Gruen, an intelligence analyst at the New York City Police Department's counter-terrorism division, notes that both Islamic extremist groups and American extremist groups use the Internet as a means for both recruitment and training.

The world of a young man recruited for jihad or holy war is a frightening one. The training he undergoes teaches hatred in the name of religious purification. They are trained to destroy with deadly weapons fashioned out of simple things from their environment.

For example, the training experiences of a group of central Asians, mostly Uzbek, by nationality, who went through local terror schools during the mid-1990s. From the content of their notebooks, which were discovered in various locations throughout Uzbekistan, it seems that the training went on in the Ferghana Valley of Uzbekistan, a center of Islamic revival in the region. The training site is less important than the content, as these young people could have received virtually identical training in Tajikistan, Afghanistan or Pakistan during these years.[29]

The Terrorist Notebooks

In 2001-2002, ten notebooks were acquired of students who attended courses during the period of 1994-1996. These notebooks were acquired through various intermediaries. The students seem to have spent the bulk of their time receiving instruction in military subjects. They heard lectures on cartography, artillery, and targeting and then spent a lot of time learning about making and laying mines, as well as preparing and using poisons.

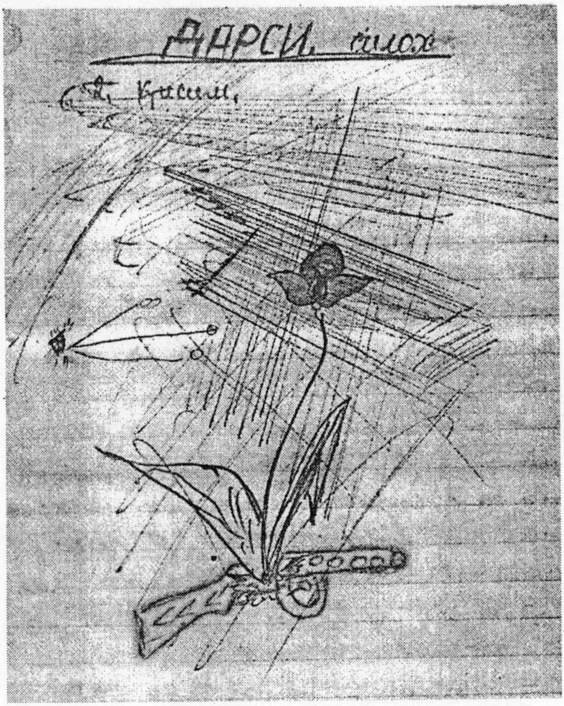

Fig 4.1: **Ayub's Notebook**

When these technical subjects were mastered, the student then went on to learn about when and how to make jihad or holy war. The students also received instruction in Arabic language and in some cases rudimentary instruction in Islam.

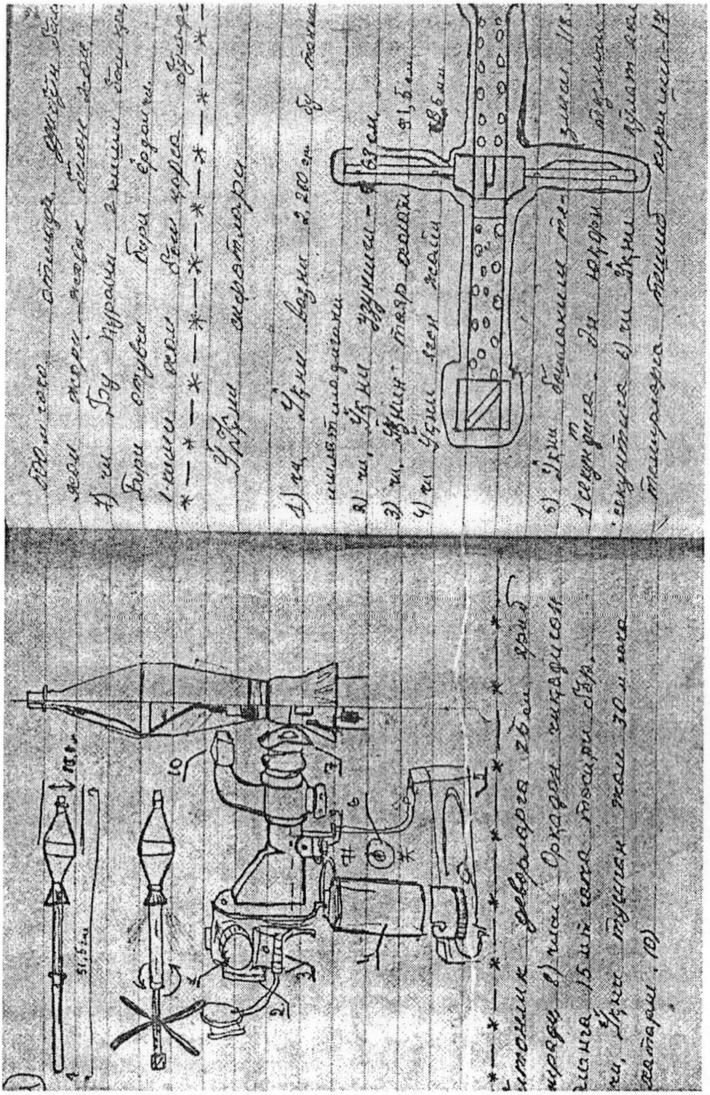

Fig 4.2: The Grenade Launcher Lesson

Ayub's Notebook

Ayub is probably a Tajik from Namangan. The text of his note book [note book 1] had many grammatical errors. The lessons begins at the end of the notebook, as is the tradition in Arabic or Persian books. On the inside cover of the notebook is written "Military Subjects" (darsi silokh), Part II, and has a drawing of a gun with a flower. (as shown in Fig 4.1).

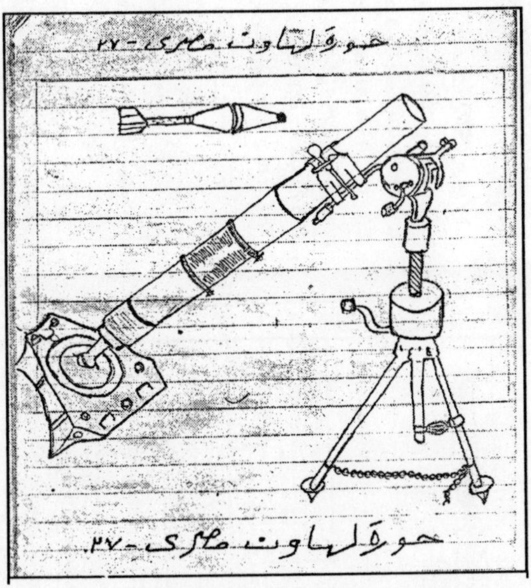

Fig 4.3: **The Mine Launcher Lesson**

All the notes contained in the notebook were from this one person, primarily on military subjects, especially artillery, rules of aiming and calculation of wind direction in launching grenades and other weapons. No humanities, no religion, holy war, or politics are represented in the lessons of Ayub's notebook.

One thing is clear, through these notebooks is that these students learned how to make some deadly weapons. All of these were "lab"-courses, and the students had hands-on

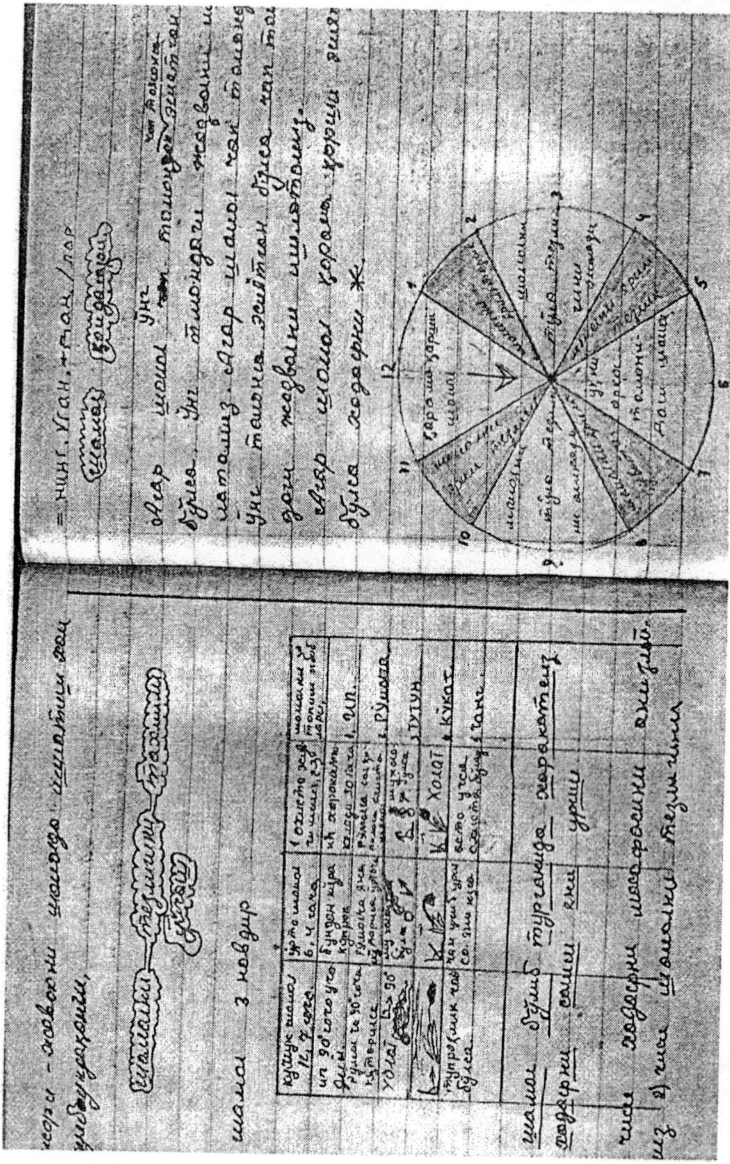

Fig 4.4: Sighting Moveable and Immoveable Targets

experience. This comes through clearly in the notes; in every field of terror, it was "learning through doing" from instructors who were proficient in their subject matter. In many cases, several different instructors taught the various military subjects.

They also taught to handle several weapons of choice from Afghanistan, including the Egyptian Rocket Propelled Grenade Launcher (Fig 4.2). "This 82-millimeter version is based on a Russian or Chinese modification of an earlier U.S. weapon," Ayub writes in Arabic with mistakes. All of these appear in illustrations, with accompanying notes on the functioning and maintenance of these weapons. This lesson of Ayub's notebook was dated on January 16 1995.[30] Another lesson covered launching mines (Fig 4.3) The subheading of these notes are in Arabic, suggesting a different teacher from the two lessons in Ayub's notebook. The description detailed in his notes is that of the Egyptian Minelauncher-27. It is not difficult to see that the student was a beginner in Arabic, because in spelling the title he copied a specially adorned

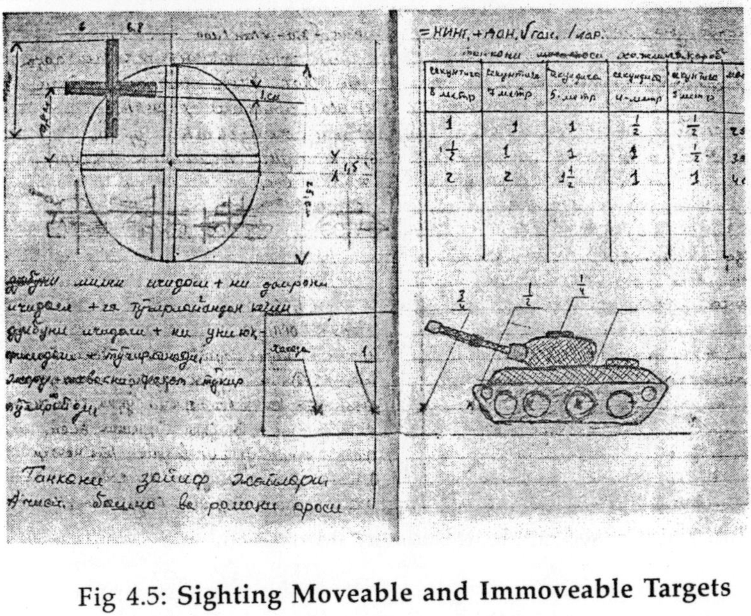

Fig 4.5: **Sighting Moveable and Immoveable Targets**

version of the letters, as they appear in slogans, ads, and posters. Their was a very detailed description of the mine launcher itself, its characteristics, and the description of the mine, as well as different ways that it can be exploded on the land, in the air, etc, depending upon the objective. There were the descriptions of setting up the weapon, calculating the aeronautics of the mine, aiming it, and tables are provided. All of the calculation formulas were in Arabic.

Ayub notebook was also diligent in learning how to target the enemy, on the ground and in the air. His notebook includes tables with elaborate calculations on how to target planes and helicopters in varying wind and weather conditions (Fig 4.4 , Fig 4.5). His teacher used both Arabic and Russian Military terminology and in the course of his lessons Ayub got to handle various forms of sighting instruments, writing in one case "the front glass reflects many colors", and "the plus sign that regulates distance is easily obscured by finger marks". One notebook includes information on making 15 different kinds of explosives devices, and the two students who prepared this notebook were taught reaction times and temperatures for blowing up buildings, bridges, railroad ties, and electricity relay stations.

Students were also taught how to make poisons with substances that were generally readily accessible, such as tobacco or toxic mushrooms. One illustration in the notebooks featured a substance made from corn flour, meat, fertilizer, alcohol, and water. Information on the precise amounts of each ingredient, how to mix them properly, and precise reaction times are included. There are also lengthy instructions on safety techniques—for example, when to wear gloves and masks—as well as how to conceal noxious odors so that potential targets are not alerted. Alongside instructions for making and using cyanide, student to writes "And the power of Allah is mightier", as if to see off his future victim, as the phrase is commonly used at deathbeds in the region.[31]

Once trained and indoctrinated, the terrorists are sent in to the action. After the operation is carried out, groups are usually quick to claim credit. This is both an achievement of their wider goals to spread fear, as well as an aid in their recruiting strategy.

Funding

Funding is an important aspect of terrorism. It serves two purposes. *Firstly,* it takes care of the long-term well being of the organization, and *secondly* it ensures logistics and operational preparedness. Funds attract youth to join militancy. Local and foreign terrorists are paid according to their status in the organization and the severity of the act performed by them. Payments are also made to the families of the terrorists killed in encounters with security forces. They are made at the time of recruitment, as monthly payment to terrorists, for their basic needs.

As per calculation 75 percent of the funding is done by Pakistan ISI and political wings of various terrorist organizations based there, 15 percent from abroad, and 10 percent from within valley.[32] Funds are collected openly in the name of jihad in Pakistan, U.K. and other countries by the radical elements and Kashmiri diasporas.

The financial support of terrorism involves both earning funds—through legal and illegal means and the illicit movement of money to terrorist groups. It is most important to note that in many cases, charities being the main example, funds transferred to terrorists are often raised legally and only acquire their relationship to terrorist financing through subsequent money laundering. In a case currently under investigation, on July 27, 2004, the Holy Land Foundation for Relief and Development, the largest Muslim Charity in the United States, was indicted on charges to provided financial support to Hamas, an Islamic terrorist group. Its finances had been frozen more than two years earlier, in December 2001. Many of the organization's donors reported no knowledge that their donations were being diverted to illegal activities. In addition to charities, apparently legitimate businesses whose profits go to terrorism are another means of earning funds. Finally, terrorists have engaged in criminal activities such as drug trafficking and smuggling cigarettes or commodities as a means of raising funds.[33]

It is known to everybody that external funding is of much greater magnitude than the collections generated from domestic internal sources. But sometime funding also picks up in response of certain domestic events. The funding may occur out of bank robberies, money laundering, counterfeiting, and hostage ransom fake currency and narcotics handlings.

It is significant that the terrorist outfits operating in the world get their financial substance from charitable donation given by Islamic organizations and also donations by other radical Islamic sympathizers. It is known to everybody that the nexus between narcotics trade and terrorism has led to lethal term called as 'narco-terrorism'. It is one of the oldest and the most dependable sources of terrorist financing as it involve huge financial back up needed for both the operations.

Another mode of financing terrorism is through front companies and hawala. Hawala system has been in existence for the last many decades in India. In Pakistan it is known as hundi, in China fei qian (flying money), in Philippines as black market Peso exchange. In Kashmir, the terrorist operate mainly through this underground channel.[34]

In addition to the complex amalgam of individuals, companies, bureaucrats and governments that contribute funds to bin Laden, U.S. efforts to trace terrorist's money is further confounded by the fact that many of the financial transactions are done in such a way that they leave nothing to be traced. Al Qaeda relies heavily on hawala (meaning "In trust" in Hindi) a paperless financial dealing system operated on the basis of trust among money brokers. In hawala activities, brokers advance funds to depositors on a odd or a hand shake, leaving no paper or electronic trail. Those involved often operate from a back of a store or, in remote areas, may not even have an office from which to conduct transactions. Furthermore, hawala's generations of existence throughout

South Asia and the Middle East make it difficult for foreign authorities to eradicate the arcane system.[35]

Before September 11, 2001 al Qaeda had no need for hawalas. It financed its activities through banks in Dubai and elsewhere, wiring lump sums to wherever it wanted. Now, it may be looking for more secretive channels.[36] Most wealthy of terrorists, Osama bin Laden Al Qaeda's leader, is seen by the United States, State Department as a Midas figure. A personal fortune of, perhaps, $ 300 million has gone in to tremendous investment—in banking, airport construction, farming, diamond dealing, and the opium trade. Funding from this store must go in to al-Qaeda coffers in possibly thirty countries. As the actual head of the business side of terrorism, it will not be too easy for Bin Laden to operate it from a remote cave-complex in Afghanistan.[37]

Osama bin laden is believed to rely on three principal sources to finance his terrorist network and its activities:

1. *Personal Investment*

Osama Bin laden is the son of a billionaire Saudi Construction magnate with close ties to the country's royalty. Bin Laden inherited an estimated $ 250-300 million from his family in the early 1990s, which he has invested in a range of business or placed in bank accounts around the world. According to FBI, bin Laden manages a portfolio of legitimate businesses across North Africa, Middle East, Europe and Asia.

Furthermore, bin Laden is believed to own investment in Mauritius, Singapore, Malaysia the Philippines, and possibly Panama. He holds bank accounts in Hong Kong, Malaysia, Vienna, Dubai and London. Hundreds of millions of dollars are secured in real estate in Paris, London and the Cote d' Azur.

2. *Arab Supporters*

According to reliable sources about $ 16 million is funneled every year from the Arab world to bin Laden's terrorist network.

Most of the amount, however, is believed to be unofficial support from wealthy Arabs in Saudi Arabia—some of whom were probably blackmailed—who either sympathize with bin Laden's cause or seek protection from terrorist activities in their countries.

3. *Charity Organizations*

Islamic Charities collect billions of dollars a year, and much of it is used for the benevolent causes the charities openly support. Some of the donations, however, are covertly handed over to Islamic terrorists and fighters by sympathizers with control of the Charities funds.[38]

As governments have begun to crack down on terrorist abuse of the formal banking sector, terrorist have increasingly turned to informal means in order to move money around. These services are cheaper than formal banking or money transfer arrangements, they can provide anonymity for all parties involved, and they can reach countries where there is no formal banking sector, in some cases even arranging for hand delivery of the cash. While most use these systems for legitimate purposes, their lack of documentation and anonymous, informal nature make them attractive for money laundering and terrorist financing purposes.

Terrorist *modus operandi* and Methods

Terrorism has been a social cancer through the ages. It has changed its pattern and way of working from time to time. Terrorist adopts unconventional methods in their operations for their success. Though their masters guide them from across the border, yet terrorist follow strict discipline to maintain secrecy of their operations, movements, and other activities. They are highly motivated for survival against all odds and with the desire to succeed in their mission.

Terrorists use whatever means are available to further their objectives, the technological advances of the modern era have made this possible and have created opportunities and vulnerabilities. The most common weapon of terrorists is threat, as well as sabotage, assassination, hostage taking, murder, kidnapping and bombing. Professional terrorists have become increasingly ruthless, sophisticated and operationally competent.

Terrorists select their targets with utmost care and caution. They often employ over-ground workers for planting bombs and for other hazardous missions. Terrorist group keep moving from place to place to avoid being traced. Organized terrorist groups like al Qaeda, Hizbul Mujahideen, Lashkar e-Toiba or Harkat ul Mujahideen are equipped with highly sophisticated communication sets. This capability makes them secure and elusive. Terrorist does not take their targets in haste. They wait with patience for the targets to become vulnerable and their 'get away' secure. A terrorist attack usually consists of several chronological subsequent phases. These are: selection of target, its observation, planning of the attack, training and trial attacks, the attack itself, escape from the scene of the attack and gaining profits from the attacks.[39]

(i) *Selection of the targets*

The main criterion for the selection of the target is its attractiveness. The more attractive the target is, from the viewpoint of terrorists, the more interested they are in attacking it. They are particularly interested in targets, which are very sensitive in the opinion of the public and the destruction of which would produce a strong and long lasting response in the media and in the minds of a large number of people. In the first planning stage, terrorist considers several targets. Then, they narrow their selection by excluding unsuitable targets, based on observation, gained information and assessment of their own powers, of the level of protection of the target and of the reliability of escape routes.

(ii) *Observation of the target*

Terrorists observe the target in order to gather data and intelligence information required for the preparation of the attack plan. The observation is done either by individuals or groups, the behaviour of which is almost identical to the behaviour of ordinary people also present at the scene. Subjects of observation include the daily course of activities within and around the building, routes of communication and information networks, access and escape routes, activity of selected persons, security and defense systems.

Basic types of observation include:

(a) *Stationary Observation*: from a steady position (restaurant, shop, apartment, parking vehicle etc.).

(b) *Observation on the move*: While Walking or driving a car.

(c) *Technical Observation*: Tapping phone calls, monitoring radio communication and computers, taking photographs or moving pictures, and other optical and technical equipment.

(d) *Segmented Observation*: based on long-term monitoring of a building, route or area and done in short time intervals. The results are reordered and evaluated, being fitted to a complex whole as a mosaic.

(iii) *Planning*

The plan contains not only the basic principles for terrorist activity; it also includes the manner, in which terrorist activity is carried out during and after the attack. Great emphasis is placed on attainment of a moment of surprise, on selection of the best time, place and conditions for the attack, on attainment of the required overpower of men and equipment on critical places, on ensuring observance posts, space to carry out the attack and escape routes, on execution of the attack and on distraction of attention.

(iv) *Training and preparatory attacks*

Training is used to test the plan in a model situation. Terrorists can verify, whether the planned means are sufficient, the time schedule is realistic and everybody understands its place and role in the attack. The training also serves the purpose of adopting the optimal tactics and coordinating activities in individual attack stages. Preparatory attacks serve the purpose of confirming the viability of the plan, material base for the attack and the level of readiness of terrorists.

(v) *The attack*

Shortly before carrying out the attack, terrorists update the gathered information, usually by observing the selected target. If necessary, they operatively update their plan. In the case of assassinations shortly before the attack the identification of the target person is confirmed to avoid any mistake. The identification is done outside the attack zone. The identification signal is usually given visually, by radio or mobile telephone.

(vi) *Escape from the scene*

In some cases, the escape after the attack might be even more important that the attack itself. This, of course, does not apply to suicide attacks. The manner of escape depends mainly on the technical base of the terrorist group, on the conditions, on the scene of the attack and the expected reaction of security forces. A part of the plan is the finding of safe shelters, where the terrorists survive the main wave of counter-terrorist measures.

(vii) *Reaping the results of the attack*

This phase serves the purpose of attaining the main object of the terrorist attack—its justification and attainment of objectives. It usually starts with the issuance of a statement, which might contain the declaration of the main goals of the group and demands, ultimatums and declarations. This statement is usually addressed to the government, to important institutions or persons. Indirectly, it is also addressed to the media. After the statement is issued, a whole series of further comments follow, with the aim to hold the media's attention and to manipulate public opinion.[40]

Methods adopts by modern terrorist reflect the idiosyncrasies of their political environment, so that no single factor explains the adoption of specific tactics by different groups. For example, some methods can become routine among a number of group but are then rarely employed by other groups. There are some of the common attack methods used by terrorists:

(a) ***Hijacking***

Hijacking can be of any form of transport, like hijacking of airlines, seagoing vessels, trains, ships and buses. It is mainly undertaken to attract media attention and maximum propaganda effect.

(b) ***Hostage taking***

Kidnapping or hostage taking are conducted for different reasons; they are sometimes to extort ransoms and at other times for purely propaganda purposes. Hostage taking may be intended to embarrass or pressure governments. This kind of activity can be hard to deal with when the location of the hostage is not known so rescue is made difficult.

Area were kidnapping is currently most prevalent are Africa, Eastern Europe, the Middle East, Pakistan, the Philippines, South America and Yemen.

(c) ***Arson***

Arson is generally used to destroy infrastructure, and shop and homes of rival ethnic or religious groups. It is easy for fire investigators to recognize an arson attack, but much harder to prove who did it.

(d) ***Fire bombing***

Side arms (pistols and rifles) are likewise commonly employed to ambush, assassinate, or otherwise inflict casualties on an enemy.

(e) ***Other attack***

Other forms of attack may include cyber attack, sabotage, poisoning, use of Chemical or biological agents.

Terrorist modus operandi is constantly changing and

evolving to take account of the response of the terrorists' adversaries and counter-terrorism capabilities—hence there are now fewer siege hostage situations or politically motivated aircraft hijacks. Terrorists will copy other group operations where these have been successful.[41]

Methods have occasionally become "Signature" of terrorist movements. These are methods that become closely affiliated with the operational activities of specific extremist groups. An example of signature methods has included kidnapping (Abu Sayyaf in the Philippines), hijacking (Popular front for the liberation of Palestine), and suicide bombings (Liberation Tigers of Tamil Eelam).

The weapons employed by terrorists are integral features of their overall methodologies. Firearms and explosives have historically been the weapons of choice for terrorists. This has not appreciably changed in the modern era, although available firepower has greatly increased, and the selection of targets has arguably become more indiscriminate. Weapons typically include small arms, commercial and military grade explosives, rocket propelled grenades, and vehicular (car and truck) bombs. Sophisticated weapons have occasionally been used, such as precision-guided munitions (shoulder-fired anti-aircraft rocket) and high-technology triggering device for bombs.

Very few examples exist of the use of weapons of mass destruction, such as chemical, biological, radiological or nuclear devices. Although the threat from terrorists acquisition of weapons of mass destruction increased during the 1990s, the overarching profile of terrorist and extremists is that they typically wield conventional firearms and explosives.

In the modern era, weaponry can be classified along a sliding scale of technological sophistication and threat potential. This scale includes a high, medium and low range, summarized as follows: [42]

1. ***High Range***

The new terrorism is defined in part by the threatened

acquisition of chemical agents, biology agents or nuclear weapons. This threat includes the development of radiological agents that spread highly toxic radioactive materials by detonating conventional explosives. The first case of widespread use of a biological agent by terrorist occurred when anthrax was deliberately sent through the mails in the United States in the aftermath of September 11, 2001, attacks.

2. *Medium Range*

Terrorists currently have extensive access to military style weaponry. These include automatic weapons, rocket launchers, and military-grade explosives of many varieties. Sympathetic state sponsorship and the international arms black market permit the procurement of a virtually unlimited array of conventional small arms and munitions. These arms have been the weapons of choice for terrorists in innumerable examples.

3. *Low Range*

Often forgotten in the discussion about the threat from medium and high-range weapon are the powerful homemade weapons that can be manufactured from commercial grade components. For example, ammonium nitrate and fuel oil (ANFO) bombs can be easily manufactured from readily available materials.

4. *Firearms*

Small arms and handheld weapons have been, and continue to be, the most common type of weapons employed by terrorist. These are light and heavy infantry weapons and include pistols rifles, submachine guns, assault rifles, machine guns, rocket-propelled grenades, mortars, and precision-guided munitions. Typical firearms found in the hands of terrorists include.

5. *Assault Rifles*

Usually capable of both automatic (repeating) and semi-automatic (single-shot) fire, assault rifles are military-grade weapons that are used extensively by terrorists and other irregular force. The AK-47, invented by Mikhail Kalashnikov for the Soviet Army, is the most successful assault rifle in terms of production number and its widespread adoption by standing armies, guerrillas and terrorists.

6. ***Rocket-Propelled Grenades***

Light self-propelled munitions are common features of modern infantry units. The RPG-7 has been used extensively by dissident forces throughout the world, particularly in Latin America, the Middle East, and Asia. It is an uncomplicated and powerful weapon that is useful against armor and fixed emplacements such as bunkers or buildings.[43]

7. ***Plastic Explosives***

Plastic explosives are putty-like explosive compounds that can be easily molded. The central component of most plastic explosives is a compound known as RDX. Nations that manufacture plastic explosives often use chemical markers to tag each batch that is made.

8. ***Timed Switches***

Time bombs are constructed from acid-activated or electronically activated triggers. They are rigged to detonate after the passage of a period of time.

Types of Bombs

Gasoline Bombs

The most easily manufactured explosive weapon used by dissidents is nothing more than a gasoline-filled bottle with a flaming rag for its trigger. It is thrown at targets after the rag is stuffed in to the mouth of the bottle and ignited. Tar, Styrofoam or other ingredients can be added to create a gelling effect for the bomb, which causes the combustible ingredient to stick to surface. These weapons are commonly called "Malotov Cocktails."

Vehicular Bombs

Ground vehicles that have been wired with explosives

are a frequent weapon in the terrorist arsenal. Vehicular bombs can include car bombs and truck bombs; they are mobile, are "covert" in the sense that they are not readily identifiable, are able to transport large amounts of explosives, and are rather easily constructed. They have been used on scores of occasions throughout the world.

Bombing and fire bombings are the most common form of terrorist incident, accounting annually, as noted earlier, for 66-75% of all international terrorist attacks. The data is not available to indicate whether this holds true for non-international terrorism but, in any case, international terrorism is a more pressing concern for western nations. The most serious threat, however, arises from the nuclear devices or weapons of mass destruction that seems to be in the possession of the stateless terrorist groups. A new nuclear era has already dawned since the extensive nuclear-smuggling operations from Pakistan have come to light. Pakistan has however, been rewarded for creating the worst menace for America and its allies.[44]

Possibilities of New Adventures

The terrorist environment in the new millennium is happed by advances in technology information, and transnational interconnectivity. This new environment has given rise to new possibilities in terrorist methodology.

The concern about chemical, biological, radiological or nuclear terrorism is based partly on the increased ease of finding pertinent information on the Internet. The principal impact of the new electronic technologies, however, has not been to move the terrorists towards more exotic method of attack, but rather to improve the efficiency of all of their activities. Computer and satellite phones have become standard equipment in terrorist groups. The possibility of proliferation of weapons of mass destruction through the innovations of modern technology is more real than it has ever been in human history. The use of these innovations for terrorist activities is limited only by the imagination of the terrorist everyone is potential target, which creates a climate of fear and suspicion within a society.

The U.S. Department of Defense (DOD) defines Weapons of Mass Destruction (WMD) as, "weapon that are capable of a high order of destruction and/or of being used in such a manner as to destroy large number of people. Weapons of mass destruction can be high explosives or nuclear, biological, chemical and radiological weapons, but exclude the means of transporting or propelling the weapon where such means is a separable and divisible part of the weapons".[45]

Conventional terrorist activities, including, assassinations, hijacking, kidnappings and bombings, are still the first choice of most terrorists. But The September 11, 2001, attack on the World Trade Center and the Pentagon demonstrated that these traditional method can be used to inflict horrifying devastation. The threat posed by contemporary terrorism is increased even further by the availability of weapons of mass destruction and the growth of cyber terrorism. Today's terrorists can choose from a potent arsenal of weapons capable of destroying large portions of our planet. WMD (made from nuclear, biological and chemical materials) and cyber terrorism (the use of computer to spread information and paralyze vital infrastructures) could cause hundreds of thousands, even millions of death and injuries.

When compared to conventional and unconventional weapons, biological agents have the greatest potential to cause mass casualties, and theoretically there could easily exceed the causalities caused by the largest nuclear weapon.

Biological Weapons

Bio-terrorism is terrorism using germ warfare, an intentional human release of a naturally occurring or human modified toxin or biological agent. These weapons are living organisms or infective material derived from them, which are intended to cause disease or death in man, animals and plants, and which depend on their ability to multiply in the person, animal or plant attacked. Viruses, fungi, and bacteria are all labeled as 'biological' weapons. Bacteria and viruses are the biological agent, which is used by terrorist.[46] These biological weapons exist in nature or can be produced in laboratories; either way, their purpose is to sicken or kill by infection or poisoning. These are highly infectious and can be produced in large quantities, and can resist antibiotics and vaccines.[47]

Biological weapons have been often called the "Poor man's atom bomb." The material equipment and infrastructure required to make them is easily available and inexpensive. There is no death of microbiologists around the world who could do it all, especially as all the required information is in the public domain. Biological weapons are easy to store, easy to deliver and extremely effective. They can be used either for an immediate effect that is within a few days—or for an effect which would be felt after a long time.[48]

Terrorist chooses to use biological weapons to achieve their goals because bio-terrorism gives the biggest "bang" for the buck. For instance, use of conventional weapons would cost an estimated $ 2,000 per square kilometer, nuclear weapon would cost $ 800, chemical weapons—$600, and biological weapons would only cost an estimated $1 per square kilometer.[49] Many of these agents would be relatively easy to prepare and easy to hide. Their use would also allow for bio terrorists to protect themselves and escape before any illness is detected. The most harmful effect of bio weapons is the tremendous psychological impact that there use or threatened use, would cause on the population. A list of material that could be used in bio-terrorism is: Bubonic plague, typhus, smallpox, botulinus toxin are classic agents. Equally dreadful is their effects are the spores of anthrax, the bacilli of smallpox, legionnaires disease, ebola, tularaemia brucellosis and cholera. Ricin is another substance that came into prominence in January 2003 when small stocks were discovered among Algerian householders in London and Manchester security forces arrested the Algerian and rendered the ricin harmless. Though never use so far on a massive scale, ricin, it is known, is an assassin's tool. One gram sprayed at a target crowd; could kill 10,000 people. Made from castor beans using low-level equipment, ricin destroys cells and there is as yet, no vaccine.[50] The prospect of terrorists using biological weapons after 9/11 was to cause unnerved Americans since the World Trade Center disaster was so closely followed by an anthrax scare. The worst seemed to have happened in Florida in October 2001. On 5th October, Robert Stevens, a Florida journalist died from inhaling anthrax. Detectives were able to isolate traces of the anthrax on the man's computer keyboard within the next few days there were reports that a similar 'potent' strain had been found in letter sent to Senator Tom Dashle, on Capitol Hill, and to Tom Brocaw, a well known television presenter at NBC News, also in Washington and to the Governor of New York State. Other spores were found in letter bins in government buildings.[51] Prompt investigation found that a number of letters being received in New York and in Washington were containing white or brown powder. There was no smell and the powder could be lethal.

If it were the spores of anthrax, then the infection could be through skin, that is cutaneous anthrax, or it could be breathed in as inhalation anthrax. The anthrax scare in October 2001 led to much anxiety intentionally. Envelop with powder turned up in more than twenty other countries including Kenya, Brazil, Japan, Pakistan, France, Morocco, Lebanon, Portugal, Hong Kong and Australia.

The result of all this does not paint a happy picture. Their people out there who were anti-life and anti-social and who were prepared both to endanger health and to induce widespread public fear.

President Bush was quick to declare his belief that Osama bin Laden and Al Qaeda were likely to be responsible both for 11 September and for the anthrax attack.[52] The anthrax incident clearly demonstrates that bio-terrorism is a psychological weapon with the potential of causing mass hysteria and feeding conspiracy theories.

Chemical Terrorism

Chemical terrorism is a terrorism in which an inorganic substance is used in warfare to attack the organs of the human body in such a way that they prevent those organs from functioning normally. They include poisons, such as arsenic and strychnine, and nerve gases, such as sarin and tabun. Mustard gases, which are blistering agents that affect the eyes, respiration, and skin, were widely used in World War I.[53]

In contrast to biological warfare, chemical warfare has already been waged on a massive scale. If there are in theory that many thousands of biological agents that terrorist could use, there are probably even more poisonous chemical substances. Most chemical agents are not gases but liquids dispensed in droplets. They can be divided according to their chemical composition. Hydrogen Cyanide and cyanogen chloride attack the respiratory system and result rapidly in coma and death. The merve gas tabun, sarin, soman and VX affect the neuromuscular system. They block the enzyme cholinesterase, causing paralysis of the neuromuscular system and thus death. Tabun and Sarin are organophosphates, discovered in Germany as a by-product of the search for new insecticides. Even more poisonous are the gases of the V (VX) series that penetrate the skin as well as the respiratory tract and bring about respiratory failure and death within a very short time.

If terrorist want, they can manufacture potent chemical poisons from such substance as isoprobyl alcohol, which is readily available, or from various pesticides and herbicides. Experts agree that the technical knowledge and experience needed to produce a chemical weapon is less than that required for manufacturing a biological weapon, probably on the level of a moderately conscientious graduate student. Some substance and compounds are, of course, more difficult to produce than others, but there is no reasons to assume that a terrorist will choose the most complicated rather than the least sophisticated weapon. Chemical terrorism poses two types of significant threats. First, in the case of mass destruction attacks, toxic substance may be released in to town centers, farmland, water supplies and crowded places such as supermarkets and railway stations. In a sense this sort of terror is as old as the history of poisoning the enemy's wells and food supplies. The other type is much more common, it is an attack planned to cause economic damage or result in blackmail. There have been sporadic and, perhaps fortunately amateurish attacks on food products, laboratories and processing plants by such as animal rights groups. A chemical substance may be introduced in to what is regarded as an offensive product.[54]

The small amount of certain chemical, sprayed left, as contaminants in a confined space will lead to numerous casualties. There are toxic dusts, which are only activated when they make contact with a moist surface such as the lungs. Terror tactics will yield a huge dividend in panic and general insecurity. Not every terrorist can feel safe, though, handling lethal chemicals.

Only one large-scale attack with WMD by non-state terrorists has been confirmed. On morning of March 20, 1995, five member of Aum Shinrikyo (which was controlled by the messianic and highly eccentric Shoko Asahara.) boarded subway trains at five different stations around Tokyo. Each member carried two sealed plastic pouches of Sarin nerve gas and a sharpened umbrella. As the train neared the center of the city, the terrorists put the plastic pouches on the floor and punctured them with the umbrellas. They then fled the subways as the liquids leaked quickly out of the bags. The effects were almost instantaneous: passengers began to sweat their noses ran, they coughed and wheezed, some vomited and other had seizure like symptoms. Twelve people died and more than 5,000 were injured. It could have been much worse. The investigation showed that Aum specialists had experimented with a variety of chemical and biological weapons.[55]

Chemical weapons are far more widely available than nuclear weapons because the technology required to produce them is far simpler. One simple fact should worry the world more about biological, than about nuclear or chemical arms; unlike either of the other two, biological weapons combine maximum destructiveness and easy availability. Nuclear arms have great killing capacity but are hard to obtain, chemical weapons are more easily available but lack such killing capacity; while biological agents have both qualities.

Nuclear Terrorism

This form of mass destruction terrorism represents the 'end of the line' in most imaginations. Nuclear terrorism is a distinct threat, and will remain one far in to the future. Nuclear terrorism poses a double danger. A nuclear device might be exploded to cause mass murder and devastation. More likely would be the threatened use of fissionable radioactive materials obtain from a nuclear reactor which would be damaged in an attack employing conventional high explosive.[56]

The attack of September 11, 2001 has provided a wake-up call for facing the threat of nuclear terrorism. The smoke over Manhattan did not reach the dimensions of a mushroom cloud, but the number of casualties was close that of a small nuclear explosion. The scenario of nuclear weapons in the hands of the terrorist is a nightmare that has been discussed from time to time, but has been considered unlikely. The Nuclear Control Institute, since its inception, has been analyzing the risks of nuclear terrorism and seeking to alert policymakers and the public to the danger. There was a solid basis for concern long before the attacks of September 11. Trial testimony has revealed that Osama Bin Laden's, al Qaeda training camps offered instruction in 'urban warfare' against 'enemies' installations including power plants. It is prudent to assume, especially after the highly coordinated, surprise attack on World Trade Center and the Pentagon, that bin Laden's soldiers have done their homework and are fully capable of attacking nuclear plants for maximum effect. It is also clear that bin laden was seeking nuclear explosive material (Plutonium or highly enriched uranium) and know how for building atomic bomb, and other dangerous nuclear materials for use in "dirty bombs" to spread radioactive contamination with conventional high explosives.

There is now intense national and international attention to the risks of nuclear terrorism. The possibilities that al

Qaeda might acquire the materials and the knowledge for building nuclear weapons or "dirty bombs" or might attack commercial nuclear-power facilities to trigger a nuclear melt down are of particular concern.[57] Although it is conceivable that terrorists could construct a nuclear device, most threat scenarios envision the acquisition of tactical nuclear weapons such as artillery shells. The soviet apparently developed several so-called suitcase bombs—nuclear weapons that are quite compact.[58]

A sophisticated terrorist group would be capable of designing and building a workable nuclear bomb from stolen plutonium or highly enriched uranium, with potential yields in the kiloton range. Less than 18 pounds of plutonium or 55 pounds of highly enriched uranium are sufficient to make a nuclear bomb. Some of the well-known nuclear weapons are: Atomic bomb, Atomic Demolition Munitions, Nuclear Warhead, Improvised Nuclear Device and Highly Enrich Uranium.[59]

Today the threat of nuclear or radiological attack by terrorist organization is clearly taken very seriously by governments. Basically, the threat of nuclear terrorism can take three forms:

1. Credible threat with a stolen nuclear weapon
2. Theft of nuclear and radioactive materials:
   - Threat with one or several radiological weapon
   - Threat with a 'home-made' explosive nuclear device.
3. Attack on, or sabotage of nuclear installation or transport.[60]

Radiological Terrorism

These weapons are materials that emit radiation that can harm living organism. In order to become threatening to life or health, these radioactive substances must be "ingested, inhaled, or absorbed through the skin" in sufficient quantities. Non weapons-grade radiological agents could theoretically be used to construct a toxic dirty bomb that would use conventional explosives to release a cloud of radioactive contaminants. Radioactive elements that could be used in a dirty bomb include Plutonium, Uranium, Cobalt 60, Strontium, and Cesium 137.[61]

Cyber Terrorism

This is another area where the terrorists have registered their presence. Like WMD, cyber terrorism can cause widespread damage. Cyber terrorists use the Internet to contact colleagues, disseminate their view to a wider audience, and tap new sources of financial support. The Internet also provides an abundance of detailed instruction for anyone interested in making bombs, rockets, flamethrowers and dozens of other lethal weapons and poisons.[62]

Cyber terrorism in the computer age is an attack on information systems rather than on people. Its consequences can be devastating. A so called 'hacker', usually a lone individual sitting at a computer keyboard, has power, inventiveness and secrecy to cause immense, sometimes irretrievable, harm to institutions & other people. Using a variety of electronic devices, such as a 'virus' or a 'worm', the hacker may access confidential records, telephone and media sources, financial and commercial data, and governmental and scientific projects. Terrorist can create a climate of fear by exploiting the information dissemination channels of its target population, reaching many by physically affecting only a few. This kind of attack is called as Information warfare (IW) and is envisioned as new dimensions of warfare, bringing conflict into the information age. By targeting or exploiting information and information processes, an attacker can use limited resources to reap disproportionate gains. Cyber terrorism is the final level of information warfare, it can be defined as a premeditated, politically motivated attack against information, computer systems, computer programme, and data which result in violence against non-combatant targets by sub-national groups or clandestine agents.

Terrorist groups are using the Internet extensively to spread their message and to communicate and coordinate action. However, there have been few computer network attack that meet the criteria for cyber terrorism.[63]

Attackers use a variety of methods to exploit numerous computer system vulnerabilities they include:

(a) ***Hard Kill***

It involves physical destruction with information systems such as mainframe computers and database servers, unlinking stations and telecommunications nodes. Even cutting telephone lines, assassinating key technical personnel and using energy weapons to destroy unshielded circuitry constitutes hard kill.

(b) ***Soft Kill***

It may be divided into sub-categories as depicted in figure 4.6.

Pest Programmes

These are software programme employing a variety of techniques for inserting codes that at a later stage endanger the working of systems. These are of various types:

Soft Kill[64]

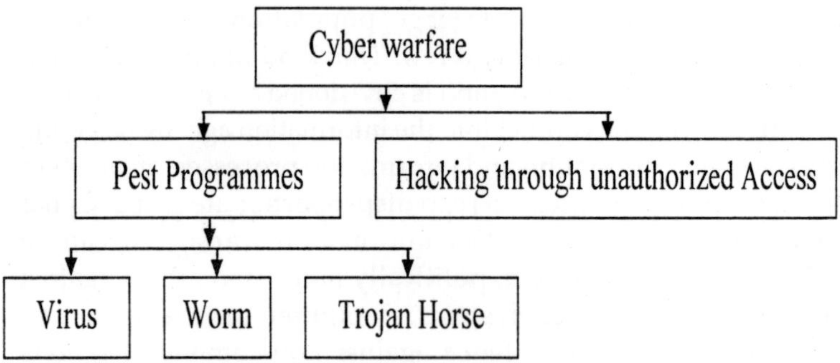

(i) *Viruses*: A virus is malicious software, which attaches itself to legitimate files, and spreads out when files or floppy disks are exchanged between computers. It could be termed as software that infect software and causes it to infect other software. A virus generally remains hidden until certain qualifying criteria are met. A virus attack on a system can erase existing files, reduce memory and disk space, slow down programme loading and running and could corrupt the database. In extreme cases it may lead to hard disc drive.

Osama bin Laden is trying, probably unknowingly to take over the world disguised as a computer virus. Thousands of messages have been posted on Internet Chat-rooms with a subject line suggesting media have discovered the leader of Al-Qaida has been found hanged. One version of the message says in the subject line: "Osama bin Laden captured." Others have longer messages offering links.[65]

(ii) *Worm:* A worm is malicious software that can replicate itself. It is an independent operating programme, which mails replicas of itself outside the host system. Worms have the capacity to slow down Internet sites and cause communication disruption by traveling around a computer network.

(iii) *Trojan Horse:* A Trojan horse is a malicious computer code located within a desirable block of code, like an application programme or operating system software. It is a seemingly innocuous programme with a concealed malevolent function. A Trojan horse remains unknown to the owner of the system, and performs functions, which are unexpected. It is capable of causing extensive damage in the form of software corruption, hardware malfunction and network destruction.

Hacking through unauthorized Access

Interconnected communication and computer systems are vulnerable to intrusion. The intruder may gather information, alter data, mutilate, delete and subvert information flowing through the network. Hackers are skilled computer users who usually break into a system. Hackers have a set of tools, basically software programmes to facilitate their activities.[66]

Due to the inherent openness of the Internet and the original design of the protocols, Internet attacks is general are quick, easy, inexpensive, and may be hard to detect or trace. An attacker does not have to be physically present to carry out the attack. In fact, many attacks can be launched readily from anywhere in the world and the location of the attacker can easily be hidden.

In general, it seems that weapons of mass destruction (WMD) may soon become a key component in the terrorist arsenal. If these threat is left unchecked, the world population may soon live under a dark cloud of constant fear; the fear that any crazy person, terrorist, or activist group has the potential to commit random act of brutal mass murder at low cost and low risk to themselves.

Maritime Terrorism

Maritime terrorism refers to the undertaking of terrorist acts and activities within the marine environment, using or against vessels or fixed platforms at sea or in port, or against any one of their passengers or personnel, against coastal facilities or settlements, including tourist resort, port areas, and port town or cities.[67] The incident that first brought the phenomenon of maritime terrorism to the world's attention was the hijacking of the cruise liner Achille Lauro by Palestinian terrorist in 1985. The incident took place in Egyptian territorial waters. The Crew and passengers were held hostage, and were threatened with death should a group of Palestinian prisoners detained in Israel not be freed. The terrorists surrendered after two days and were captured through U.S. military intervention when they were fleeing on board a commercial jetliner.

Other high-profile maritime terrorist attacks have been the suicide attack on the USS Cope on October 12, 2000 when two Al Qaeda suicide bombers rammed an explosive—Laden Skiff into the US Arleigh-Burke-Class destroyer, USS code. The attack killed 17 US Navy personnel and injured 42 others and rendered the vessel inoperable.[68] Although these attacks have been well-documented, attention is only now starting to turn to the implications these attacks have for international maritime security in general. Apart from these somewhat isolated incidents of maritime terrorism, terrorist attacks against maritime targets are quite rare. Terrorist groups that are known to have a maritime capability include Polisario, the Abu Sayyaf Group (ASG), Palestinian groups, Al Qaeda, the Moro Islamic liberation front (MILF) and the Liberation Tigers of Tamil Eelam (LTTE).

Over the years maritime terrorist attacks have taken different forms. They have been committed on board vessels or fixed platforms. The vessel itself may be used as a weapon against another. Maritime attacks can be carried out from land, sea, and air. Terrorist tactics range from employment of land-based teams—trained to place improvised explosive devices

(IED) on ships—to terrorist divers, attack craft, and sea mines. Maritime terrorist technologies range from scuba, sea scooters, and speedboats to GPS (Global Positioning System), all of which are available on the open market. By far the high-profileest maritime terrorist group is the LTTE, which has been employing maritime terrorist tactics since the 1980s in their ongoing war against the Sri Lankan govenrment. Since July 1990 they have carried out over forty sea-borne suicide attacks against the Sri Lankan navy.[69] The LTTE is at the cutting edge of maritime terrorism, and their activities are potentially copycat models for other groups. The LTTE also has 'Black Sea Tigers' (BST), a squad that includes women.

The September 11, 2001 attack demonstrated that ordinary means of transportation could be turned in to lethal weapons of terror in the hands of determined terrorists. The fear of mass destruction threat such as biological, chemical or nuclear attack has revealed an oversight in international security, one that has failed to see that this type of attack, using ordinary means of transportation, is a possibility. This new strategy was made evident in a statement by Al Qaeda: "We, the fighters of the holy war, in general are hoping to enter the next phase ... it will be a war of killing, a war against businesses, which will hit the enemy where he does not expect us to." Thus, the targeting of maritime infrastructure is now a real possibility.[70]

The devastating attack on the U.S. on September 11, 2001 clearly demonstrated two things: Firstly, a terrorist's next move is very hard to predict. Secondly, terrorists should never be underestimated. However fantastical some of the possible scenarios of a terrorist attack may be, they must be treated as though they may one day become a reality. Most importantly, we cannot afford to wait for the terrorist next attack. We must now respond quickly to their new developments and trends.

REFERENCES

1. James J.F. Forest, *The making of A Terrorist, Recruitment, Training and Root Causes*, Vol. II, Training; Praeger Security International, London, 2006, p. 2.

2. Lius S.R. Vas; *Osama bin Laden, king of Terror or Saviour of Islam?* Pustak Mahal, Publication, Delhi, October 2001; p. 5.

3. Loyd Pettiford and David Harding, *Terrorism the New World War*, Arcturus Publication, London, 2003; p. 144.

4. Joseph Von Hammer, Bernard Lewis, 'The History of Assassin'; Burt Franklin Publishers, New York.; Basic Book 2002, p. 6.

5. www.Pc world.com/news/article/o, aid, 116822, tk.asp.

6. Adam Gadahn, "Becoming Muslim" 2004 online at http://www.USC.edu/dept/MSA/new/Yohiye.html

7. Paul M. Rodriguez, "Iranian Group Seeks Recruits for 'Martyrdom Operation," Insight online, 8 June 2004, online at http://www.insight mag.com/global_ user_ elements/printpage.cfm ? Storyid—684918.

8. J.M. Berger, "Online Videos Shows Children Training for Jihad"; Intelwire (2004), online at http://www.interwire.com/2004_10_13.exclusives.html.

9. Yariv Tzfati and Gabrol Weimann, www.terrorism.com.Terror on the Internet.

10. James J.F. Forest, *The Making of A Terrorist, Recruitment, Training and Root Causes*, volume I: Training; Praeger Security International, London, 2006, p. 64.

11. www.Pc world.com/news/article/o, aid, 116822 tk.asp.-P.W. Singer

12. Ami Pedahzur; *Suicide Terrorism*, Polity Press, Cambridge, U.K.; 2005. p. 165.

13. http://www.satp.org/sat porgtp/South asia/Samain.html.

14. Ami Pedahzur; *Suicide Terrorism*, Polity Press Cambridge U.K.; 2005, p. 167

15. *The Hindu*; 2 March 2003, p. 11.

16. Adluri Subramanyam Raju; *Terrorism in South Asia view from India*; Indian Research Press New Delhi; 2004, p. 108.

17. James J.F. Forest, *op.cit.*, p. 153.

18. Clara Beyler, "Messenger of Death" 12 February 2003 online

at http://www.inightmag.com/Messengers_Death_elements/printpage.cfm

19. James J.F. Forest, *op. cit.,* p. 155
20. Yoram Schweitzer, "Suicide Bombing—The ultimate weapon"? Online at http://www.ict.org.il/articles/article det.cfm? arti cleid=373.
21. James J.F. Forest, *op. cit.,* p. 114.
22. Amira hes, "Floating to Paradise", Ha'aretz Daily newspaper, 14 July 2003.
23. James J.F. Forest, *op. cit.,* p. 115.
24. Ami Pedahzur, *op. cit.,* p. 173.
25. James J.F. Forest, *op. cit.,* p. 162.
26. Rohan Gunaratha, *Suicide Terrorism in Sri Lanka and India,* in countering suicide terrorism;
27. Shaul Shay; *The Shahids Islam and Suicide Attacks;* Transaction Publishers, USA & London, 2004, p. 19.
28. R.C. Mishra; *Terrorism Implication of Tactics and Technology;* Authorspress Delhi; 2004; p. 68
29. James J.F. Forest; *op. cit.,* p. 137.
30. James J.F. Forest, *The Making of a Terrorist,* Vol. II: Training; Praegar Security International London; 2006; p. 142.
31. *Ibid.,* p. 147.
32. N.S. Jamwal, Terrorist Financing and Support Structures in Jammu and Kashmir; *Strategic Analysis,* Jan-March 2002; Vol 26 No.1; Institute for Defence Studies & Analysis; New Delhi.
33. Anna Sabasteanlki, *Patterns of Global Terrorism;* 1985-2005 Volume one; Berkshira Publishing Group; U.S.A; 2005, p. 128.
34. http://www.cdi.org/terrorism/financial_pr. cfm.
35. *Ibid.*
36. 'Al Qaeda operations are rather Cheap, *The Economist;* October 4th 2003.

37. David J. Whittaker, *Terrorism Understanding the Global Threat;* Longman Publishers, London; 2002, p. 145.

38. http://www.Cdi.arg/terrorism/financial_pr. cfm.

39. R.C. Mishra, *op. cit.,* pp. 74-77.

40. *Ibid.*

41. Clive Williams, *Terrorism Explained the Fact about Terrorism and Terrorist Groups;* New Holland Publishers, 2004; p. 155.

42. Gus Martin, *Understanding Terrorism Challenges, Perspective and Issues;* Sage Publication, London; 2003, p. 254.

43. Gus Martin, *op. cit.,* p. 256.

44. Clive Williams, *op. cit.,* p. 165.

45. Eric A. Goddy, *Weapons of Mass Destruction-An Encyclopedia of Worldwide Policy, technology and history*: Vol. I: Chemical & Biological Weapons; ABC Clio Publication, California; 2005; p. XXV.

46. Rajpal Kaur; Bio-Terrorism, Threats and Challenges Deep & Deep Publications, New Delhi; Year 2006; p. IX.

47. K.R. Gupta; *Global Terrorism;* Atlantic Publication New Delhi; 2004, p. 95.

48. Adluri Subramanyam Raju, *Terrorism in South Asia;* India Research Press, New Delhi, 2004; p. 118.

49. Rajpal Kaur; *Bio-Terrorism, Threats & Challenges,* Deep & Deep Publications New Delhi, 2006; p. 3.

50. David J. Whittaker; Terrorists and Terrorism in the contemporary world; Routledge Taylor and Francis Group, New York, 2004; p. 118.

51. David J. Whittaker; Terrorism understanding the Global threat; longman publishers, New York; Year 2002; Pg 151.

52. Ibid Pg 153.

53. Squardon leader Rahul Monga; "Use of chemical and Biological Weapons by Terrorist"; *U.S.I. Journal;* January-March 2002.

54. David J. Whittaker, *op. cit.,* p. 157.

55. Pamala L. Griset, Sue Mohan, *Terrorism in Perspective*; Sage Publications, London; 2003; p. 232.

56. David J. Whittaker, *op. cti.*, p. 122.

57. Chronology of State use and biological & Chemical Weapons; Monterey Institute, California; refer to http ://www. cns. miis.edu.

58. Gus Martin, *op. cit.*, p. 259.

59. R.C. Mishra, *op. cit.*, p. 95.

60. K.R. Gupta, *op. cit.*, p. 119.

61. Gus Martin, *op. cit.*, p. 259.

62. Pamala L. Griset, Sue Mahan, *Terrorism in Perspective* Sage Publications, London; 2003, p. 230.

63. R.C. Mishra, *op. cit.*, p. 125.

64. Verinder Grover; *Encylopedia of International Terrorism,* Deep & Deep Publishers New Delhi; 2002, p. 69.

65. 'Osama e-Virus': *Hindustan Times*; 25 Sunday July 2004, p. 13.

66. Verinder Grover, *op. cit.*, p. 70.

67. 'Council for security cooperation in the Asia Pacific' refer to http://www. escape. org/

68. Catherine Zara Raymond, *Maritime Terrorism in Southeast Asia: A Risk Assessment;* Routledge Taylor Rubtrert, 2006; p. 240.

69. *Ibid.*, p. 241.

70. Rohan Gunaratan, *Terrorism in the Asia-Pacific: Threat & Response,* Eastern University Press, London, 2003, p. 79.

5

Fighting Terrorism on Global Front

Since the terrible event of September 11, 2001, with the attacks on the World Trade Center and the Pentagon, the subject of terrorism has exploded on the World Stage. President George W. Bush has declared a war against terrorism. The vast resources of the United States and other countries have been directed toward ending terrorism around the world. From New York to Bali, and with further attacks in London, India and Madrid, terrorism has become a global phenomenon requiring a concerted, ongoing international response. In recent years, the fight against terrorism has become an international priority and a major issue for debate in virtually every international organization: the United Nations, the European Union, the Council of Europe, North Atlantic Treaty Organization (NATO) and Organization for Security and Cooperation in Europe (OSCE).

The fight against terrorism encompasses an extremely diverse range of concerns. Discussion and cooperation in European and international bodies have covered many different issues such as police and judicial cooperation, the fight against funding networks, increased measures to protect citizens and infrastructure against terrorist attacks, particularly in public transport, the fight against radicalism and recruitment and improved support for victims of terrorist acts.

It is clearly impossible for one country to deal with all these aspects indepth on its own. International cooperation is required and all the more so since the countries involved in the fight against terrorism are all interested in the same issues.

With much of the homeland counter-terrorism efforts post 9/11 directed towards enhancing physiological preparation and response mechanisms, the psychological angle (communicating the terrorism threat, and engaging with the public, etc.) has arguably not been fully explored with the same urgency by government. Understanding the psychological and behavioural responses of citizens is important for anticipating how the general public may respond to pre and post incident planning. Most responses to terrorist threats are however, at the national level. This is for several reasons: national security is seen as a matter for the sovereign government; responses are faster and more flexible; and cooperation on matters involving intelligence is sensitive, and therefore difficult. National responses tend to be shaped with reference to a country's traditions, history and experience; experience of immigration and minorities; geopolitical situation; and threat perception.

Panic is rare following an attack with the public generally reacting in a calm and calculated way, but this is partly dependent on the effectiveness of the information provided by authorities and their level of engagement with the public. Panic occurs in situations where there is an immediate and clear threat of death, and in which escape routes will not accommodate all those in danger in the minutes before death comes to those left behind.

To investigate these difficulties some of the example will examine the psychological and behavioural responses of the public. Like after 9/11 a number of mental health studies have been published providing valuable empirical evidence on the extent a major mass casualty conventional attack can have on the targeted population and the nation as a whole. Evidence suggests that there was no overt panic in the self-evacuation of the World Trade Center although this might have been because the people concerned largely knew each other beforehand. Furthermore very few of those trapped above the impact zone, believing they had a chance of making their way out alive of the WTC, exhibited panic.[1]

While Americans believed that ordinary citizens behaved responsibly rather than panicked, the attacks left a psychological scar that exhibited itself with many changing their behaviour to minimize the risk of terrorism to themselves. There are also likely to be long-term mental health problems for a segment of the population suffering from conditions including depression and PTSD.

9/11 caused an increased in levels of depression, stress and in many cases PTSD among New Yorkers and to a lesser extent the rest of the nation. According to mental health study by William E. Schlenger the prevalence of PTSD 1-2 months after the attack in the New York Metropolitan area was 11.2%, in Washington DC 2.7%, and the rest of the country around 4%.[2]

To make a direct comparison between the PTSD levels in New York and the rest of the nation requires taking in to account the socio-demographic conditions of the New York area compared to the national average. Once this is factored in, the New York PTSD level decline to 9.4% still significantly higher than the rest of the nation of around 3-4%. Research by Sandro Galea, calculates PTSD level in New York at 7.5% and those expressing symptoms of depressions at 9.7%. Based on the number residing in Manhattan within seven miles from the WTC, it is estimated that 67,000 persons had PTSD and 87,000 depressions.[3] Therefore 'probable PTSD' is associated with direct exposure to the terrorist attack among adults.

A study found that two months after the attacks nearly two third (64%) of the national population reported fears of future terrorism at least sometimes and 59% reported fear of harm to family as a result of terrorism. A separate national survey found that 50% of Americans were very concerned that there would be another attack on U.S. soil in the near future and 11% are there who are not very concerned, while others were concerned of becoming a victim of terrorism.

This suggests that population believed the risk of further attacks against the nation was greater than being personally threatened by terrorism.

A survey of national trends discovered that in January 2002 13-14% of Americans had altered their travel plans since 9/11 and 5-7% had stopped flying altogether out of fear. A year after the attacks a survey conducted by the New York *Daily News* in August 2002 found that almost a year on New Yorkers continued to alter their daily lives. 11% were making an effort to avoid potential terror targets, such as subways; 23% avoiding tourist sight, and 20% tall buildings.[4]

Chemical, Biological and Radiological weapons are traditionally viewed as destroying an individual's sense of security and trust in their environment, causing shock, horror, helplessness and panic. The fear of the unknown caused by a CBR device with often the inability to see or smell the agent may exacerbate this. Thus the more threat by terrorist to use such weapons is viewed as potentially breeding 'panic'. Assessment of the 1995 Sarin attack in Tokyo and 2001 anthrax attack suggests the systemic fear and anxiety.

The 1995 Sarin attack on Tokyo

The religious cult Aum Shinrikyo successfully released sarin against its own people with their attacks on Tokyo subway on March 12, 1995. One of the passenger on the Hibya line reported that when someone came walking from the next carriage where the gas had been released shouting "Sarin Sarin", those around him stood up but were not running to escape. When the public address system announced that poison gas had been detected and passengers were advised to head for the safety of above ground, "passengers stood up and got off the train, but there wasn't any panic. They walked little faster than normal, but there was no pushing or anything. Some put handkerchief to their mouths or were coughing." A firefighter who attended the incident later recalled that people coming out of the contaminated subway remained silent. He had never experienced such a scene: "Just Victims' coughing heard in the perplexing for scene". The same scene was reported to have occurred in hospitals where victims waited patiently to be treated.[5]

A surveys of 610 victims (who were hospitalized) conducted within weeks of the incident revealed that 60% of the 475 respondents reported symptoms of PTSD. Symptoms victims noted included nightmares, numerous flashbacks that included unusual odours, ambulance sirens, and the sound of coughing when using the subways, seeing depictions of the attack on television, and news of other terrorist attack. 20% had fear of using the subway.

The 2001 Anthrax Attack

The use of the US postal system to attack media and government institutions with anthrax, killing five people in October to November 2001, exposed America to a type of threat they were not fully prepared. Proximity to the reported anthrax cases influenced the risk perception of contracting anthrax with 26% of Washington DC residents whose workplaces had been closed believing it was likely they would contract the disease, compared to 15% of area residents without any direct experience of the threat, and the general US population. Nationally 57% of Americans changed their behaviour to minimize their risk of contracting anthrax. Behavioural changes included 12% avoiding public events, one-third exercised caution when opening mail, including 30% who washed their hands afterward, and 6% who wore gloves. In the New York area 55% reported handling the mail at home more carefully as a consequences of the news of anthrax contamination.[6]

Although mental health data and research survey can explain to some extent the terror of terrorism through measuring the levels of fear and anxiety, and for a minority mental health problems like depression, stress on even PTSD, this does not provide sufficient explanation for the behavioural changes observed in the rest of the population. For instance, the fear of flying, taking extra precution when opening mail during the antrax attack or avoiding taking taxi. Although behavioural changes are recognized as one of the symptoms of certain mental health disorder (for instance the avoidance symptomatology criteria of PTSD), changes in an individual's daily routine or attitude does not necessarily mean they have a mental health problem-however there is arguably no distinct line between clinically diagnosed psychological disorder and those changing their behaviour. Changes are classed as one of several symptoms of psychological disorders.

An individual's perception of personal risk by terrorism is likely to be influenced by the perceived level of certainty and control they have over a situation. Lack of certainty over when, where and by what means an attack could take place leads to the perception of unknown risk involved in carrying out their daily lives. For instance, Tokyo citizens were concerned over taking the subway following the sarin attack fearful of further their strikes by Aum, and Americans taking precautions when opening their mail during the anthrax attacks. Lack of control is the belief that one lacks the ability to influence a situation imposed by terrorism. This causes individuals to change their routines to ones that they believe they have greater control over.

The attack on Indian Parliament then on Ayodhya followed by that in London along with continuous attacks in Iraq and Jammu & Kashmir and more recently 28/11 attack on Mumbai are clear indications of the role of International terrorism in today's world. No part of the country is entirely safe, yet it is nobody's case that it cannot be countered through effective collective action. To successfully counter this international threat the nations of the world need to come together; accept it as the common threat to mankind and to the safety and security of humanity.

Essential to the global response to terrorism is that it not fracture the unity of September 11 while the world must recognize that there are enemies common to all societies, it must equally understand that they are not, are never defined by religion or national descent. No people, no region and no religion should be targeted because of the unspeakable acts of individuals.

Terrorism threatens every society. As the world takes action against it, we have all been reminded of the need to address the conditions that permit the growth of hatred and depravity. We must confront violence, bigotry and hatred even more resolutely.

Doing so will not remove every source of hatred or prevent every act of violence. There are those who will hate and who will kill even if every injustice is ended. But if the world can show that it will carry on, that it will persevere in creating a stronger, more just, more benevolent and more genuine international community across all lines of religion and race, then terrorism will rotted out. And now it is a right and ripe time that all countries should face the challenge and talk concerted action to counter this onslaught against humanity, without adopting a policy of shifting convenience. So, all countries should draw up a common plan to fight against terrorism.

An Analysis on World Public Response

Everyday special services need to invent something new for effective fight against terrorism. Today countries across the world increasingly turn their attention and resources to counter-terrorism measures, and it is essential to reaffirm states obligation to protect human rights in this work. The recently released report of the UN High level panel on threats noted that the global counter-terrorism effort "has in some instance corroded the value that terrorist target: human rights and the rule of law" and has called attention to the vital need for a legal framework that is respectful of civil liberties and human rights in this international effort. Government have the right and obligation to protect the citizens from terrorism and to conduct investigation into terrorist act in order to identify those responsible and bring them to justice. In that effort, governments must defend the very principles that terrorism and violence assault. Universally now, it is said that terrorism requires a global response in Counter-Terrorism.

Counter-Terrorism

Counter-terrorism refers to the practices, tactics, techniques and strategies that governments, militaries and other groups adopt in order to fight terrorism. Counter-terrorism is not specific to any one field or organization; rather, it involves entities from all levels of society. Building a counter-terrorism plan involves all segments of a society or many government agencies. Because propaganda and indoctrination lie at the core of terrorism, understanding their profile and functions increases the ability to counter-terrorism more effectively.

Although there is no simple standard, any assessment of counter-terrorist policies should bear in mind that the purpose of counter-terrorism is to save lives, limbs and property without unduly compromising other national interests and objectives. Counter-terrorist programs will prevent many terrorist attacks but will not prevent them all. Terrorism happens. It should never be accepted but it should always be expected.

The impossibility of winning a "war" or inflicting an overall defeat raises the question of what standard to use in assessing the success or failure of counter-terrorist programs. Terrorist attacks, and people getting killed or wounded in them are obvious but as noted, zero attacks would be an impossible standard.

The War on Terrorism, the War against Terror: War on Terror is an umbrella term used by the Bush administration to refer to the various military, political and legal action taken to "curb the spread of terrorism". The stated goal of the war is to "end international terrorism" it was launched in response to the September 11, 2001 attacks on the U.S. for which al-Qaeda claimed responsibility. President George W. Bush defined the "War on Terror" : "Our war on terror begins with al-Qaeda, but it does not end there. It will not end until every terrorist group of global reach has been found, stopped and defeated."[7]

The war on terrorism was launched by US President George W. Bush, with support from NATO and other allies. The "War on Terror" has taken many forms, such as diplomacy, going after `terrorist financing", domestic provisions aiming to prevent future attacks and joint training and peacekeeping operations with a wide variety of nations.

The phrase Global War on Terrorism (or GWOT) is the official name used by the US military for operations designated as part of the campaign. Thus, the "War on Terror" as defined by this article is largely a military effort, and has been compared in both its unspecified, continuing duration and its multiple theaters of operation, to the cold war. The war is also characterized as an ideological struggle, "involving both a battle of arms and a battle of ideas," and some have characterized it as a "Clash of Civilizations.[8] Although the US-led coalition that invaded Iraq in 2003 and fall President Saddam Hussein was made up of allies in the "war on Terror", the current Iraq war and its alleged links to the larger campaign against terrorism have been highly controversial.

In addition, according to the US government's own measures, international terrorist incidents have been on the rise since the campaign began. However, the US and allies have claimed victories, such as democratic elections in Afghanistan and Iraq, and the capture of alleged 9/11 planner Khalid Sheikh Mohammed. The War on Terrorism has resulted in high military casualties on both sides as well as high civilian casualties, although very few United States civilians have been killed other than those who died on 9/11, and is a "Long War" whose planners expect it to continue for the foreseeable future.

Today, many countries have special units designated to handle terrorist threats. Besides various security agencies, there are elite tactical units whose role is to directly engage terrorist and prevent terrorist attacks, such units perform bath in preventive actions, hostage rescue and responding to ongoing attacks.

Africa (Horn of Africa)

This extension of Operation Enduring Freedom, titled OEA-HOA, was initiated in response to the September 11, 2001 attacks on the United States. Unlike other operations contained in operation Enduring Freedom OEF-HOA does not have a specific terrorist organization as a target. OEF-HOA instead focuses its efforts to disrupt and detect terrorist activities in the region and to work with host nations to prevent the reemergence of terrorist cells and activities.

In October 2002, the Combined Joint Task Force, Horn of Africa (CJTF-HOA) was established in Djibouti at Camp Le Monier. It contains approximately 2,000 personal including U.S Military and Special Operation Force (SOF) and coalition force members, Coalition Task force 150 (CTF-150). The Coalition force members, consist of ships from Australia, Canada, France, Germany, Italy, Netherland, Pakistan, New Zealand, Spain and the United Kingdom. The primary goal of the coalition force is to monitor, inspect, board and stop suspected shipments from entering the Horn of Africa region and areas of operation Iraqi Freedom.[9] Included in the operation is the training of selected armed forced units of the countries of Djibouti, Kenya and Ethiopia in counter-terrorism and counter-insurgency tactics.

Humanitarian efforts conducted by CJTF-HOA include rebuilding of schools and medical clinics as well as providing medical services to those countries whose forces are being trained. The program expands as part of the Trans-Saharan Counter-Terrorism Initiative as CJTF personnel also assist in training the force of Chad, Niger, Mauritania and Mali.

Only July 1, 2006, a web-posted message purportedly written by Osama bin Laden urged Somalis to build an Islamic State in the country and warned western states that his al-Qaeda network would fight against them if they intervened there.

Somalia has been considered a "failed state" because its official central government was weak, dominated by warlords and unable to exert effective control over the country. Beginning in mid-2006, the Islamic Courts Union (ICV), an Islamist faction campaigning on a restoration of "Law and order" through Sharia law, had rapidly taken control of much of Southern Somalia. On December 14, 2006, the U.S. Assistant Secretary of State Jendayi Frazer claimed al-Qaeda cell operative were controlling the Islamic Court union, a claim denied by the ICU.[10]

By late 2006, the UN-backed Transitional Federal Government (TFG) of Somalia had seen its power effectively limited to Boidoa, while the Islamic courts union controlled the majority of Southern Somalia, including the capital of Mogadishu. On December 20, the Islamic courts union launched an offensive on the government stronghold of Baidoa, and saw early gains before Ethiopia intervened in favour of the government: By December 26, the Islamic court union went into a "tactical retreat" towards Mogadishu; before again retreating as TFG/Ethiopian troop neared, leading them to take Mogadishu, with no resistance. The ICU then fled to Kismayo, Where they are currently fighting Ethiopian/TFG forces in the Battle of Jilib. The Prime Minister of Somalia claims that 3 terror suspects from the 1998 Embassy Bombings are being sheltered in Kismayo.

On 30 December 2006, al-Qaeda deputy leader Ayman al-Zawahiri called upon Muslims Worldwide to fight against Ethiopia and the TFG in Somalia. On January 8, 2007, the US launched a strike in Somalia against the suspects using AC-130 gunships.[11]

Europe

Terrorism is a scourge with which European nations, from Ireland to Spain, are only too familiar. Islamist terrorism, of the kind that hit Washington and New York on September 11, 2001 and Madrid on March 11, 2004, is new however. Neither America nor Europe was prepared for this kind of indiscriminate, wanton violence against the civilian population unleashed by al-Qaeda and it followers.

This explains that individual nation conduct risk based assessments of Critical National Infrastructures-those assets and activities, which if damaged or destroyed, would affect a country's ability to continue normal life. It recommends that all European countries adopt a range of action intended to prevent terrorist action, to pursue those responsible, to protect against attacks and to develop resilience against them.

European Union (EU) member states have adopted a wide range of policies to defend themselves against terrorism. As part of their response they have strengthened the role of the European union. Since 2001 and Home Affairs council—has adopted important legislative measures and policies to facilities Cross-border cooperation by national law-enforcement authorities and intelligence agencies. In June 2005, the European Council adopted a plan of action containing well over 100 initiatives to be taken during the Dutch, Luxembourg and British presidencies. It also identified four priority areas: information sharing, combating terrorist financing, mainstreaming counter-terrorism in the EU's external relations, and improving civil protection and the protection of critical infrastructure.

Information Sharing

Timely and accurate information—its collection, analysis and dissemination—is essential to prevent acts of terrorism and to bring terrorist suspects to justice. Progress is being made in implementing the decisions of the council to improve the exchange of terrorism-related information. In June 2005 the council decided to stimulate cooperation among Europe's security and intelligence services by reinforcing the Situation Centre (Sitcen) in the council secretariat. Cooperation between the security services in the Counter-Terrorist Group and the Chiefs of Police Task force has also been enhanced.

Combating Terrorist Financing

Terrorists need money to prepare and carry out attacks. Identifying and disrupting the mechanisms through which terrorism is financed are therefore key elements of the Union's counter-terrorism strategy. As well as reducing the financial flows to terrorists and disrupting their activities, action to counter-terrorist financing can provide vital information on terrorists and their networks. In accordance with resolutions adopted by the Security Council, the union has established lists of individuals and groups designated as being involved in terrorist acts, whose assets must be frozen. In part as a result of increased attention by governments and the financial sector, the methods involved in terrorism financing appear to have changed since September 11, 2001; intelligence indicates that there is now less use of the regular banking system.

The European Council will shortly be presented with additional proposals from the Secretary-General/High Representative (SG/HR) and the commission. Their aim is to provide the Union with a coordinated, cross-pillar strategy, based on an intelligence-led approach including input from the Sitcen, and in close cooperation with international bodies such as the UN and the Financial Action Task Force.

External Relations

Terrorism is global phenomenon that requires a global response. Terrorism poses a serious threat to international peace and security, including the security of the European Union, as was recognized in the European Security Strategy proposed by Javier Solana. The United Nation is a key partner of the union in many fields, including the fight against terrorism. UN Security Council resolution 1267, 1373, 1540 and 1566 have considerably enhanced the role of the UN in countering terrorism. The UN and the EU share a strong commitment to the protection and promotion of human rights in the world. Based on this shared approach, there are three areas that offer much scope for cooperation.

First, promoting the universal ratification of all twelve UN conventions in the fight against terrorism.

Second, cooperation between the EU and the UN is the provision of aid and technical assistance to countries lacking the capability to implement this common legal framework. Counter-terrorism assistance is already part of the aid strategy of the EU and its member states, and the council has resolved to further enhance the contribution of the Union.

Third, the UN and the EU have similar agenda in addressing the factors underlying recruitment and support for terrorism. There is general recognition that regional conflicts, bad governance and state failure can provide fertile ground for recruitment in to terrorism. Efforts to resolve regional conflicts and to promote human rights and good governance must therefore be at the heart of international counter-terrorism strategies.

Civil Protection

The main objective of the EU's counter-terrorism strategy is to help the member states prevent terrorist attack. Member-states need to ensure that essential public services are maintained or restored as soon as possible and that emergency relief is provided to citizens and businesses. Civil protection and emergency response management for the most part fall under the national competence of member states. Nevertheless, in March the union's heads of state and government declared their firm intention to 'act jointly in a spirit of solidarity if one of them is the victim of a terrorist attack' and pledged to mobilize all the instruments at their disposal, including military resources, to assist a member state affected by such an attack.

The European Union as a whole should develop a comprehensive strategy as well as a stronger operational and tactical structure. The EU should also work with important partner countries to develop links between terrorism analysis centers and share analysis of risks and counter-measures.

MIDDLE EAST

Iraq

Iraq had been listed as a state, sponsoring terrorism, by the United States since 1990, and maintained poor relations with the United States since the Gulf War. Tensions were high throughout the 1990s with the United States launching operation 'Desert Fox' against Iraq in 1998 after it failed to meet demands of "unconditional cooperation" in weapons inspections.[12] After the September 11 attacks, the U.S government claimed that Iraq was a threat to the United States because Iraq could begin to use its alleged Weapons of Mass Destruction to aid terrorist groups. However, Iraq had no role in the September 11 attacks and had no known history of a significant working relationship with al-Qaeda.

The George W. Bush administration called for the United Nation Security Council (UNSC) to send weapons inspectors to Iraq to find and destroy alleged weapons of mass destruction and for a UNSC resolution. UNSC Resolution 1441 was passed unanimously, which offered Iraq "a final opportunity to comply with its disarmament obligations" or face "serious consequences". Resolution 1441 did not authorize the use of force by member states, thus Resolution 1441 had no effect on the UN charter's prohibition on the use of force by member states against fellow member states. Saddam Hussein subsequently allowed UN inspectors to access Iraqi sites, while the U.S. government continued to assert that Iraq was being obstructionist.[13] The burden of proof was on Iraq to show it had no weapons and not the US due to the nature of the regime. Before the 2nd Iraq war, Hussein got 100% of the vote in Iraq's presidential election. In October 2002, the United States Congress authorized the president to use force if necessary to disarm Iraq in order to "Prosecute the war on terrorism."

On March 20th, 2003, the invasion of Iraq was launched in what the Bush Administration said were the "serious consequences" spoken of in UNSC Resolution 1441. Iraq had violated 17 different UN resolutions up to that point since the end of the 1991 Gulf war.

Saddam Hussein's regime was quickly toppled and on May 1, 2003, George W. Bush Stated major combat operations in Iraq had ended and claimed victory over in Iraq. But the war continued on as an insurgency against the U.S-led coalition forces and the Iraqi police units and governing structures the installed. Elements of the insurgency are led by Sunni loyalists, who are Iraqi nationalists and pan Arabists Some insurgency leaders are strict Muslims and see themselves as fighting a religious war to liberate Iraq of foreign non-Muslim occupiers and their Iraqi collaborators.[14] Over 3,000 soldiers from the coalition have been killed with an estimated 67,000 Insurgents killed or detained.[15]

At a news conference with the British Prime Minister Tony Blair in Washington on December 6, 2006, President George W. Bush commented the Iraq study Group's report and admitted for the first time that a "new approach" is needed in Iraq, that the situation in Iraq is "bad there" and that the task ahead was "daunting". Mr. Bush said he would not accept every recommendation by the ISG panel but promised that he would take the report seriously. Mr. Bush is expected to wait for three other studies from the Pentagon, the U.S. State Department and the National Security Council before charting the new course on Iraq.

Lebanon

In July 2006, following the killing of three Israeli soldiers and the taking prisoner of two more by Hezbollah, Israel invaded Southern Lebanon, intent on the destruction of Hezbollah. The conflict lasted over a month and caused the deaths of between 845 and 1300 Lebanese and 163 Israelis and wounding thousands more Israelis and Lebanese. Both the Lebanese government (including Hezbollah) and the Israeli government have agreed to the term of the ceasefire agreement created by the United Nations that began on August 14, 2006. While the conflict is associated with the longer running Arab-Israeli conflict, prior to the declaration of the ceasefire, Israel stated it was fighting a war against terror, the U.S. government stated the conflict was also a front in the "War on Terrorism" and President Bush reiterated it in a speech the day, the ceasefire came into effect.

ASIA

India

India has had to deal with a slow but steady rise in

Islamist terrorism over the course of the 1990s and the 21st century. The recent rise in prominence of several terror groups, such as Lashkar-e-Toiba, Jaish-e-Mohammed, Hizbul Mujahideen and others in Kashmir has created grave problem for the country. Major terrorist incidents in India include the 1993 Mumbai bombings as well as Terrorism in Kashmir. Terrorist attack in the rest of the country include the 2001 Indian Parliament attack, Akshardham Temple attack, October 29, 2005 Delhi bombings, 2005 Ram Janmabhoomi attack in Ayodhya, 2005 Jaunpur train bombing, July 11, 2006 Mumbai train bombings, and 2007 Samjhauta Express bombings. In the aftermath of the 2001 Indian Parliament attack, massive troop build-ups occurred in the Kashmir region by both India and Pakistan and fire was exchange. This incident is called the 2001-2002 India-Pakistan standoff.

On January 12, 2002, Pakistani President Pervez Musharraf gave a speech intended to reduce tensions with India. He declared the Pakistan would combat extremism on its own soil, but said that Pakistan had a right to Kashmir. Indian leaders reacted with skepticism. The then Minister of State for External Affairs Omar Abdullah said that the speech was nothing new, and others said that it would not make any change in the Indian stand.

Afghanistan

In October 2001, in the wake of the September 11, 2001 attacks on the United States, the U.S. and some of its allies invaded the country of Afghanistan to remove al-Qaeda forces and oust the Taliban regime that had control of the country. On September 20, 2001 George W. Bush delivered an ultimatum to the Taliban regime to turn over Osama bin Laden and al Qaeda leaders operating in the country. The Taliban demanded evidence of bin Laden's link to the September 11 attacks and, if such evidence warranted a trial, they offered to handle such a trial in an Islamic court. On October 7, 2001 the official invasion began with British and American forces conducting aerial bombing campaigns which is still going on in 2009.

Pakistan

The Saudi born zayn al-Abidn Muhammed Hasayn Abu Zubaydah was arrested by Pakistani officials during a series of joint U.S. and Pakistani raids during the week of March 23, 2002. During the raid the suspect was shot three times while trying to escape capture by military personnel. Zubaydah is said to be a high-ranking al-Qaeda official with the title of operation's chief and In-charge of running al-Qaeda training camps.

Later that year on September 14, 2002, Ramzi Binalshibh was arrested in Pakistan after a three-hour gunfight with police forces. Binalshibh is known to have shared a room with Mohammed Atta in Hamburg, Germany and, to be a financial backer of al-Qaeda operations. It is said Binalshibh was supposed to be another hijacker, however the U.S. Citizenship and Immigration services rejected his visa application three times, leaving him to role of financier. The trail of money transferred by Binalshibh from Germany to the United States links both Mohammed Atta and Zacarias Maussaoui.[16]

On March 1, 2003, Khalid Shaikh Mohammed was arrested during CIA-led raids on the Suburb of Rawalpindi, nine miles outside of the Pakistani Capital of Islamabad. Mohammed at the time of his capture was the third highest-ranking official in al-Qaeda and had been directly in charge of the planning for the September 11 attacks. Escaping capture the week before during a previous raid, the Pakistani government was able to use information gathered from other suspects captured to locate and detain Mohammed.

During all this, Pakistan has been accused by NATO commanding officers of aiding and abetting, the Taliban in Afghanistan. India, meanwhile continues to accuse Pakistan's Inter-Services Intelligence of planning several terrorist attacks in occupied Kashmir and elsewhere in the India, including the July 11, 2006 Mumbai train bombings and more recently attack on Mumbai on 26-11-2008.

Phillippines

In January, 2002 the United States Special Operations Command, Pacific to the Philippines to advise and assist the Armed Forces of the Philippines in combating terrorism. The operations were mainly focused on removing the Abu Sayyaf Group (ASG) and Jemaah Islamiyah (JI) from their stronghold on the Island of Basilan. The United States Military has reported that they have removed over 80% of the Abu Sayyaf Group members from the region.

United States of America

The Bush administration said it intended to base its counter-terrorism strategy on several steps:

First, the United States seeks to destroy terrorist organizations, particularly those of global reach. Such destruction may come from direct military strikes on terrorist cells and infrastructure. More commonly it involves the use of intelligence and law enforcement services to arrest, hound, and disrupt terrorists, making it hard for them to recruit, organize, proselytize, and plan as well as to conduct attacks.

Second, the United States opposes states that sponsor terrorists or offer them sanctuary. Washington presses for zero tolerance of terrorism, pushing all states to work together to deny terrorists financing and a place to recruit, to say nothing of open sponsorship. Washington also presses countries to improve their internal security to prevent Al Qaeda from operating below the radar screen. As appropriate, the United States also try to improve the capacity of weak states that might fall host to terrorists despite the regime's best efforts to suppress them.

Third, although US leaders consistently speak of a war on terrorism, in practice this efforts has focused on Al Qaeda and its affiliates. After 9/11, the United States has significantly changed its policies regarding Hizbullah, Hamas, and the Liberation of Tamil Eelam or other leading terrorist groups.

Fourth, Much of the effort in the war on terrorism is linked to efforts against large Islamist insurgent movements, which employ guerrilla warfare, as well as terrorist cells. Much of the global war on terrorism is focused effort against Islamist insurgencies.

Al Qaeda's training camps in Afghanistan were previously a key stage in the radicalization and recruitment of terrorists such as those who led the 9/11 attacks. The terrorist infrastructure was destroyed in the 2001 Afghan war, along with the sponsoring Taliban regime. A significant part of al-Qaeda's leaders and members will killed or scattered—and the campaign against the organization and its top leaders continues in Afghanistan and Pakistan. However, al-Qaeda remains a significant threat, even though as an organization it is now harder to define.

United Nations to Counter-Terrorism

The United Nations Global Counter-Terrorism Strategy was adopted by Member States on September 8, 2006. The strategy in the form of a resolution and an annexed Plan of Action is a unique global instrument that will enhance national, regional and international efforts to counter-terrorism. This is the first time that all member-states have agreed to a common strategic approach to fight terrorism, not only sending a clear message that terrorism is unacceptable in all and manifestation but also resolving to take practical steps individually and collectively to prevent and combat it. Those practical steps include a wide array of measures ranging from strength state capacity to counter-terrorist threats to better coordinating United Nation's system's counter-terrorism activities. The adoption of the strength fulfils the commitment made by world leaders at the 2005 September summit and builds on many of the elements proposed by the Secretary General in his May 2, 2006 report, entitled Uniting Against Terrorism : (Recommendation for a global counter-Terrorism Strategy).

The State Members of the United Nations Resolve

1. To consistently, unequivocally and strongly condemn terrorism in all its forms and manifestations, committed

by who wherever and for whatever purposes, as it constitutes one of the most serious threat to international peace and security.

2. To take urgent action to prevent and combat terrorism in all its forms and manifestation and in particular:

   (a) To consider becoming parties without delay to the existing international conventions and protocols against terrorism and implementing them, and to make every effort to reach an agreement on and conclude a comprehensive convention on international terrorism.

   (b) To implement all resolutions adopted by the Security Council related to international terrorism and to cooperate fully with the counter-terrorism subsidiary bodies of the security council in the fulfillment of their tasks, recognizing that many states continue to require assistance in implementing these resolutions.

   (c) To implement all General Assembly resolution's on measures to eliminate international terrorism, and relevant General Assembly resolution on the protection of human rights and fundamental freedoms while countering terrorism.

3. To recognize the international cooperation and any measures that we undertake to prevent and combat terrorism must comply with our obligations under international law, including the charter of the United Nations and relevant international conventions and protocols, in particular human rights law, refugee law and international humanitarian law.

UN resolve to undertake the following measures to prevent and combat terrorism, in particular by denying terrorists access to the means to carry out their attacks, to their targets and to the desired impact of their attack:

1. To refrain from organizing, instigating, facilitating participating in, financing, encouraging or tolerating terrorist

activities and take appropriate practical measures to ensure that our respective territories are not used for terrorist installations or training camps, or for the preparation or organization of terrorist acts intended to be committed against other states.

2. To cooperate fully in the fight against terrorism, in accordance with our obligations under international law, in order to find, deny safe heaven and bring to justice, on the basis of the principle of extradite or prosecute any person who supports, facilitates participates or attempts to participate in the financing, planning, preparation or perpetration of terrorist acts or providing safe havens.

3. To ensure the apprehension and prosecution or extradition of perpetrator of terrorist acts, in accordance with the relevant provisions of national and international law, in particular human right law, refugee law and international humanitarian law. UN will endeavour to conclude and implement to that effect mutual judicial assistance and extradition agreements, and to strength cooperation between law enforcement agencies.

4. To intensify cooperation, as appropriate, in exchanging timely and accurate information concerning the prevention and combating of terrorism.

5. To strength coordination and cooperation among states in combating crimes that might be connected with terrorism, including drug trafficking in all its aspects, unlawful arms trade, in particular of small arms and light weapons, money laundering and smuggling of nuclear, chemical, biological, and other potential materials.

Measures Against Terrorism

Different terrorists have different *modus operandi* and tactics, which keep changing with improvisation depending upon the response of the police and security forces to their actions. Hence, the struggle for one-upmanship is always there. However, irrespective of terrorist techniques and tactics, the administration must take certain basic steps to strengthen the security measures and to pre-empt the actions of terrorists before they strike in order to always keep them guessing and put them on the defensive.

Any state measures to counter-terrorism has, therefore, to be a mixture of political, social, economic and administrative and military actions. It is rather impossible to defeat terrorism simply by military action alone. Defeating terrorism, thus, demands of taking number of measures.

Some basic important measures which can help counter-terrorism are as follows:

1. Study of terrain and topography of the entire area is important before making any definite plan of action and before deploying the forces. The deployment of forces will be different in a hilly area as compared to the deployment of the forces and tactics to be used in a city/town of the plains.
2. The entry and exit points to the city/town concerned should be checked. This must be done regularly and, if there is a shortage of force, this should be done at different times so as to surprise the terrorist and be a deterrent for them.
3. Proper security to essential services like Malls, banks, petrol pumps, public places, hospitals, schools, and market places should be ensured.
4. Proper security arrangements must be made in the location of Police Stations/Police Posts. Each police units should have proper fire fighting equipments. Bushes and trees disturbing the sentry's view should be cut.
5. There should be proper security arrangements in the Government offices like: courts, Municipality office, offices of government officials, secretariat etc. The police should deploy plain-clothes men to mingle with crowd to see if someone is up to mischief.
6. There should be proper intelligence system around the

hideouts of the terrorists.

7. Strong administrative measures are most essential to counter-terrorism. The local administration should neither be humiliated nor ignored. Officers of local police should command their own forces and should not abdicate their responsibilities and bask under the protection and performance of some other force.

8. All organs of the state function at their optimum of efficiency. Individually as well as collectively.

9. Efforts should be made to be normalizing the relations between civilian and the police force. It will generate confidence among the people. They will not only trust on the local police but also help the authorities to counter-terrorists. Even the constitutional authority cannot defeat the terrorist's movement without the popular support; they should mix with the public by playing games, etc. with them, by this people loose their inhibition and fear and come out and give good information.

10. VIP and officers should always keep changing their position in the convoy in which they travel. For example, officers should sometimes even sit in the escort or pilot vehicles or travel in one of two identical Ambassador cars.

11. Counter measures should be designed to reduce terrorist resources, their propensity to strike and the damage they intend to cause. Border security should be improved. Infiltration and exfitration should be checked.

12. As accurate information and timely intelligence are most essential to counter-terrorism, there should be proper and meaningful coordination between various intelligences agencies working in the field. There is also a need for the establishment of the composite intelligence gathering and dissemination center like joint Interrogation centres.

Global Efforts to Fight Terrorism

1. On September 11, 2001, only two nations had adhered to

all 12 international anti-terrorism conventions and protocols. Now more than 30 nations belong to all 12, and many more have become parties to most of the conventions and protocols and have passed implementing legislation to put them into effect.

2. The United Nations Security Council, through its counter-terrorism committee (CTC), has taken on a new, important role under Resolution 1373 as the coordination of UN member states in efforts to raise the global level of counter-terrorism capability, cooperation and effectiveness.

3. On June 26, 2002, President Bush secured agreement on a US sponsored plan for G-8 action on transport security. The G-8 committed to accelerated action on pre-screening people and cargo, increasing security on ships, planes and trucks, and enhancing security in airports and seaports. The G-8 initiative also enhances transport security through better intelligence, coordinated national efforts, and international cooperation against terrorist threats.

4. The G-8 leaders took significant steps to expand international cooperation on projects to prevent the proliferation of weapons of mass destruction in the first year of the Global Partnership Against the Spread of Weapons and Materials of Mass Destruction Launched by leaders in June 2002. The partnership has been broadened to include Finland, Norway Poland, Sweden and Switzerland. The G-8 also launched an initiative to improve the security of radioactive sources and prevent their use by terrorists in so-called "dirty bombs."

5. On May 31, 2003, the US President announced the Proliferation Security Initiative (PSI), designed to combat the trade in weapons of mass destruction, their delivery systems, and related materials to and from states and non-states actors of proliferation concern. This proliferation, together with terrorism, constitutes the greatest threat to international security. On September 4, 2003, Australia, France, Germany, Italy, Japan, the Netherland, Poland,

Spain and the UK joined the United States in announcing the PSI statement of the interdiction principles, consistent with national legal authorities and International law.

6. The International Atomic Energy Agency's (IAEA) Nuclear Security Action Plan provides advice, training and equipment to its 136 Member States to combat nuclear terrorism. The United States has contributed $ 15.9 million since the Action Plan's inception in March 2002. The IAEA coordinates its nuclear security activities with the United States and other donor states to mutually reinforce our nuclear security goals.

7. The Department of Defense established the Regional Defense Counter-terrorism fellowship program, funded at $ 20 million per year, to provide coalition counterparts with the training and education necessary to establish and maintain effective counter terrorism programs in their home countries.

Regional Efforts to Fight Terrorism

1. On June 26, 2003, the President announced a $ 100 million Eastern Africa counter-terrorism Initiative to expand and accelerate counter-terrorism efforts with Kenya, Ethiopia, Djibouti, Uganda, Tanzania and other countries, as appropriate.

2. On October 26, 2002, President Bush obtained agreement for an Asia-Pacific Economic cooperation (APEC) Leaders plan on fighting terrorism and promoting growth that contains specific commitments to secure key pacific Rim infrastructure-transport, finance, and communications-from exploitation or attack by terrorists.

3. The North Atlantic Treaty Organization (NATO) has endorsed an ambitious transformation agenda designed to enhance its capabilities by increasing deployment speed and agility to address new threats of terrorism. Other organizations, including the Organization of American State (OAS), the European Union (EU), the Organization

for Security and Cooperation in Europe (OSCE), the Association of South East Asian Nations (ASEAN), the Australia, New Zealand and United States (ANZUS) Treaty members, took concrete steps to combat terrorism more effectively and to cooperate with each other in the fight.

4. The Department of State initiated a counter-terrorism and law Enforcement Joint Working Group with Pakistan and greatly enhanced counter-terrorism cooperation with India, Japan and China. It has also launched an intensive training program for Pakistan counter-terrorism units in Crisis Response Team and investigation techniques.

5. Colombia has developed a democratic security strategy as a blueprint for waging an aggressive campaign against designated Foreign terrorist organization (FTO) such as Revolutionary Armed Forces of Colombia (FARC), National Liberation Army (ELN) and other illegal armed groups. U.S. Congressional passage of new authorities for Colombia, in July 2002, enhanced the flexibility of U.S. security assistance against illicit drugs and terrorism.

6. In 2003, Argentina, Brazil, Paraguay, and the United States established a regional counter-terrorism mechanism to focus on practical steps to strengthen financial and border controls, legislation and enhance law enforcement and intelligence sharing. The mechanism is built on the framework of the "Tripartite Commission of the Triple Frontier", creating the "3+1" format.

Success in the global war against terrorism depends on the actions of a powerful coalition of nations maintaining a united front against terror. Over 170 nations continue to participate in the war on terrorism by taking terrorists in to custody, freezing terrorist assets and providing military forces and other support. International organizations are becoming more agile, adapting their structures to meet changing threats. We must support the action of our partners because terrorist strikes will continue and so will the killings unabated, till we really, honestly, sincerely and unselfishly decide to protect mankind and abhor the ambition for one-upmanship.

REFERENCES

1. Jim Dwyer, Kevin Flynn & Ford Fessenden, "Fighting to live as the Towers Dies", *The New York Times*, 26 May 2002 (www.nytimes.com)
2. William E. Schlenger, "Psychological Reaction to terrorist attacks. 'Finding from the National Study of Americans' Reaction to September 11", *Journal of American Medical Association*, Vol. 288, No. 5 August 7, 2002, pp. 581-588.
3. Sandro Galea, "Psychological Seqwelae of the September 11 Terrorist Attacks in New York City."*The New England Journal of Medicine*, Vol. 346, No. 13 March 28, 2002 p. 982.
4. Russ Hoyle, "A year later, a city is still on edge," *New York Daily News*, September 1, 2002, p. 1.
5. Nozomu Asukai and Kazuhiko Maekawa; "*Psychological and Physical health effects of the 1995 Sarin Attack in the Tokyo Subway System*" Plenum Publishers, New York; Year 2002, p. 153.
6. http://www. hsph. Harvard.edu/press/releases/report 2.pdf.
7. http://www. white house.gov/news/releases/2001/09/print/20010920-8.html, "President Declares Freedom at war with fear."
8. The White House. National Strategy for Combating Terrorism. (http://www. White house. gov/infocus/national security/index.html)
9. http://www. guardian. Co. UK/USa/Story/O, 1710062, oo.html.
10. US says al Qaeda behind Somali Islamists; *Times of India*, Dec 16, 2006.
11. http://www. fox news.com/story/0,2933, 242460,00. html.
12. http://en.wiki/war-on-Terrorism
13. http://www. Pbs. Org/newshour/bb/middle_east/Iraq/resolution 2_2_24-03.html)
14. http://www. time.com/time/magazine/arti /0,9171, 1101040705-658290,00 html).
15. http://www. brookings. edu/fp/Saban/iraq/index.BIF
16. http://english.provda.ru/main/2002/09/14/36623.html.

6

Conclusion and Suggestions

No exaggeration 'National Security' is concern for everyone, and as we enter the 21st century, it is appropriate to take stock of the security situation around us and assess what the future holds for succeeding generations. There are six cluster of threats with which the world must be concerned now in the decades ahead.

1. War between States.
2. Violence within states, including civil wars; large-scale human rights abuses and genocide.
3. Poverty, infectious diseases and environmental degradation.
4. Nuclear, radiological, chemical and biological weapons.
5. Transnational organized crime, and
6. Terrorism.

The grief or tragedy, which accompanies a terrorist attack, can lead to a rather uni-dimensional view of terrorism. For those personally affected by the loss of loved ones and friends this uni-dimensionality focuses on their loss, and not, we suspect on bloodlust and revenge. But for those not directly linked to events, the feeling is perhaps entirely understandable that someone ought to be held accountable and that someone be made to pay. But despite the powerful and simple emotions that can overcome people at times of personal, national or global tragedy the reality of terror is, alas, much more complicated: 'Terrorism is a complex problem: It origins are diverse; and so are those who engage in it'.

Though terrorism is not a new activity as an opponent is using it as means to destablise political stability, economic growth, Nations morale and peace to another rival state.

But the attack on U.S. World Trade Center on September 11, 2001, was a turning point in the history of terrorism. Bin Laden a recognized name as a superman of terrorism has challenged U.S.A and the world. The 9/11 attacks on the United States pushed terrorism to the international agenda.

In the autumn of 2001 the word 'terrorism' was on all lips. Everybody use it but nobody explain it. Hundreds of definitions of terrorism are offered in the literature. No definition can possibly cover all varieties of terrorism that have appeared throughout the history. How we define terrorism profoundly influence how we respond to it.

In short, terrorism may be defined as a surprise attack, generally on innocent civilians, historical monuments, means of transportation, crowded markets and center of entertainment for terrorising a much larger group of people to obtain their goal.

Terrorism is not a term that terrorists own to; for the main part their intentions and actions define a duty they feel they must discharge. Most terrorists claim to be delivering a political message and few calls themselves as 'freedom fighters'. Here once more we meet with a generalisation that fogs a clear meaning.

Today there are more than fifty to sixty terrorist groups whose organization ranges from simple to complex and long-lasting. There are highly feared organizations with dynamic leaders propitiating consistently dreaded strategies.

Though almost all active terrorist organizations are

discussed at length in the second Chapter of the book, however, few more dangerous organizations are being explained continental wise.

AFRICA

(a) Armed Islamic Group

This is a group that aims to overthrow the secular Algerian regime and replace it with an Islamic State. It has attacked civilians, journalists and foreigners and conducted a campaign of massacres. It is believed to have around 100 members and Algiers has accused Iran and Sudan of backing the group. The group uses assassination and bombings including car bombs, and it is known to favour kidnapping victims and slitting their throats.

(b) Al Gama'a Al Islamiyya (GAI)

The GAI, Egypt's largest militant group, has been active since the late 1970's. The group main aim is to overthrow the Egyptian government and replace it with a Islamic State in Egypt. After the 1997 cease-fire the faction led by Taha Musa launched attack on tourists in Egypt, most notably the attack in November 1997 at Luxor. This group operates mainly in al-Minya, Asyut, Qina of Southern Egypt. Osama bin Laden and Afghan militant groups support the organization. They also obtain some funding through various Islamic non-governmental organization (NGOs).

(c) Libyan Islamic Fighting Group (LIFG)

The Libyan Islamic fighting group emerged in the 1990s among Libyans who had fought against Soviet forces in Afghanistan and against the Qadhafi regime in Libya. LIFG is a group, which planned the Casablanca suicide bombing in May 2003. It is believed to have several hundred active members and supporters. This group obtains funds through private donations, and criminal acts. Probably maintain a clandestine presence in Libya, Persian Gulf, African and European countries.

ASIA

(a) Harakat Ul-Mujahadin

This is an Islamic militant group based in Pakistan that operates primarily in Kashmir. It was believed to have close links with al-Qaeda. Its attacks include a number on Indian troops and civilian targets in the disputed region of Kashmir. In December 1999 it pulled off its most notable attack when it hijacked an Indian airlines and forced the release of Masood Azhar. The group collected donations from Saudi Arabia and Pakistan. At its peak it was thought to have several thousand armed supporters. HUM trained its militants in Afghanistan and also in Pakistan.

(b) Jaish-e-Mohammed (JEM)

When Masood Azhar was released from prison he formed Jaish-e-Mohammed. The group's aim is to unite Kashmir with Pakistan. On October 1, 2001, JEM claimed responsibility for a suicide attack on J&K legislative assembly building in Srinagar that killed 31 persons. It is thought to have broad support in the Kashmir area of Pakistan as well as the Southern Kashmir area of India. Osama bin Laden is suspected to giving funding to JEM.

(c) Liberation Tigers of Tamil Eelam (LTTE)

Better known as Tamil Tigers, had the highest rate of suicide mission in the world. LTTE was founded in 1976; the LTTE is the most powerful Tamil group in Sri Lanka. In May 21, 1991 the LTTE murdered the Indian Prime Minister Rajiv Gandhi at an election campaign rally in India. Tamil Tigers have also been known to carry cyanide capsules in case they are caught. At full strength it was thought to have around 10,000 armed combatants. Fundings is thought to have come through the large displaced Tamil population throughout Europe and North America.

EUROPE

Basque Fatherland and Liberty (ETA)

Basque Fatherland and Liberty is the English translation of Euskadi ta Askatasuna (ETA). It is a group formed in northern part of Spain. The group was formed in 1959. Primarily involved in bombing and assassination of Spanish government officials, security and military forces, politicians, and judicial figures also targeted journalists and tourists areas operates primarily in Northern Spain and South Western France.

MIDDLE EAST

(a) Al-Qaeda

Al-Qaeda was established by Osama bin Laden in 1988 with Arabs who fought in Afghanistan against the Soviet Union. Their main goal is to Unite Muslims to fight the United States as a means of defeating Israel, overthrowing regimes it deems "Non-Islamic" and expelling westerners and non-Muslims from Muslim countries. They had done many attacks, but the most horrified attack was on September 11, 2001 on WTC and Pentagon. Currently al-Qaeda is thought to have several thousand members and supporters. It is funded through the murky connections of the Bin Laden group; a construction empire that is said to be worth billions of pounds and from which Osama bin Laden has poured his own money into the organization. It seems however that al-Qaeda has enough resources to continue its operations. Generally operates in Middle East, Asia, Europe, North America and South America.

(b) HAMAS

The Hamas group has gained international notoriety in its long-standing armed struggle to create an Islamic Palestinian State in Middle East. It was founded in 1987 and its strength is concentrated in the West Bank and Gaza Strip. It raised funds from neighbouring Arab Countries, Europe and United States. In November 2002, they claimed responsibility for a suicide attack on an Israeli bus in residential Jerusalem. Hamas currently limits its terrorist operations to Israeli military and civilian targets in the West Bank, Gaza Strip, Israel and Lebanon.

(c) Hizballah

Its name means the 'Party of God'; it was formed in June 1982 in Lebanon as the militant wing of a religious group. It has several thousand supporters and is thought to have over a hundred terrorist operatives. It continues to receive financial and other support from Iran. Among the attacks it has claimed responsibility for include the three suicide truck bombing of 1983 in Lebanon. Hizballah also attacked the Israeli Embassy in Argentina in 1992. They have established cells in Europe, Africa, South America, North America and Asia.

SOUTH AMERICA

Shining Path (SL)

It is also known as Sendero Luminoso People's Liberation Army. Former University professor Abimael Guzman formed SL in Peru in the late 1960s and his teachings created the foundation of SL's Militant Maoist doctrine. Its goal is to destroy existing Peruvian institution and replace them with a communist peasant revolutionary regime. Approximately 30,000 persons have died since shining path took up arms in 1980. They conducted indiscriminate bombings campaigns and selective assassinations. It is believe to have around 300-armed Militant. SL's are mostly active in Peru and rural areas. The group gets their funds through cocaine trafficking.

Terrorists are insane and inhuman. Their motives initiate, direct and sustain behaviour for leaders of a group or a movement, motives must be proclaimed to make intentions clear to acolytes and to a wider audience, even to those who will contest intention and goals.

The first and foremost objective of the terrorist is to draw worldwide attention for their cause. Terrorism inflicts immediate damage in destroying lives and property, but terrorists hope that the long-term costs will be much greater.

They want to create fear and uncertainty far beyond the victims and those close to them. They want their enemy to spend time and money on security.

Another main motive of terrorists is to cripple normal functioning of the government by undermines the faith of the people in the government and in the role of law.

Terrorism is the illegal use or threatened use of violence by groups with political or ideological motives. Their goal is to coerce societies or governments by inducing fear in their population. The central goal of terrorism, in other words is to create a climate of fear, uncertainty and vulnerability.

Terrorism intentionally hits emotional "hot buttons". Victims of terrorism experience a peculiar sense of insecurity, which is often painful and intolerable.

The effect of captivity on the mind or attitude or outlook is far more damaging. It destroys the morale of the people, the will to live, shatter faith in the living beings, in the surrounding and in humanity in general.

A minority of respondents also reported symptoms linked to depression a distinct but related psychological response to the event. The more directly a person is affected by a terrorist act, the greater is the risk of developing post-traumatic stress disorder (PTSD) and other disorders. Financial markets have also been directly and indirectly the victims of terrorist attack. The impact of the September 11 attacks was visible worldwide on the major equity markets, which experienced sharp and rapid declines, demonstrating that market participants perceived the event as a global shock.

It is an indication that despite all the efforts deployed by the security and intelligence services, they have failed to find answers to all the challenges posed by the new terrorist actors.

Terrorism has been a social cancer through the ages. It has changed its pattern and way of working from time to time. Terrorists adopt unconventional methods in their operations for their success. They are highly motivated for survival against all odds and with the desire to succeed in their mission.

A method adopts by modern terrorist reflect the idiosyncrasies of their political environment, so that no single factor explains the adoption of specific tactics by different groups. Some of the methods that terrorist have used—arson, assassination or targeted murders, bombing, chemical substance, hijacking, kidnapping, grenades, gun, letter bombs, suicide bombers, mortars and rocket launchers.

The terrorist incident most difficult to anticipate is the one, which leads to mass murder and widespread damages. The destruction of New York's World Trade Center on September 11, 2001 was a new method in that using of jet aircraft and all their passengers, as suicide bombers had never been tried before.

After 9/11 everything is possible, new threat for 21st century is Chemical, Biological, Radiological and Nuclear terrorism, which have been already discuss in detail in Chapter 4 of this work. Another possibilities of new type of terrorism are Eco-terrorism, Cyber-terrorism and Maritime terrorism. Today's terrorists can choose from a potent arsenal of weapons capable of destroying large portions of our planet. Weapons of Mass Destruction (WMD) and cyber terrorism (the use of computer to spread information and paralyze vital infrastructures) could cause hundred of thousands, even millions, of death and injuries.

Everyday there was a fresh incident, usually that of a car bomb or suicide bomber decimating civilians and triggering the hardest of responses from a government feeling itself beleaguered. Now it is right and ripe time that all countries should face the challenges and talk-concerted action to counter this onslaught against humanity, without adopting a policy of shifting convenience.

The fight against terrorism encompasses an extremely

diverse range of concerns, and it is clearly impossible for one country to deal with all the aspects in depth on its own. International cooperation is required and all the more so since the countries involved in the fight against terrorism are all interested in the same issues.

Today, many countries have special units designated to handle terrorist threats. Besides various security agencies, there are elite tactical units perform both in preventive actions, hostage rescue and responding to on-going attacks. Hence, the purpose of counter terrorism is to save lives, limbs and property without unduly compromising other national interests and objectives. Dealing effectively with terrorism thus demands of taking various strong measures.

Some important measures that can help counter-terrorism are as follows:

1. Study of terrain and topography of the entire area is important before making any definite plan of action and before deploying the force.
2. Proper security arrangements must be made in the locations like, public places, schools, market places, airports and banks.
3. There should be proper intelligence system around the hideouts of the terrorists.
4. Counter measures should be designed to reduce terrorist resources, their propensity to strike and the damage they intend to cause. Border security should be improved. Infiltration and exhilaration should be checked.

Success in the global war against terrorism depends on the actions of a powerful coalition of nations maintaining a united front against terror.

Suggestions

Terrorist requires means to carry out their attacks. The

ability to generate and move finances, to acquire weapons, to recruit and train cadres, and to communicate, particularly through use of the Internet, is essential to terrorists. They seek easy access to their intended targets and increasingly look for greater impact—both in numbers killed and in media exposure. Denying them access to these means and targets can help to prevent future attack.

(1)Terrorists generate funds in many ways, with moneys moved through both formal and informal sector. Whereas some terrorist groups may fund their activities from drug cultivation and trafficking, terrorist operating though decentralized networks that once raised and moved money through formal channels and otherwise legitimate sources such as private business and charities are turning to methods that are more difficult to monitor, such as the use of cash couriers. In addition, we cannot overlook the fact that certain acts of terrorism require relatively minor funding—Low-budget terrorism.

All states should take the necessary measures and steps to eliminate the financing of terrorism.

Terrorists cash and property are to be seized and forfeited, suspected financial transactions must be frozen.

(2) Once a terrorist has money, with which, to plan an a atrocity, he will next turn to what practical means he can use—how to get hold of a weapon. While most terrorist attacks so far have used conventional weapons, no one can disregard the enormously destructive potential of terrorists using nuclear, biological, chemical or radiological weapons. Several terrorist groups have professed a determination to obtain weapons of mass destruction (WMD) and some have even used them, fortunately without catastrophic impact. Denying them access to these materials must be a serious part of the international effort.

(3)A nuclear, biological, chemical or radiological terrorist attack would have a devastatingly far-reaching impact. In addition to causing widespread death and destruction, it could deal a crippling blow, to the world economy and drive millions of people in to dire poverty. An ensuring effect on infant mortality could unleash a second wave of deaths throughout the developing world.

Our common goal must be to secure, and, wherever possible eliminate, nuclear, biological, chemical, and radiological weapons and implement effective domestic and export controls on dual-use materials related to weapons of mass destruction.

To prevent terrorist from acquiring chemical, biological or nuclear materials, states should ensure that security at chemical, biological or nuclear plant is kept to the highest standard of high alert at all the tunes.

(4)Terrorists network rely on communication to build support and recruit members. We must deny them this access, particularly by countering their use of the Internet—a rapidly growing vehicle for terrorist recruitment and dissemination of information and propaganda. In 1998, there were fewer than 20 terrorist websites. By 2005, that number was estimated by experts to have surged into the hundreds.

Member States that have not already done so should take the necessary steps to impede the use of information and communications technologies for promoting and carrying out terrorist activities. All States should work hard to control the power of the Internet to counter-terrorism.

(5) Much of international terrorist activity still relies on physical movement—using regular transportation to reach another country in order to promote their message, recruit new members, and provide explosive training or transfer money. We need to do more in transport security, and to assist states in developing tools to tackle identity theft and fraudulent travel documents.

(6) We must also work to strengthen border control, in particular in developing countries with long, poorly defined and often mountainous frontiers. Their should be a modernization of 'border management' systems, facilities, and institutions,

at the national regional and international levels. It is also suggested that statesmen should further work in this area, and highlight the need for political support within relevant countries to implement improved border management practices.

(7) One of the most harmful aspects of modern terrorism is the intent to cause mass casualties in public places, including those related to tourism and recreational facilities. We must work to improve the protection of soft targets as well as the security and safety of civilians affected by their attacks. In addition, we must not forget the importance of ensuring the safety of peacetime security personnel from similar attacks.

(8) The outcome of the 2005 World Summit on terrorism reiterated the call upon states to refrain from organizing, financing, encouraging providing training for or otherwise supporting terrorist activities and to take appropriate measures to ensure that their territories are not used for such activities.

(9) At the same time, in the fight against terrorism, we must never sacrifice our values and lower our standards to those of the terrorists. Because if we sacrifice them in our response, we are handing a victory to the terrorist. International cooperation to fight terrorism must be conducted in full conformity with international law, including the charter of the United Nations and relevant international conventions and protocols.

(10) Intelligence and law enforcement go hand in hand. Arresting a terrorist is usually better than killing him/her, as a successful interrogation can led the location of other terrorists or additional knowledge of the organization.

(11) States should also refrain from providing any form of support to entities or persons involved in terrorist acts; deny safe haven to those who finance, support, commit terrorist acts, and provide safe haven as well.

(12) All States should enhance the coordination of national, sub regional, regional and international efforts to strengthen a global response to the threat posed by these activities.

(13) No strategy to curb terrorism would be complete without clear provisions for development. To combat terrorism, a more just international economic and political order has to be established, which would take into account the interests of as many people as possible. It is obvious that extreme poverty, injustice and frustration could lead to further terrorist acts, which is a threat to all of humanity.

(14) There is a primary need of proper equipping and marshalling of the police and para-military forces. There is also a vital need of professional anti-terrorist force in the full combat readiness. They should also be supplied with sophisticated weapons to fight back terrorists who have already equipped with them. (It is rightly said that 99% victory depends upon superior armaments) Gen. Fuller.

(15) Last, but far from least, all effort should be made to eradicate corruption. Administration must be fair and transparent and all armed forces including Para-military forces must be more alert in managing their duties.

There is a need to develop national character leading towards International brotherhood because terrorism is a threat to all nation-states and to all people, which can strike anytime and anywhere. We all must involve in countering it and we must be at the forefront in fighting it and involve in countering it, proclaiming loud and clear that terrorism can never be accepted justified, in any case whatsoever must be the motto of the present world.

Bibliography

Abu Khalil, Asad. *Bin Laden, Islam, and America's New War on Terrorism*. New York: Seven Stories, 2002.

Adams, James. *The Financing of Terror*. New York: Simon & Schuster, 1986.

Alali, A. Odasuo, and Kenoye Kelvin Eke, eds. *Media Coverage of Terrorism: Methods of Diffusion*. Newbury Park, CA: Sage, 1991.

Alexander, Yonah, and Michael S. Swetnam, eds. *Cyber Terrorism and Information Warfare: Threats and Responses*. Ardsley, NY: Transnational, 2001.

Alexander, Yonah, and Michael S. Swetnam, *Usama bin Laden's al-Qaida: Profile of a Terrorist Network*. Ardsley, NY: Transnational, 2001.

Alexander, Yonah, Michael S. Swetnam, and Herbert M. Levine. *ETA: Profile of a Terrorist Group*. Ardsley, NY: Transnational, 2001.

Anonymous, *Imperial Hubris: Why the West is Losing the War on Terror,* Washington DC: Brassey's, 2004

Aquilla, J. and D. Ronfeldt, eds. *Networks and Netwars*.

Bhattacharjee, J.B., *Roots of Insurgency in Northeast India,* New Delhi, Akansha, 2007.

Byrne, Brendan T., 'Foreword', in Marius H. Livingston, Lee Bruce Kress and Marie G. Wanek (eds), *International Terrorism in the Contemporary World, (Contributions in Political Science: 3,)* Westport, CT: Greenwood Press, 1987.

Barnhurst, Kevin. 'Contemporary Terrorism in Peru: Sendero-Luminoso and the Media'. *Journal of Communication*. 1991.

Barnhurst, Stephen R. *International Terrorism and Political Violence*. Victoria, BC: Trafford 2002.

Bjorgo, T. *Terror from the Extreme Right*. London: Cassell, 1995.

Bremer, L.P. *Terrorism: Its Evolving Nature*, Washington. D.C.: Bureau of Public Affairs, 1989.

Burton, Anthony. *Urban Terrorism: Theory, Practice, and Response*. London: Cooper, 1975.

Byman, Daniel, *Deadly Dynamics: States that Sponsor Terrorism* (New York: Cambridge UP 2005).

Carr, Caleb, *'Terrorism as Warfare: The Lessons of Military History'*, World Policy Journal, 1996.

Cerny, Philip G., 'France: Non-terrorism and the politics of repressive tolerance', in Juliet Lodge (ed.), *Terrorism: A Challenge to the State*, Oxford: Martin Robertson, 1981.

Chand, Attar. *Pakistan Terrorism in Punjab and Kashmir*. Delhi: Amar Prakashan, 1991.

Change, Nancy. *Silencing Political Dissent: How Post-September 11 Anti-Terrorism Measures Threaten Our Civil Liberties*. New York: Seven Stories Press, 2002.

Chomsky, Noam, 'International terrorism: image and reality', in Alexander George (ed.), *Western State Terrorism*, Cambridge: Polity Press, 1991.

Chomsky, Noam. 9/11. New York: Seven Stories, 2001.

Clark, Ian. *Globalization and International Relations Theory*. Oxford: Oxford University Press, 1999.

Clarke, Richard and Barry McCaffrey, 'NATO's Role in Confronting International Terrorism', *The Atlantic Council* (June 2004).

Clutterbuck, Richard. *Guerrillas and Terrorists*. Chicago: Ohio University Press, 1980.

Clutterbuck, Richard. *Terrorism in an Unstable World*. New York: Routledge, 1994.

Cooley, John K. *Unholy Wars: Afghanistan, America and International Terrorism*. Sterling, VA: Pluto, 1999.

Crelinsten, Ronald D., 'Power and meaning: terrorism as a struggle over access in the communication structure', in Paul Wilkinson and Alasdair M. Stewart (eds), *Contemporary Research on Terrorism*, Aberdeen: Aberdeen University Press, 1987.

Crenshaw, Martha, ed. *Terrorism in Africa*. New York: G. K. Hall; Toronto, Ontario: Maxwell Macmillan Canada, 1994.

Dobkin, Bethami A., *Tales of Terror: Television News and the Construction of the Terrorist Threat*. New York: Praeger, 1992.

Dutta, A. & Triveni, *Women Rebels: Stories, from Nepal and Nagaland*, New Delhi, Akansha Publishing House, 2009.

Fair, C. Christine, 'Militant Recruitment in Pakistan: Implications for Al Qaeda and Other Organizations', *Studies in Conflict and Terrorism* 27/6 (Nov./Dec. 2004).

Falkenrath, Richard A., Robert Newman, and Bradley A. Thayer. *America's Achilles' Heel: Nuclear, Biological, and Chemical Terrorism and Covert Attack*. Cambridge MIT Press, 1998.

Frey, R.G. and Christopher W. Morris, eds. *Violence, Terrorism and Justice*. New York: Cambridge University Press, 1991.

George, A. *Western State Terrorism*. New York: Routledge, 1991.

George, Alexander, ed. *Western State Terrorism*. New York: Routledge, 1991.

Greenberg, Bradley S. and Marcia Thomson, *Communication and Terrorism: Public and Media Responses to 9/11*. Hampton Press, 2002.

Guelke, Adrian, *The Age of Terrorism and the International Political System*, (Library of International Relations: 2), London: Tauris Academic Studies, 1995.

Gunaratna, Rohan. *Inside Al Qaeda: Global Network of Terror*. New York: Columbia University Press, 2002.

Han, Henry H., ed. *Terrorism & Political Violence: Limits & Possibilities of Legal Control*. New York: Oceana, 1993.

Harclerode, Peter. *Secret Soldiers: Special Forces in the War Against Terrorism*. London: Cassell, 2000.

Harris, Daniel C. *Combating Terrorism: FBI's Use of Federal Funds for Counterterrorism and Related Activities*, 1995-98. Collingdale, PA: Diane Publishing, 1998.

Herman, Edward S. and Gerry O' Sullivan. *The Terrorism Industry: The Experts and Institutions that Shape our View of Terror*. New York: Pantheon, 1989.

Heskin, Ken. *Northern Ireland: A Psychological Analysis*. New York: Columbia University Press, 1980.

Hochschild, Adam, *King Leopold's Ghost: A Story of Greed, Terror, and Heroism in Colonial Africa*. New York: Houghton Mifflin, 1998.

Hoffman, Bruce, *Inside Terrorism*. New York: Columbia University Press, 1998.

Hoffman, Bruce. *Terrorism and Weapons of Mass Destruction: An Analysis of Trends and Motivations*. Santa Monica, CA: RAND, 1999.

Howard, Russell D., and Reid L. Sawyer. *Terrorism and Counter terrorism*. Guilford, Conn: McGraw-Hill/Dushkin, 2003.

Joshi, Hargovind, *Defence Administration in India* (2 Vols.), New Delhi, Akansha, 2002.

Kaplan, David E. and Andrew Marshall. *The Cult at the End of the World: The Incredible Story of Aum*. London: Hutchinson, 1996.

Kushner, Harvey W. *Terrorism in America: A Structured Approach to Understanding the Terrorist Threat*. Springfield, IL: Charles C Thomas, 1998.

Laqueur, Walter. *History of Terrorism*. New York: Transaction Publishers, 2001.

Laqueur, Walter. *The New Terrorism: Fanaticism and the Arms of Mass Destruction*. New York: Oxford University Press, 1999.

Lee, Alfred McLung. *Terrorism in Northern Ireland*. New York: General Hall, 1983.

Levitt, Geoffrey M. *Democracies Against Terror: The Western Response to State-Sponsored Terrorism*. New York: Praeger, 1988.

MacWillson, Alastair C. *Hostage-Taking Terrorism: Incident-Response Strategy*. New York: St. Martin's, 1992.

Mahajan Rahul. *The New Crusade: America's War on Terrorism*. New York: Monthly Review, 2002.

Melman, Yossi. *The Master Terrorist: The True Story Behind Abu Nidal*. New York: Adama, 1986.

Merkl, Peter H., ed. *Political Violence and Terror: Motifs and Motivations*. Berkeley: University of California Press, 1986.

Mickolus, Edward F., *International Terrorism: Attributes of Terrorist Events*, 1968-1977, ICPSR 7947, Code book to data set, n.p, 1991.

Mishra, R.C., *Terrorism Implications of Tactics and Technology*, New Delhi, AuthorsPress, 2004.

Netanyahu, Benjamin. *The Terrorism Reader*, New York: Meridian, 1986.

O' Connell, Joseph T., et al. *Sikh History and Religion in the Twentieth Century*. Toronto, Ontario: University of Toronto, 1988.

O' Neill Bard E. *Insurgency and Terrorism: Inside Modern Revolutionary Warfare*. Washington, DC: Brassey's, 1990.

Oliverio, Annamarie. *The State of Terror: SUNY Series in Deviance and Social Control*. Albany: State University of New York Press, 1998.

Oliverio, Annemarie., *The State of Terror*. Albany, NY: State University of New York Press, 1998.

Palmer, Nancy, (editor) *Terrorism, War and the Press*. The Joan Shorenstein Center on the Press, Politics and Public Policy, John F. Kennedy School of Government, Harvard University, 2003.

Parry, Albert. *Terrorism From Robespierre to Arafat*. New York: Vanguard, 1976.

Picard, Robert G. *Media Portrayal of Terrorism: Functions and Meaning of News Coverage*. Ames: Iowa State University Press, 1993.

Reeve, Simon. *The New Jackals: Ramzi Yousef. Osama bin Laden, and the Future of Terrorism*. Boston : Northeastern University Press, 1999.

Reich, Walter. ed., *Origins of Terrorism: Psychologies, Ideologies, Theologies*, States of Mind. Washington, D.C.: Woodrow Wilson Center Press, 1988.

Reid, E.O.F., 'Evolution of a Body of Knowledge: An Analysis of Terrorism Research.' *Information Processing and Management*. 1997.

Ritter, Scott. *Frontier Justice: Weapons of Mass Destruction and the Bush-whacking of America*. New York: Context, 2003.

Robertson, Roland. *Globalization: Social Theory and Global Culture*, London: Sage, 1992.

Robinson, Adam, *Bin Laden: Behind the Mask of Terrorism*. New York: Arcade, 2002.

Rosen, Jay, "When the Networks Ran in Reverse: Reflections on the Terror in New York." *Journalism: Theory, Practice and Criticism* 3 (1) 2002.

Rosenberg, Tina. *Children of Cain: Violence and the Violent in Latin America*. New York: Penguin, 1992.

Rubin, Barry, and Judith Colp Rubin. *Anti-American Terrorism in the Middle East*. New York: Oxford University Press, 2002.

Satloff, Robert B. *War on Terror: The Middle East Dimension*. Washington, DC: Washington Institute for Near East Policy, 2002.

Schmid, Alex P., and Janny de Graaf. *Violence as Communication: Insurgent Terrorism and the Western News Media*. London: Sage, 1982.

Shulsky, Abram N. *Silent Warfare: Understanding the World of Intelligence*. 2nd ed., rev./revised by Gary J. Schmitt. Washington, DC: Brassey's, 1993.

Singh, T. Hemo (Col.), *Manipur Imbroiglio: Insurgency, Ethnic Politics, Sociocultural Dimensions*, New Delhi, Akansha, 2009.

Sloan, Stephen, *Simulating Terrorism*. Norman: University of Oklahoma Press, 1981.

Stern, Jessica. *The Ultimate Terrorists*. Cambridge, MA: Harvard University Press, 1999.

Strong, Simon. *Shining Path: Terror and Revolution in Peru*. New York: Times Books, 1992.

Tanter, Raymond, *Rogue Regimes: Terrorism & Proliferation*. New York: St. Martin's, 1998.

The Future of Terror, Crime and Militancy. Santa Monica, CA: RAND, 2001.

Vercher, Antonio, *Terrorism in Europe: An International Comparative Legal Analysis*. Oxford, UK: Clarendon; New York: Oxford University Press, 1992.

Whittacker, David, ed. *The Terrorism Reader*. London: Routledge, 1995.

Williams, Paul. *Al Qaeda: The Brotherhood of Terror*. New York: Alpha, 2002.

Wolf, John B. *Fear of Fear: A Survey of Terrorist Operations and Controls in Open Societies*. New York: Plenum, 1981.

Yallop, H.J. *Protection Against Terrorism*. Chichester, UK: Barry Rose, 1980.

Zinn, Howard. *A People's History of the United States: 1492-Present*. New York: Harper Perennial, 1999.

Zinn, Howard. *Declarations of Independence: Cross-examining American Ideology*. New York: Harper Perennial, 1991.

Zinn, Howard. *Terrorism and War*, New York: Seven Stories Press, 2002.

Primary Sources

Annual Reports Ministry of Defence.

Annual Reports Ministry of Home Affairs.

Annual Report Ministry of External Affairs.

National Human Rights Commission Reports.

POTA.

Study Reports Originated by Corps and Command HQs (only unclassified material).

United Nation Website on Human Rights.

NHRC Website.

Amazon Website (www.amazon.co.uk)

United Nations (www.un.org)

Terrorism Research Council (www.terrorism.com)

International Policy Institute for Counter Terrorism (www.ict.org.il)

National Memorial Institute for the Prevention of Terrorism (www.mipt.org)

Journals

1. *Aakrosh*
2. *Asian Survey.*
3. *Armed Forces and Society.*
4. *Armed Forces Journal.*
5. *Combat.*
6. *Current History.*
7. *Comparative Strategy.*
8. *Defence Watch.*
9. *Defence Management.*
10. *Defence Digest.*
11. *Defence and Security Analysis.*
12. *Foreign Affairs.*
13. *Indian Defence Review.*
14. *I.C.W.A. Foreign Affairs Report.*
15. *Janes Defence Weekly.*
16. *Journal of Peace Studies.*

17. *Journal of Strategic Studies.*
18. *Manistream.*
19. *Pinnacle.*
20. *Small Wars and Insurgencies.*
21. *Strategic Analysis.*
22. *Strategic Digest.*
23. *Seminar.*
24. *Survival.*
25. *The Defence Monitor.*
26. *The Journal of Parliamentary Information.*
27. *USI Digest.*
28. *USI Journal.*
29. *Vidura.*
30. *World Focus.*

Newspapers and Magazines

1. *The Times of India.*
2. *The Indian Express*
3. *The Hindu.*
4. *The Asian Age.*
5. *The Pioneer.*
6. *The Statesman.*
7. *Kashmir Times.*
8. *India Today.*
9. *Frontline.*
10. *Out Look.*
11. *The Week.*
12. *Time.*
13. *News Week.*
14. *Alive.*
15. *Sahara Times.*
16. *The Economist*
17. *New York Times*

Index

***